# ECCE ROMANI

**A Latin Reading Course**
**Prepared by The Scottish Classics Group**

## 5
## Domi Militiaeque

*Second Edition*

Oliver & Boyd

# Contents

| Roman Government | Kings | Republic | Empire | Later divides into Western and Eastern | Empire disintegrates into separate nations |
|---|---|---|---|---|---|
| Literature | Legends / Literature begins | Golden Age | Silver Age | Latin written in monasteries (Medieval Latin) | European settlers bring their language and literature to all parts of the world |
| Language | Spread of Latin — In Italy | | Throughout Europe, North Africa, Middle East | Development of French, Spanish and Italian from Latin / English from Latin and Anglo-Saxon | |
| Dates | 700 600 500 400 300 200 100 **BC** | | 100 200 300 400 500 600 700 800 900 1000 1100 1200 1300 1400 1500 1600 1700 1800 1900 2000 **AD** | | |

Most of the Latin we read was written between 100 BC and AD 100, when there was a wealth of great writers. These works of early writers were preserved in the Christian monasteries where the monks themselves wrote history and poetry in Latin, in addition to editing the Scriptures. For a thousand years, Latin was spoken throughout Europe, and all business and diplomacy was conducted in Latin. As the nations developed separately, their languages also separated, but wherever English, French, Spanish, Italian are spoken, the language is based on Latin.

A more detailed time-chart is available on page 280. It is not in scale but shows when the more famous Latin authors lived.

# 55
# The King's Treasure

This story is adapted from a version of the tale written about AD 1200 by a monk called John of Alta Silva who lived in France. The general theme of the story (the builder of a treasure-house leaves a secret entrance through which he gradually steals the contents, is trapped and, to avoid being recognised, is beheaded by his companion) is to be found in other literatures. The Greek historian Herodotus (5th century BC) gives a version in which the thief employs quite different ruses to recover the headless body and is, in fact, finally reconciled to the king and given his daughter in marriage.

### A prodigal son

fuit antiquo tempore rex quidam magnus et potens qui, maximam thesauri cupiditatem habens, turrim magnae altitudinis latitudinisque auro et argento et pretiosis rebus usque ad summum compleverat.

habebat autem rex militem qui in multis rebus fidelis fuerat cui claves thesauri sui commisit. at miles, cum thesaurum multos annos custodivisset, labore et senectute confectus, regem rogavit ut claves thesauri reciperet ac se sineret domum redire et inter filios reliquum vitae suae tempus quiete agere. rex vero, ratus militem rem iustam petere, tristis eum magnis muneribus donatum domum abire sivit. receptis igitur clavibus, rex alteri custodi thesaurum commisit.

| | |
|---|---|
| **potens, -entis,** powerful | **autem,** now |
| **thesaurus, -i** (*m*), treasure | **fidelis, -is, -e,** faithful, |
| **cupiditas, -atis** (*f*), desire |    trustworthy |
| **turris, -is** (*f*), tower | **clavis, -is** (*f*), key |
| **latitudo, -inis** (*f*), width | **senectus, -utis** (*f*), old age |
| **argentum, -i** (*n*), silver | **confectus, -a, -um,** worn out |
| **pretiosus, -a, -um,** precious | **munus, -eris** (*n*), gift |
| **usque ad,** right up to | **dono** (1), to present |

**compleo, -ere** (2), **complevi, completum,** to fill
**reor, reri** (2), **ratus sum,** to think

miles autem multos filios habebat ex quibus unum nimis diligebat. cui omnes suas divitias exposuit iussitque eum large expendere ut famam et amicos sibi compararet. filius igitur equos, arma, vestes ceteraque quibus adulescentes saepe delectari solent, comparavit. brevi tempore exhausta pecunia, ad patrem regressus dixit pecuniam iam defecisse.

tum pater "quoniam" inquit "te, fili, nimis et stulte dilexi, omnes divitias meas tibi dedi. at tu temperantiae immemor ita omnia consumpsisti ut nihil mihi praeter solam domum reliqueris. quid ergo tibi magis faciam? hoc unum superest consilium, sed periculosum. si large, ut prius, vivere vis, ad turrim in qua regis thesaurus positus est silentio noctis adeamus."

quo audito, filius "at gloria nominis nostri non peribit. omnia pericula tecum libenter subibo, si divitias comparabimus."

consurgunt igitur ambo nocte, turrim adeunt, perforant murum. intrat pater, sublataque magna thesauri parte, exit obstruitque foramen. revertuntur domum onusti regis divitiis,

**nimis,** too much
**divitiae, -arum** (*f.pl*), riches
**large,** lavishly
**fama, -ae** (*f*), fame, reputation
**comparo** (1), to obtain, acquire

**temperantia, -ae** (*f*), self-restraint
**ergo,** therefore
**adeamus,** let us go to
**perforo** (1), to bore through
**foramen, -inis** (*n*), hole
**onustus, -a, -um,** loaded, laden

**diligo, -ere** (3), **dilexi, dilectum,** to love
**expono, -ere** (3), **-posui, -positum,** to make available
**expendo, -ere** (3), **-pendi, -pensum,** to spend
**deficio, -ere** (3), **-feci, -fectum,** to run out, fail, disappear
**consumo, -ere,** (3), **-sumpsi, -sumptum,** to use up
**supersum, superesse, superfui,** to remain, be left
**pereo, -ire, perii, peritum,** to pass away, perish, be lost
**subeo, -ire, subii, subitum,** to undergo
**tollo, -ere** (3), **sustuli, sublatum,** to lift, raise, remove
**obstruo, -ere** (3), **-struxi, -structum,** to block up
**revertor, -ti** (3), **reversus sum,** to return

et iuvenis iterum sua utitur largitate. quandocunque iterum opus erat pecunia, ad thesaurum revertebantur.

### To catch a thief

accidit autem ut rex thesaurum suum videre vellet. custode igitur arcessito, intrat turrim videtque magnam thesauri partem sublatam esse. ira igitur commotus, dissimulans tamen, egreditur venitque ad senem quendam ut consilium quaereret. fuerat hic senex olim famosissimus praedo quem comprehensum rex oculis privaverat eique de mensa sua cibum cotidie dabat. hic regi consilium bonum et utile saepe praebebat.

narrat ei rex rem totam quaeritque quomodo perdita recuperare possit. cui senex tale dat consilium: "si," inquit "o rex, scire cupis quis hoc egerit, iube aliquid herbae viridis in turrim inferri ignemque supponi. deinde est tibi egrediendum. ianua clausa, circum turrim iterum atque iterum tibi est ambulandum exspectandumque si fumum per aliquam muri rimam egredientem videas. hoc facto, ad me redi ut te doceam quid posthac tibi agendum sit."

rex igitur, herba viridi incensa, clausit ianuam et tacitus turrim circumire coepit. ecce autem fumus, ex calore ignis et herbae humore maxime excitatus, adeo replevit turrim ut per locum foraminis egrederetur, quod ibi lapide modo sine caemento obstructum erat.

---

**sua largitate,** his usual extravagance
**quandocunque,** whenever
**opus est** ( + *abl.*), there is need (of)
**dissimulo** (1), to keep secret
**privo** ( + *abl.*), to deprive (of)
**praebeo** (2), to provide, give
**perditus, -a, -um,** lost
**herba, -ae** (*f*), grass
**viridis, -is, -e,** green

**ignis, -is** (*m*), fire
**tibi est egrediendum,** you must go out
**posthac,** after this
**quid tibi agendum sit,** what you must do
**tacitus, -a, -um,** silent(ly)
**humor, -oris** (*m*), moisture, dampness
**modo,** only
**caementum, -i** (*n*), mortar

**utor, uti** (3), **usus sum** ( + *abl.*) to use, employ
**suppono, -ere** (3), **supposui, suppositum,** to place under
**repleo, -ere** (2), **replevi, repletum,** to fill

quo viso, ad senem rex festinat et nuntiat quid viderit. quibus rebus auditis, senex "fures," ait "o rex, thesaurum tuum per locum ubi fumus egreditur tibi abstulerunt. nisi aliqua arte eos ceperis, non cessabunt donec totum thesaurum auferant. tu igitur comple cupam latam et profundam resina et glutine ! eam prope foramen intra turrim pone ut fur, cum more solito nihil suspicans ad thesaurum revenerit, repente in cupam cadat et glutine captus prima luce inveniatur."

rex, astutum senis consilium miratus, cupam glutine impletam prope foramen posuit. quo facto, discessit.

### A desperate remedy

ecce autem eadem nocte miser pater cum filio ad turrim rediit. remoto a foramine lapide, intrat pater nihil suspicatus. incautus in cupam desilit mento tenus statimque glutine captus haeret immobilis ita ut nec manum nec pedem vel aliquod membrorum movere posset, excepta lingua quae tantum libera remanserat. gemens igitur filium advocatum orat ut cito caput amputet et abscedat ne forte per caput cognitus aeternam suo generi maculam inferat.

**incautus, -a, -um,** not taking care
**mento tenus,** up to his chin
**membrum, -i** (*n*), limb
**aliquod membrorum,** any of his limbs
**tantum,** only, alone

**liber, -era, -erum,** free
**cito,** quickly
**forte,** by chance, perchance
**aeternus, -a, -um,** everlasting
**genus, -eris** (*n*), family
**macula, -ae** (*f*), stain, disgrace

**remaneo, -ere** (2), **-mansi,** to remain
**abscedo, -ere** (3), **-cessi, -cessum,** to go away

filius ei parere diu dubitavit, sed tandem invitus caput patris cultro amputavit et fugiens asportavit.

## The search begins

postridie autem rex, cum prima luce e lecto surrexisset, intravit turrim cucurritque ad cupam invenitque murum perforatum terramque sanguine maculatam. furem quoque suum conspexit, sed truncato capite.

rex ad senem festinavit; nuntiavit captum quidem esse furem, sed truncato capite. quod cum audivisset, senex paulisper subridens "miror" inquit "huius furis astutiam. quia enim nobilis erat nec voluit vel se vel genus suum prodere, socium iussit caput suum amputare. quare tibi difficile erit aut thesaurum recuperare aut cognoscere furem."

tum rex vehementer persuadebat seni ut melius consilium daret. cui senex "iube furem de cupa extractum caudae equi fortissimi alligari trahique per vias vicorum regni tui. milites armati subsequantur; qui, si viderint viros vel mulieres ad aspectum cadaveris lacrimantes, eos ad te ducant. nam si fuerit ibi socius aut uxor aut filii, nullo modo poterunt lacrimas retinere."

bonum rex ratus senis consilium, iubet statim truncum equo fortissimo pedibus alligatum cum armatis militibus trahi per proximos vicos. dum miser trahitur, accidit ut ante fores domus suae perveniret.

---

**dubito** (1), to hesitate
**culter, cultri** (*m*), knife
**asporto** (1), to carry off
**maculatus, -a, -um,** stained
**trunco** (1), to cut off
**subridens,** smiling
**quia,** because
**socius, -i** (*m*), ally, accomplice
**quare,** therefore
**alligo** (1), to tie to

**vicus, -i** (*m*), village
**regnum, -i** (*n*), kingdom
**subsequantur,** let (them) follow closely
**aspectus, -us** (*m*), sight
**cadaver, -eris** (*n*), corpse
**ducant,** let them bring
**truncus, -i** (*m*), headless body
**proximus, -a, -um,** nearest
**fores, -um** (*f.pl*), door

**prodo, -ere** (3), **prodidi, proditum,** to betray

## Quick thinking

stabat autem ille filius eius, qui ei in furto fuerat socius, ante ipsas fores. qui cum videret patrem sic miserabiliter trahi, quamquam flere non audebat, retinere tamen lacrimas non poterat. itaque, occasione reperta, cultrum lignumque arripit, quasi aliquid incisurus, sinistraeque manus pollicem de industria amputat. vocem emittit luctuosam; erumpunt lacrimae. ad eum accurrit mater. fratres et sorores dilacerant manibus vestes oraque et capillos. quamquam filium lamentari videntur, re vera patrem miserum lamentantur.

adfuerunt statim milites qui eos caperent ducerentque ad regem. at vero rex tanto gaudio commotus est ut promiserit illis vitam si thesaurum suum redderent.

cui iuvenis ille audacissimus "o rex, non quia hic miser truncus ad nos pertinet lacrimas effundimus sed quia hic dies infelix mihi sinistrae manus pollicem abstulit."

rex vero, cum pollicem adhuc fluentem sanguine videret, misericordia commotus "non est" ait "mirum si doles quod hoc tibi accidit. vade in pace!" sic ergo ille astutia sua se suosque liberans domum rediit; et regressus est rex ad senem ut consilium iterum quaereret.

---

**furtum, -i** (*n*), theft
**sic miserabiliter,** in such a pitiful state
**occasio, -onis** (*f*), opportunity
**lignum, -i** (*n*), piece of wood
**quasi incisurus,** as if intending to carve
**pollex, -icis** (*m*), thumb
**de industria,** deliberately
**luctuosus, -a, -um,** mournful

**dilacero** (1), to tear apart
**os, oris** (*n*), face
**qui eos caperent,** to arrest them
**gaudium, -i** (*n*), joy
**pertinere ad** ( + *acc.*), to concern
**infelix, -icis,** unlucky
**misericordia, -ae** (*f*), pity
**pax, pacis** (*f*), peace

**fleo, -ere** (2), **flevi, fletum,** to weep
**reperio, -ire** (4), **repperi, repertum,** to find
**lamentor, -ari** (1), **lamentatus sum,** to weep over
**promitto, -ere** (3), **-misi, -missum,** to promise
**effundo, -ere** (3), **-fudi, -fusum,** to pour out
**fluo, -ere** (3), **fluxi, fluxum,** to flow
**vado, -ere** (3), to go

## The search continues

senex regi suasit ut cadaver iterum per eosdem traheretur vicos. quod factum est. cum, ut prius, ventum esset ad domum eius, fur dolorem non ferens, parvum filium suum in puteum, qui pro foribus erat, clam proiecit. tum voce lacrimosa populum quasi ad liberandum filium convocat. accurrit iterum mater cum filiis. puteum circumstant. lacrimant omnes. alii funibus ad extrahendum puerum in puteum se demittunt, alii eos iterum sursum extrahunt. quid plura? capitur iterum ille solus duciturque ad regem.

rex, cum vidisset hunc iterum captum esse quem antea dimiserat "cur dissimulas?" ait. "furta tua te accusant. redde ergo thesaurum et te liberum dimittam."

tum fur, suspiria ab imo pectore trahens "o me" inquit "omnium infelicissimum hominum! heri mihi dies infelix pollicem abstulit; hic dies infelicior filium unicum demersit in puteum et ecce de thesauro regis requiror. beneficium mihi misero praebueris, si me ab hac vita subtraxeris."

rex autem, cum iuvenem lacrimis perfusum mortem quaerere videret audiretque eum illo ipso die filium perdidisse, hesterno die pollicem, hominem abire sivit, magnam pecuniam pro solatio tribuens.

**ventum esset,** they came
**dolor, -oris** (*m*), grief, anguish
**puteus, -i** (*m*), well
**pro** ( + *abl.*), in front of
**ad liberandum filium,** to free his son
**funis, -is** (*m*), rope
**ad extrahendum puerum,** to drag out the boy
**sursum,** upwards
**quid plura?** to cut a long story short
**suspirium, -i** (*n*), sigh
**imus, -a, -um,** bottom of
**pectus, pectoris** (*n*), chest, breast
**unicus, -a, -um,** only
**beneficium, -i** (*n*), act of kindness, favour
**praebueris,** you will have granted
**perfusus, -a, -um,** drenched
**hesternus, -a, -um,** of yesterday
**pro solatio,** as compensation

**suadeo, -ere** (2), **suasi, suasum** ( + *dat.*) to advise
**proicio, -ere** (3), **-ieci, -iectum,** to throw, cast
**demergo, -ere** (3), **-mersi, -mersum,** to plunge into
**requiro, -ere** (3), **requisivi, requisitum,** to question
**subtraho, -ere** (3), **-traxi, -tractum,** to take away, remove
**tribuo, -ere** (3), **tribui, tributum,** to give, bestow

## Scot-free!

sic iterum rex deceptus senem adiit, rem totam narravit. qua re audita, senex regi "unum" ait "adhuc superest agendum: elige tibi milites fortissimos quadraginta, quorum viginti nigris armis nigrisque equis sint armati, aliique viginti albis equis armisque eiusdem coloris. cadaver ligno pedibus suspensum nocte ac die his militibus custodiendum est, viginti albis hinc, illinc viginti nigris circa cadaver ipsum ordinatis. hi profecto, si vigilanter custodierint, tuum capient furem quia non sinet ipse socium diutius pendere, etiamsi sciat se mortem protinus subiturum esse.

**agendum,** to be done
**quadraginta,** forty
**lignum, -i** (*n*), a tree
**custodiendum est,** must be guarded
**hinc ... illinc,** on one side ..., on the other side

**circa** ( + *acc.*), around
**ordino** (1), to draw up
**profecto,** certainly
**vigilanter,** vigilantly
**etiamsi,** even if
**protinus,** immediately

**decipio, -ere** (3), **-cepi, -ceptum,** to deceive
**eligo, -ere** (3), **elegi, electum,** to choose
**pendeo, -ere** (2), **pependi,** to hang

rex autem, ut dixerat senex, milites circa cadaver ordinavit.
at vero fur, qui opprobrium suum patrisque ferre non poterat,
malebat mori quam diu infeliciter vivere. deliberavit igitur in
animo quomodo aut patrem turpi ludibrio subtraheret aut ipse
una cum eo moreretur. fabricare ergo constituit arma, ab
altera parte alba, nigra ab altera. quibus armatus equum hinc
albo, illinc nigro panno coopertum ascendit, et sic lucente luna
per medios transiit milites ita ut nigra pars armorum eius
viginti albos deciperet et alba pars deciperet nigros, putarent-
que nigri unum esse ex albis, et albi unum ex nigris.

sic ergo venit ad patrem depositumque a ligno asportavit.
milites, cum mane vidissent corpus sublatum esse, confusi
redierunt ad regem narrantes quomodo se miles albis nigrisque
armis partitis decepisset. desperans ergo iam rex perdita
recuperari posse, neque furem neque thesaurum diutius
quaerebat.

**opprobrium, -i** (*n*), insult
**infeliciter,** unhappily, in
  misery
**turpis, -is, -e,** shameful
**ludibrium, -i** (*n*), mockery
**fabrico** (1), to make

**pannus, -i** (*m*), cloth
**coopertus, -a, -um,** covered
**luna, -ae** (*f*), moon
**confusus, -a, -um,** bewildered
**partio** (4), to divide
**despero** (1), to give up hope

# VERBS: Gerundives

1 Look at these sentences:

| | |
|---|---|
| puer **est** lauda**ndus**. | *The boy* **must be** *praised.* |
| discipuli **sunt** punie**ndi**. | *The pupils* **should be** *punished.* |
| urbs **erat** defende**nda**. | *The city* **had to be** *defended.* |
| epistola **erit** scribe**nda**. | *A letter* **will have to be** *written.* |

In these sentences **laudandus, puniendi, defendenda** and **scribenda** are gerundives (verbal adjectives which are passive). You will recognise this part of the verb by **-nd-** at the end of the stem. When used with a part of **esse**, gerundives are translated "must be . . .", "has to be . . .", "should be . . .", "had to be . . ." etc.

2 Compare the following two sentences:

| | |
|---|---|
| vestimenta custodienda sunt. | *The clothes must be guarded.* |
| vestimenta **tibi** custodienda sunt. | *The clothes must be guarded* **by you.** |

In English, the second sentence may also be translated

**You** *must guard the clothes.*

The dative **tibi** has become the subject in English, and the verb has become active.

3 Look at the following sentences:

| | |
|---|---|
| nobis eundum est ad Thermas. | *We must go to the Baths.* |
| tibi egrediendum est. | *You must go out.* |
| furi fugiendum erat. | *The thief had to run away.* |

The best way to translate these sentences is in the active, with the dative supplying the English subject. In such sentences, the gerundive will always end in **-um** (neuter singular).

14

# Exercise 55a

*Paying special attention to the **-nd-** words, translate the following sentences which are based on "The King's Treasure":*

1 rex militi fideli "thesaurus meus" inquit "tibi diligentissime custodiendus est."
2 turris magna regi aedificanda erat.
3 post multos annos miles regi "iam mihi" ait "domum redeundum est."
4 cum plus pecuniae comparare vellent, seni et filio ad turrim silentio noctis adeundum erat.
5 herba viridis in turre incendenda erat.
6 "eheu!" ait pater. "cum me extrahere non possis, tibi caput meum amputandum est."
7 rex dixit melius consilium seni dandum esse.
8 cadaver ad equum fortissimum pedibus alligatum per vicos trahendum erat.
9 viginti milites nigris armis erant armandi.
10 cadaver ex arbore suspensum militibus nocte ac die custodiendum erat.

# Exercise 55b

*Translate:*

1 Papirius propter prudentiam laudandus est.
2 ianua et postes coronis ornandi sunt; dies nuptialis venit.
3 tabulae nuptiales obsignandae sunt.
4 nova nupta super limen tollenda est ne labatur.
5 lectica, in qua iacebat Titus, in domum maxima cum cura ferenda erat; medicus statim arcessendus erat.
6 die Liberalium toga praetexta et bulla consecrandae sunt.
7 Marcus ad Tabularium patri deducendus erat et nomen eius in tabulis publicis inscribendum erat.
8 aestate nobis omnibus ex urbe ad villam eundum erit.

# VERBS: Future Perfect Tense

Look at the following sentences:

> nisi eos **ceperis,** non cessabunt.
> *Unless you catch them, they will not stop.*

> beneficium mihi **praebueris,** si me ab hac vita **subtraxeris.**
> *You will have done me a favour, if you remove me from this life.*

> si vigilanter **custodierint,** furem capient.
> *If they watch carefully, they will capture the thief.*

**ceperis, praebueris, subtraxeris** and **custodierint** are all examples of the future perfect indicative active. You will meet this tense mostly in clauses introduced by **si** (*if*), **nisi** (*unless*), **cum** (*when*), where the verb in the main clause is future tense. You will note that English tends to translate the future perfect, not by its literal meaning "will have . . .", but by a present tense.

The full form of the future perfect indicative active is:

|       |   | Group 1 | Group 2 | Group 3 | Group 4 |
|-------|---|---------|---------|---------|---------|
|       | 1 | portavero | movero | misero | audivero |
| Sing. | 2 | portaveris | moveris | miseris | audiveris |
|       | 3 | portaverit | moverit | miserit | audiverit |
|       | 1 | portaverimus | moverimus | miserimus | audiverimus |
| Plur. | 2 | portaveritis | moveritis | miseritis | audiveritis |
|       | 3 | portaverint | moverint | miserint | audiverint |

It is very similar in form to the perfect subjunctive active. The context will help you decide which it is.

# C. Julius Caesar

*(Photo: The Mansell Collection)*

The final dramatic events of Julius Caesar's life are well known: his crossing of the River Rubicon, the defeat he inflicted on his great rival, Pompey, his meeting with Cleopatra, his victories in Syria, Africa and Spain, his attainment of supreme power, his assassination on the Ides of March, 44 BC.

There was not much hint of this greatness to come, however, until 61 BC when, at the age of thirty-nine, he became Governor of Further Spain and suddenly displayed a genius for generalship. He returned to Rome in 60 BC to stand for the consulship of 59 BC, expecting that he would be given the usual provincial command in the year after his consulship and hoping that it would be one where he would find scope for military conquest.

The Senate, however, was determined to frustrate these dangerous ambitions and decreed that the proconsular responsibility of the consuls of 59 BC was to be "the superintendence of the forests and cattle-drifts of Italy".

Caesar's immediate reaction when he became consul was to team up with the financier, Crassus, and the general, Pompey. Through their influence—their three-man group was known as the First Triumvirate—he obtained as his proconsular province Cisalpine Gaul combined with Illyricum. By a turn of events fortunate for Caesar—in time his luck became proverbial—the Governor of Transalpine Gaul, which was often called simply **Provincia** ("The Province"), died just then and this area was added to Caesar's command.

17

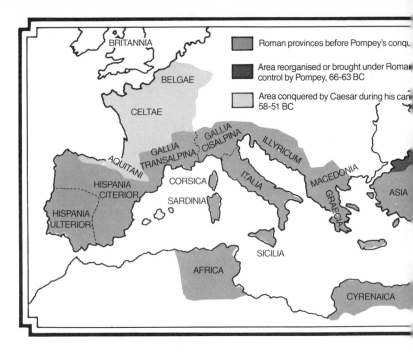

Roman provinces before Pompey's conqu...

Area reorganised or brought under Roma...
control by Pompey, 66-63 BC

Area conquered by Caesar during his can...
58-51 BC

### Commentarii Rerum Gestarum

This was the title given by Caesar to his writings which describe his military campaigns—"Summary Notes of My Campaigns".

The word **commentarii** means notes made at the time of the event, intended by the author to be expanded, by himself or a professional writer, into a full history at a later date; but these "commentaries" of Caesar became so famous in themselves that they have come down to us in their original form.

In the first chapter of Book I of **Commentarii De Bello Gallico** Caesar sketches in the geographical background of Gaul and the way in which the migration of the Helvetii made it necessary, in his view, for him to intervene.

The **Commentarii** are also skilful propaganda. Caesar does not use the pronoun "I" but describes himself as "Caesar" throughout, thus making his exploits more believable since they appear to have been written by a neutral observer. He justifies his every action and describes his own contribution in the best possible light. He does not falsify the facts but he interprets them in such a way that he always seems to be defending Roman interests rather than indulging in conquest for its own sake—which is exactly what his enemies in Rome continually accused him of.

*Map 1* Regions under Roman control.
This map indicates the extent of Roman power
and influence in the Mediterranean area when
Caesar took up his provincial command in
58 BC.

*Map 2* Gaul, 58 BC

BELGAE

Rhenus Fl. (Rhine)

Sequana Fl. (Seine)

Matrona Fl. (Marne)

GERMANI

LATOBRIGI

TULINGI

SEQUANI

RAURACI

BOII

CELTAE (GALLI)

Jura Mons

HELVETII

Lacus
Lemannus

Genava

A l p e s

ALLOBROGES

Garumna Fl. (Garonne)

Rhodanus Fl. (Rhone)

TRANSALPINA

GALLIA
CISALPINA

AQUITANI

GALLIA

- - - - - - Boundary of The Province

| 0 | 50 | 100 | 150 Roman miles |

| 0 | 50 | 100 | 150 | 200 kilometres |

The year is 58 BC. Caesar has just taken over his command of the two Roman provinces—Cisalpine Gaul (north Italy) and Transalpine Gaul (the part of France roughly equivalent to what is now Provence). By studying Map 2, you will see that what he here refers to as **Gallia** covers the rest of France, Belgium and part of Germany and Switzerland.

*line*

1 **omnis:** *(taken) as a whole.*

   **unam:** Supply **partem.** (Compare **aliam** and **tertiam.**) Note how the Latin sentence is condensed:

> **unam (partem) incolunt Belgae**
> **aliam (partem incolunt) Aquitani**
> **tertiam (partem incolunt) (ei) qui . . .**

2 **qui:** Supply **ei.**

   **ipsorum lingua:** *in their own language.*

3 **nostra:** Supply **lingua.**

   **lingua:** *in language.*

4 In the sentence **Gallos . . . dividit,** there is again balance. The verb **dividit** must be understood after **flumen,** and **Gallos** is supplied before **a Belgis.** Although **Matrona et Sequana** is a double subject, **dividit** is singular because the two rivers form a single boundary.

8 **qua de causa:** *for* (literally *from*) *this reason.* "Linking Relative", as usual, refers the reader to previous sentence for an explanation.

9 **Gallos:** Caesar is here thinking of "Gauls" in the wider sense, whereas in the two previous uses he was thinking only of the Celtic Gauls.

12 **M. Messala . . . consulibus:** *in the consulship of Marcus Messala and Marcus Piso.* The Romans had two ways of dating the years in which events happened: one method used the founding of the city as the starting point; the other named the two men who held the consulship in that particular year. Messala and Piso were consuls in 61 BC. Note that the Latin words are in the ablative case, the construction used being the Ablative Absolute. (Compare **me duce,** *under my leadership.*)

13 **regni:** *of royal power.*

14 **civitati:** literally *the state,* i.e. all the people in the state. That is why the verb **exirent** is plural.

15 **perfacile esse:** This is an Accusative and Infinitive depending on **persuasit** (understood). Where the indirect speech is continued beyond the first sentence, it is normal practice for the "speaking" or "thinking" verb not to be repeated. Sometimes, as here, a colon gives a clue to this usage.

# 56
# Caesar's Gallic War

### Description of Gaul

Gallia est omnis divisa in partes tres, quarum unam
incolunt Belgae, aliam Aquitani, tertiam qui ipsorum
lingua Celtae, nostra Galli appellantur. hi omnes lingua,
institutis, legibus inter se differunt. Gallos ab Aquitanis
5   Garumna flumen, a Belgis Matrona et Sequana dividit.
horum omnium fortissimi sunt Belgae proximique sunt
Germanis qui trans Rhenum incolunt, quibuscum continenter bellum gerunt. qua de causa Helvetii quoque
reliquos Gallos virtute praecedunt quod fere cotidianis
10  proeliis cum Germanis contendunt.

### The situation of the Helvetii

apud Helvetios longe nobilissimus fuit et ditissimus
Orgetorix. is, M. Messala et M. Pupio Pisone consulibus,
regni cupiditate inductus coniurationem nobilitatis fecit
et civitati persuasit ut de finibus suis cum omnibus copiis
15  exirent: perfacile esse, cum virtute omnibus praestarent,

| | |
|---|---|
| **appello** (1), to call, name | **cotidianus, -a, -um,** daily |
| **institutum, -i** (*n*), custom | **proelium, -i** (*n*), battle |
| **lex, legis** (*f*), law | **apud** (*+ acc.*), among |
| **flumen, -inis** (*n*), river | **ditissimus, -a, -um,** richest |
| **Garumna, -ae** (*m*), Garonne | **coniuratio, -onis** (*f*), conspiracy |
| **Matrona, -ae** (*m*), Marne | **nobilitas, -atis** (*f*), the nobles |
| **Sequana, -ae** (*m*), Seine | **civitas, -atis** (*f*), state |
| **Rhenus, -i** (*m*), Rhine | **fines, -ium** (*m.pl*), territory |
| **continenter,** continually | **copiae, -arum** (*f.pl*), forces |
| **bellum gerere,** to wage war | **perfacilis, -is, -e,** very easy |
| **virtus, -utis** (*f*), courage | |

**divido, -ere** (3), **-visi, -visum,** to divide, separate
**incolo, -ere** (3), **-colui, -cultum,** to inhabit
**differo, -ferre, distuli, dilatum,** to differ
**praecedo, -ere** (3). **-cessi, -cessum,** to excel, surpass
**contendo, -ere** (3), **-di, -tentum,** to fight
**praesto, -are** (1), **-stiti, -statum** (*+ dat.*), to be superior (to)

16 **imperio potiri:** *to gain control*, in the sense that other tribes would have to do what they ordered. The infinitive **potiri** depends on **perfacile esse**.

**id persuasit:** The pronoun **id** sums up all that was stated in the previous sentence, i.e. the Indirect Command and the Accusative and Infinitive depending on **persuasit** in line 14. Translate *he persuaded them (to follow) that course of action.*

**hoc facilius . . . quod:** *all the more easily because.* **hoc** is ablative case: literally *by this much.*

17 **loci natura:** literally *by the nature of the place*, i.e. *by natural barriers.* Study the details in the map on page 19.

**una ex parte:** *on the one side.*

18 **atque altissimo: atque** is a stronger link than **et**; it joins two words of which the stronger/more important is the one which follows **atque**, whereas **et** joins two words/ideas of equal value. Translate *and also very deep.*

19 **monte Iura:** Note that English calls this mountain range *the Jura Mountains.*

20 **tertia:** Supply **ex parte**.

23 **his rebus fiebat ut:** literally *from these things it came about that*, i.e. *the consequence of this was that.*

**minus late:** *less widely.*

24 **qua ex parte:** *for this reason.*

25 **homines afficiebantur: homines** is not the subject of the sentence, but stands in apposition to *they.* Translate *being people.*

**bellandi:** genitive of the gerund depending on **cupidi**: literally *desirous of going to war*, i.e. *eager to go to war.*

**pro multitudine:** *in proportion to the number.* The comparison is with **angustos**. According to Caesar, there were 360 000 Helvetians.

26 **pro gloria belli:** Latin, as usual, uses the genitive to link the two nouns, but English would say *glory in war*, i.e. their *military prestige.*

27 **in longitudinem patebant:** (*they*) *extended in length*, i.e. North to South. **milia passuum CCXL:** literally *240 000 paces*, i.e. *240 miles.* Note that, although 1000 is expressed by the adjective **mille**, the plural *thousands* is expressed by the noun **milia** and, as usual, the noun depending on it (**passuum**) is in the genitive case (compare line 26).

A *pace* (**passus**) was approximately 5 feet, being the distance a Roman soldier would cover in two steps (i.e. the distance between the point where one foot landed to the point where it came down again). The Roman mile was therefore roughly 100 yards shorter than the British mile.

totius Galliae imperio potiri. id hoc facilius eis persuasit quod undique loci natura Helvetii continentur; una ex parte flumine Rheno latissimo atque altissimo, qui agrum Helvetium a Germanis dividit; altera ex parte monte Iura
20 altissimo, qui est inter Sequanos et Helvetios; tertia lacu Lemanno et flumine Rhodano, qui provinciam nostram ab Helvetiis dividit.

his rebus fiebat ut et minus late vagarentur et minus facile finitimis bellum inferre possent. qua ex parte
25 homines bellandi cupidi magno dolore afficiebantur. pro multitudine autem hominum et pro gloria belli angustos se fines habere arbitrabantur, qui in longitudinem milia passuum CCXL, in latitudinem CLXXX patebant.

**imperium, -i** (*n*), command
**mons, montis** (*m*), mountain
**lacus Lemannus,** Lake Geneva
**Rhodanus, -i** (*m*), Rhône
**provincia, -ae** (*f*), province
**finitimus, -i** (*m*), neighbour

**bello** (1), to make war
**angustus, -a, -um,** narrow
**pateo** (2), to lie open, extend

**potior, -iri** (4), **potitus sum** ( + *abl.*), to gain possession (of)
**vagor, -ari** (1), **-atus sum,** to wander
**arbitror, -ari,** (1), **-atus sum,** to think
**afficio, -ere** (3), **affeci, affectum,** to affect, fill

29 **auctoritate: auctoritas** is the *influence, ability to persuade* which a leader
can bring to bear on other people, mainly through the strength of his
personality or the esteem which people attach to his position.

30 **ad proficiscendum pertinerent:** literally *had reference to setting out*, i.e.
*were necessary for setting out*. The word **proficiscendum** is not the
gerundive, but a verbal noun called the gerund, the use of which is
explained on page 26. (Cf. **bellandi** in line 25.)
**pertinerent:** The use of the subjunctive shows that this clause was part
of what the Helvetii were thinking when they came to their decision
(subordinate clause in indirect speech). Contrast line 28 above where
the use of the indicative **patebant** indicates that it is Caesar (the author)
who is making the point and not the Helvetii.

31 **comparare:** This and the three other infinitives all depend on
**constituerunt.**

34 **ad eas res conficiendas:** *to complete those preparations*. This method of
expressing Purpose is explained on page 36.

35 **duxerunt:** *they thought*.
**in tertium annum confirmant:** literally *they put it firmly into the third
year*, i.e. *they fixed it for two years later*. Caesar has slipped into the
present tense (**confirmant**). He frequently does this in his narrative.

36 **lege:** By passing a law they made certain that the leaders two years
later could not change their minds about migrating.

37 **ad eam rem:** *for that undertaking*. Caesar uses the word **res** frequently
and with various meanings. The reader must rely on the context to
decide on the best translation.

38 **oppida . . . vicos:** The **oppida** would be fortified, whereas the **vici** would
be open villages.
**ad duodecim:** When used with numerals, **ad** means *about, up to*.

39 **reliqua privata aedificia:** In this context, **reliqua** means, not *the
remaining*, but *as well as*. These private buildings would probably be
standing on their own, outside the towns and villages.
**incendunt:** Note how this sentence is balanced, with the verb **incendunt**
having to be understood with each of the objects:

| | | |
|---|---|---|
| oppida sua omnia | numero ad duodecim | (incendunt) |
| vicos | (numero) ad quadringentos | (incendunt) |
| reliqua privata aedificia | | incendunt. |

42 **ad omnia pericula subeunda:** Compare line 34 for this way of expressing
Purpose. Translate *to undergo all the dangers (which awaited them)*.

43 **eodem usi consilio:** Although separated from it by **usi, eodem** agrees
with **consilio**. The perfect participle **usi** (literally *having used*) and the
Ablative Absolute (**oppidis ... exustis**) should be translated in the same
way as the main verb **proficiscantur**. Translate *to adopt the same plan,
to burn . . ., and to set out*.

### They prepare to migrate

his rebus adducti et auctoritate Orgetorigis permoti
30  constituerunt ea quae ad proficiscendum pertinerent
comparare, iumentorum et carrorum quam maximum
numerum coemere, sementes quam maximas facere ut in
itinere copia frumenti suppeteret, cum proximis civitatibus pacem et amicitiam confirmare. ad eas res conficien-
35  das biennium sibi satis esse duxerunt. in tertium annum
profectionem lege confirmant.

ubi iam se ad eam rem paratos esse arbitrati sunt,
oppida sua omnia numero ad duodecim, vicos ad
quadringentos, reliqua privata aedificia incendunt; frum-
40  entum omne praeterquam quod secum portaturi erant
comburunt ut, domum reditionis spe sublata, paratiores
ad omnia pericula subeunda essent. persuadent Rauracis
et Tulingis et Latobrigis finitimis ut, eodem usi consilio,
oppidis suis vicisque exustis, una cum eis proficiscantur.
45  Boiosque, qui trans Rhenum incoluerant et in agrum
Noricum transierant Noreiamque oppugnarant, receptos
ad se socios sibi adsciscunt.

| | |
|---|---|
| **auctoritas, -atis** (*f*), influence | **confirmo** (1), to establish |
| **permotus, -a, -um,** persuaded | **biennium, -i** (*n*), (a period of) |
| **iumentum, -i** (*n*), a beast of | two years |
| burden | **profectio, -onis** (*f*), departure |
| **carrus, -i** (*m*), (two-wheeled) | **praeterquam quod,** apart from what |
| wagon | **reditio, -onis** (*f*), return |
| **sementis, -is** (*f*), sowing | **spes, spei** (*f*), hope |
| **copia, -ae** (*f*), supply | **oppugno** (1), to attack |
| **frumentum, -i** (*n*), corn | **sibi,** to themselves |

**coemo, -ere** (3), **coemi, coemptum,** to buy up
**suppeto, -ere** (3), **-petivi, -petitum,** to be sufficient
**duco, -ere** (3), **duxi, ductum,** to think, consider
**tollo, -ere** (3), **sustuli, sublatum,** to lift, raise, remove
**exuro, -ere** (3), **exussi, exustum,** to burn up
**adscisco, -ere** (3), **adscivi, adscitum,** to attach

---

46  **oppugnarant:** This is a contracted form of **oppugnaverant.**

**receptos ad se socios sibi adsciscunt: socios** is used in apposition to
**receptos,** i.e. *having been received as allies.* English would more
naturally treat **receptos** as an active main verb in parallel with
**adsciscunt,** i.e. *they welcomed . . . and added.*

# VERBS: Gerunds (Verbal Nouns)

Look at the following examples:

> quis creabitur arbiter **bibendi**?
> *Who will be made master* **of drinking**?

> nunc tempus est **bibendi**.
> *Now is the time* **for drinking**.

> finem **recitandi** fecit.
> *She made an end* **of reciting** (i.e. she stopped reciting).

> homines **bellandi** cupidi
> *men desirous* **of fighting** (*keen* **on fighting**)

The words **bibendi, recitandi** and **bellandi** are examples of the gerund (verbal noun). You will recognise this form by the **-nd-** at the end of the verb stem. The gerund is active and has the same endings as those of the neuter nouns of Group 2.

The gerund is used:

1  In the *genitive case*, often in a phrase with another noun or an adjective. It should be translated by the English verbal noun ending in -*ing* or by the English infinitive, e.g.

> tempus **bibendi**, "time for drinking" or "time to drink"
> **bellandi** cupidi, "keen on fighting" or "keen to fight"
> **praedandi** causa, "for the purpose of plundering" or "to plunder"

2  In the *accusative case* with **ad** to express Purpose. This can often be translated by the English infinitive, e.g.

> respondit se diem **ad deliberandum** sumpturum.
> *He said he would take a day* **to consider**.

> ea quae **ad proficiscendum** pertinebant.
> *the things which related* **to setting out**.

3  In the *ablative case*, e.g.

> unus homo nobis **cunctando** restituit rem.
> *One man* **by delaying** *restored the state to us*.

> (said of Q. Fabius Maximus Cunctator, who successfully used delaying tactics against Hannibal.)

Note that, in translating a gerund, English tends to use either the verbal noun ending in *-ing* or the English infinitive:

**signum progrediendi,** the signal to advance (for advancing)
**tempus proficiscendi,** time to set out (for setting out)
**laborando,** by working
**occasio effugiendi,** a chance to escape (of escaping)
**paratus ad resistendum,** ready to resist (for resisting)

## Exercise 56a

*Translate:*

1 iam omnia parata sunt ad proficiscendum.
2 "mox tempus erit exeundi" inquit Orgetorix.
3 occasionem petebat finitimis persuadendi.
4 brevi tempore ad castra celeriter ambulando pervenimus.
5 milites laborando defessi fiebant.
6 pauci discipuli discendi cupidi sunt.
7 milites flumen natando transire non poterant.
8 occasio redeundi ad urbem ei data est.
9 imperator signum proficiscendi dedit.
10 perseverando omnia vinces.

*Map 3* The alternative routes of the Helvetii and attacks of Ariovistus

48 **erant:** Standing as it does at the beginning of the sentence, this word means *there were*.

**itinera duo, quibus itineribus possent:** Caesar frequently repeats the antecedent noun. Translate *two routes by which they could*.

50 **vix:** Although put in front of **qua** for emphasis, **vix** should be taken with **ducerentur**.

**singuli:** *in single file*.

**ducerentur:** *could be taken*.

51 **ut:** *with the result that*.

53 **expeditius** is the neuter of the comparative adjective: *presenting fewer obstacles*.

54 **nuper:** They had rebelled in 61 BC and had been defeated by Cn. Pontinus, the **praetor** (governor) in charge of the Province.

55 **vado transitur:** *is crossed by a ford*, i.e. *can be forded*.

**nonnullis:** literally *not none*, i.e. *some* or *several*. (Compare **nonnumquam**, *sometimes*, **non nemo**, *someone*.)

56 **extremum:** *last*, i.e. for someone travelling north towards the territory of the Helvetii (see map on page 27).

58 **sese vel persuasuros:** Supply **esse**. This is an Accusative and Infinitive depending on **existimabant**. The word **vel** warns you to look for another Accusative and Infinitive to balance this one: **(sese) vi coacturos (esse)**, also depending on **existimabant**.

59 **bono animo (esse) in:** *to be well-disposed towards*.

**viderentur:** The use of the subjunctive indicates that this clause was part of what the Helvetii thought (subordinate clause in indirect speech), and not a comment from the writer. (Compare line 30.)

60 **suos** refers to the Allobroges, **eos** to the Helvetii.

**ut ... paterentur:** This clause depends on both **persuasuros** and **coacturos**.

62 **omnibus rebus:** Note again the use of **res**. As usual, the context will help you to decide on the best English translation. (Compare line 37.)

**diem dicunt, qua die:** Compare line 48 for the repetition of the antecedent noun. When **dies** is used to denote a fixed day or date, it is feminine. In line 64, where it is used in the normal sense of *day*, it is masculine.

63 **conveniant:** Although the clause does not begin with **ut**, it has the force of an Indirect Command depending on the notion "instructing them to" contained in the phrase **diem dicunt**. Translate *(a date on which) they were to assemble*.

## The alternative routes

erant omnino itinera duo, quibus itineribus domo exire
possent: unum per Sequanos angustum et difficile, inter
50　Iuram et flumen Rhodanum, vix qua singuli carri ducerentur; mons autem altissimus impendebat ut facile perpauci prohibere possent; alterum per provinciam nostram
multo facilius atque expeditius, propterea quod inter fines
Helvetiorum et Allobrogum, qui nuper pacati erant,
55　Rhodanus fluit isque nonnullis locis vado transitur.

extremum oppidum Allobrogum est proximumque
Helvetiorum finibus Genava. ex eo oppido pons ad
Helvetios pertinet. Allobrogibus sese vel persuasuros,
quod nondum bono animo in populum Romanum vider-
60　entur, existimabant, vel vi coacturos ut per suos fines eos
ire paterentur.

omnibus rebus ad profectionem comparatis, diem
dicunt, qua die ad ripam Rhodani omnes conveniant.
is dies erat a.d. V Kal.Apr. L.Pisone, A. Gabinio
65　consulibus.

| | |
|---|---|
| **omnino,** altogether | **propterea quod,** because, |
| **singuli, -ae, -a,** singly, one at | inasmuch as |
| a time | **paco** (1), to pacify |
| **impendeo** (2), to hang over | **vadum, -i** (*n*), ford |
| **prohibeo** (2), to prevent | **extremus, -a, -um,** last |
| **expeditus, -a, -um,** | **existimo** (1), to think, |
| unencumbered | consider |
| | **ripa, -ae** (*f*), bank (of a river) |

**cogo, -ere** (3), **coegi, coactum,** to compel, force
**patior, pati** (3), **passus sum,** to allow

---

64　**a.d. V Kal.Apr.:** Shortened version of **ante diem quintum Kalendas
Apriles,** *the fifth day before the Kalends of April,* which, by inclusive
reckoning, is 28th March.

**L.Pisone A.Gabinio consulibus:** See line 12 for this method used by the
Romans to record dates. The year is 58 BC.

66 **Caesari:** Note the emphatic position of this word. So far, Caesar has been describing the background to his taking over command in Gaul. In this chapter, he suddenly throws himself into the limelight as far as the reader is concerned. Note too that he refers to himself as "Caesar" and not "I" or "me".

**id** refers to what has been said in the previous section, but the idea is summarised in the Accusative and Infinitive (**eos . . . conari**) which follows and is in apposition to **id**. Translate the Accusative and Infinitive as *namely, that they . . ..*

67 **maturat:** The subject is "he", i.e. Caesar.

**ab urbe:** *from the vicinity of the city,* i.e. Rome.

68 **quam maximis potest itineribus: iter** is used for the normal distance covered by a Roman army in one day—a fairly standard figure of 32 kilometres, because of the existence of paved roadways constructed to facilitate the movement of the army from place to place. A **magnum iter** was a *forced march,* i.e. the army covered a greater distance than usual because of some emergency. There was no limit to a *forced march,* and we are told here that Caesar marched his troops as far as he possibly could each day. One writer says he covered the distance in seven days, averaging 144 kilometres (90 miles) per day.

**quam** with a superlative means *as . . . as possible.* The expression used by Caesar here indicates how this use came into being. It is contracted from a much longer expression, e.g. **contendit itineribus tam maximis quam potest contendere**—*he hastened by marches as great as he was able to hasten.*

**in Galliam ulteriorem:** This was the province beyond the Alps (as seen from the Italian side) and was sometimes called **Gallia Transalpina**.

69 **ad Genavam:** *in the vicinity of Geneva,* the usual meaning when **ad** is used with the **name** of a town.

**provinciae . . . numerum imperat:** Caesar frequently uses **imperare** in the same way as English uses *to order goods from.* The person to whom the instruction is given appears in the dative case, and what he is ordered to provide is put in the accusative.

**quam maximum potest numerum:** Compare line 68.

71 **legio una:** This was the Tenth Legion, Caesar's favourite legion.

72 **iubet:** The paragraph which you have just translated illustrates very well how fond Caesar is of the Historic Present (**maturat, contendit, pervenit, imperat, iubet**) which he uses to add vividness to his narrative.

## Caesar reacts

Caesari cum id nuntiatum esset eos per provinciam nostram iter facere conari, maturat ab urbe proficisci et quam maximis potest itineribus in Galliam ulteriorem contendit et ad Genavam pervenit. provinciae toti quam
70    maximum potest militum numerum imperat (erat omnino in Gallia ulteriore legio una), pontem qui erat ad Genavam iubet rescindi.

ubi de eius adventu Helvetii certiores facti sunt, legatos ad eum mittunt nobilissimos civitatis qui dicerent sibi esse
75    in animo sine ullo maleficio iter per provinciam facere, propterea quod aliud iter haberent nullum: rogare ut eius voluntate id sibi facere liceat.

**maturo** (1), to hasten
**ulterior, -oris,** farther
**legio, -onis** (*f*), legion
**adventus, -us** (*m*), arrival
**certiorem facere,** to inform

**legatus, -i,** (*m*), ambassador
**maleficium, -i** (*n*), causing of
    damage, mischief
**voluntas, -atis** (*f*), wish,
    willingness, good will

**rescindo, -ere** (3), **-scidi, -scissum,** to break down

---

73 **legatos:** Either take this as the object of **mittunt** with **nobilissimos** in apposition, or regard **nobilissimos** as the object and translate **legatos** in apposition: *as ambassadors.*

74 **qui dicerent:** This is a Purpose clause in which **qui** replaces **ut**, a very common use where the relative refers back to someone or some people "who were to" do something.

    **sibi** refers to the Helvetii. **sibi esse in animo** is an Indirect Statement depending on **dicerent.**

76 **haberent:** The use of the subjunctive indicates that this clause is part of what they were to say (subordinate clause in indirect speech). (Compare lines 30 and 59.)

    **nullum:** Note the very emphatic position given to this word.

    **rogare:** Supply **se**—an Accusative and Infinitive depending on **dicerent.** As usual, when indirect speech is continued into a second sentence, the verb of "speaking" is not repeated. (Compare line 15, and again note the clue supplied by the colon.)

78 **memoria tenebat . . . concedendum non putabat:** Caesar deliberately emphasises his personal attitude, one which would find favour with Roman opinion. It must be remembered that Caesar was a politician and it is therefore not surprising that he should use his military writings to promote his own political reputation. (Compare the reference to **homines inimico animo** in line 81.)

**L. Cassium occisum:** This had happened in 107 BC. Note that **esse** must be supplied with **occisum, pulsum** and **missum**.

79 **sub iugum:** The "yoke" consisted of two spears stuck in the ground with a third strapped across the top. A conquered army was forced to pass unarmed under the yoke, as a sign of complete submission. Caesar was intent on wiping out the disgrace that had been inflicted on Cassius by the Helvetii.

80 **concedendum:** Supply **esse**. It means literally *that it should (not) be conceded*, i.e. *permission should (not) be given*.

**neque:** Take this with **existimabat** (line 83)—*nor did he think that*. The Accusative and Infinitive **homines . . . temperaturos (esse)** depends on **existimabat**.

81 **inimico animo:** an Ablative of Description to be taken with **homines**, *men of hostile intent*.

**data facultate:** This Ablative Absolute is best translated by an "if" clause.

83 **dum . . . convenirent:** yet another way of expressing Purpose—*until (they) might assemble*, i.e. *to give them time to assemble*.

84 **imperaverat** is used here in the same sense as it was in line 70. Translate *he had levied*.

85 **diem:** not *a day* here, but *time*. It is the object of **sumpturum (esse)**.

**ad deliberandum:** another Purpose expression involving a gerund.

**quid:** As usual, after **si, quid** means *anything*.

**ad Id.Apr. = ad Idus Apriles**—on the Ides (13th) of April.

86 **reverterentur:** The verb **respondit** is followed by
      (a) the Accusative and Infinitive **se . . . sumpturum (esse)**
      (b) the Indirect Command **(ut) reverterentur**.

Caesar, quod memoria tenebat L. Cassium consulem occisum exercitumque eius ab Helvetiis pulsum et sub

80 iugum missum, concedendum non putabat; neque homines inimico animo, data facultate per provinciam itineris faciendi, temperaturos ab iniuria et maleficio existimabat. tamen, ut spatium intercedere posset dum milites quos imperaverat convenirent, legatis respondit

85 diem se ad deliberandum sumpturum; si quid vellent, ad Id.Apr. reverterentur.

**exercitus, -us** (*m*), army
**iugum, -i** (*n*), yoke
**inimicus, -a, -um,** hostile
**facultas, -atis** (*f*), opportunity

**tempero** (1), to refrain
**iniuria, -ae** (*f*), injury, wrong-doing
**spatium, -i** (*n*), space, interval

**occido, -ere** (3), **occidi, occisum,** to kill
**concedo, -ere** (3), **-cessi, -cessum,** to yield, give permission
**intercedo, -ere** (3), **-cessi, -cessum,** to intervene

Roman soldiers suffering the humiliation of being sent, unarmed, "under the yoke"

33

87 **ea legione:** *with that legion,* i.e. *using that legion.* (Compare **militibus.**)
No preposition is used since the legion and the soldiers are regarded as
the *instruments* used to construct these defences, rather than as people.

90 **perducit:** The usual phrase for building a wall is **murum ducere.** The
verb **perducere** is used here to indicate that the defences were complete
all the way. In actual fact, it was not necessary to construct nineteen
miles of defences since (apart from 3–4 miles) the south bank of the
Rhône is so steep that no man-made defences were necessary.

91 **praesidia disponit:** The prefix **dis-**, as often, means *at intervals* or *at
various points.*

**quo facilius:** When a Purpose clause contains a comparative adjective
or adverb, it is introduced by **quo** rather than **ut.**

92 **se invito:** an Ablative Absolute meaning *against his wishes.*

93 **ea dies: dies** is again feminine, since it refers to *the appointed day.*
(Compare line 63.)

94 **negat se posse:** *he said that he could not.*

**more et exemplo:** *in accordance with the tradition and practice.*

96 **vim facere:** *to use force.*

**prohibiturum:** Supply **se** and **esse.**

98 **alii:** Caesar has condensed the description. Implicit in the Ablative
Absolute (**navibus . . . factis**) is the idea that the majority of them used
boats or rafts. When he writes **alii** (in line 98), he seems to assume that
the Ablative Absolute also represents an **alii** clause: *some . . . others . . .*

**qua:** *where.*

99 **nonnumquam:** Compare line 55.

100 **operis munitione:** literally *by fortification (consisting) of the work,* i.e.
*the rampart which they had erected.*

101 **concursu:** The soldiers rushed to reinforce the point where the Helvetii
were making the attack.

## Invasion repelled

interea ea legione, quam secum habebat, militibusque, qui ex provincia convenerant, a lacu Lemanno ad montem Iuram milia passuum decem novem murum in altitu-
90 dinem pedum sedecim fossamque perducit. eo opere perfecto, praesidia disponit, castella communit quo facilius, si se invito transire conarentur, prohibere posset.

ubi ea dies, quam constituerat cum legatis, venit et legati ad eum reverterunt, negat se more et exemplo
95 populi Romani posse iter ulli per provinciam dare; et, si vim facere conentur, prohibiturum ostendit.

Helvetii ea spe deiecti, navibus iunctis ratibusque compluribus factis, alii vadis Rhodani, qua minima altitudo fluminis erat, nonnumquam interdiu, saepius
100 noctu perrumpere conati sunt. operis tamen munitione et militum concursu et telis repulsi, hoc conatu destiterunt.

**fossa, -ae** (*f*), ditch
**opus, operis** (*n*), work
**praesidium, -i** (*n*), garrison
**castellum, -i** (*n*), fort
**communio** (4), to fortify
**exemplum, -i** (*n*), example

**ratis, -is** (*f*), raft
**munitio, -onis** (*f*), fortification
**concursus, -us** (*m*), rushing
  together, massing
**telum, -i** (*n*), weapon
**conatus, -us** (*m*), attempt

**perficio, -ere** (3), **-feci, -fectum,** to finish
**dispono, -ere** (3), **-posui, -positum,** to station at intervals
**ostendo, -ere** (3), **-endi, -entum,** to show
**deicio, -ere** (3), **-ieci, -iectum,** to cast down
**desisto, -ere** (3), **destiti,** to cease, give up

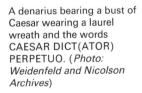

A denarius bearing a bust of Caesar wearing a laurel wreath and the words CAESAR DICT(ATOR) PERPETUO. (*Photo: Weidenfeld and Nicolson Archives*)

# VERBS: Gerunds and Gerundives

Sometimes the type of expression mentioned on page 26 is expanded by the insertion of yet another noun, e.g.

occasio **scribendi**             *a chance* **of writing**
occasio **epistolae scribendae**    *a chance* **of writing a letter**

Note that in the second example the noun and verbal adjective (gerundive) form a phrase in the genitive depending on **occasio**. When translating such a phrase into English, make the noun the object of the English verbal noun or infinitive. Compare the following examples:

**paratus ad scribendum**
*prepared to write (for writing)*

**paratus ad epistolas scribendas**
*prepared to write letters (for writing letters)*

**ars scribendi**
*the art of writing*

**ars libri scribendi**
*the art of writing a book*

**facultas itineris faciendi**
*an opportunity to make a journey*

**ad eas res conficiendas**
*(with a view) to completing those preparations*

**ad omnia pericula subeunda**
*to undergo all the dangers*

**proelii committendi signum**
*the signal for joining (to join) battle*

**pacis petendae causa**
*to ask for peace* (literally *for the sake of seeking peace*)

## Exercise 56b

*Translate:*

1 miles cupidus erat pugnandi.
2 rex thesauri custodiendi cupidus erat.
3 rex ad senem quendam venit ad consilium quaerendum.

4 pater populum convocavit quasi ad filium parvum liberandum.
5 occasio pacis petendae Helvetiis non dabitur.
6 hostes facultatem regrediendi non dederunt.
7 Caesar milites suos itinere defessos procedere ad oppugnanda castra iubere noluit.
8 sumus ad dimicandum parati.
9 tam altum est flumen ut id transire natando non possimus.
10 occasionem thesauri auferendi petebant.

# How to translate Gerunds and Gerundives

The following strategy should help you to translate phrases which contain gerunds or gerundives.

1 If the "gerund/gerundive word" is in the nominative case or in the accusative case without **ad**, translate it as *must be, have to be*, etc., e.g.

**puer laudandus est.**
*The boy must be praised.*

**scimus puerum laudandum esse.**
*We know that the boy must be praised.*

Note that the verb **esse** is usually in this construction, or is understood.

2 If the "gerund/gerundive word" is in the accusative with **ad**, or in the genitive, dative or ablative, translate it as *to* or *-ing*, e.g.

**ad cohortandos milites**
*to encourage the soldiers*

**signum pugnandi**
*the signal for fighting*

**signum proelii committendi**
*the signal to join battle*

**ambulando**
*by walking*

37

# Exercise 56c

*Translate into English, first checking the case of the gerund or gerundive:*

1 Helvetiis, quod proximi erant Germanis, bellum continenter erat gerendum.
2 bello continenter gerendo Helvetii fortissimi facti sunt.
3 ad amicitiam confirmandam legatos per proximas civitates mittebant.
4 arbitrati sunt pacem et amicitiam cum proximis civitatibus esse confirmandam.
5 Caesari, cum id nuntiatum esset, putabat provinciam esse defendendam.
6 provinciae defendendae causa in Galliam ulteriorem contendit.
7 murus in altitudinem sedecim pedum a lacu Lemanno militibus perducendus erat.
8 muro alto perducendo sperabant se Helvetios transire prohibituros esse.
9 ad flumen transeundum Helvetiis rates quam plurimae erant faciendae.
10 Caesar non putabat facultatem itineris per provinciam faciendi Helvetiis esse concedendam.

# The Roman Army

The smallest self-supporting and independent unit in the Roman army was the legion (**legio**) containing nominally 6000 men, split up into ten cohorts (**cohortes**), each cohort into three maniples (**manipuli**), and each maniple into two centuries (**centuriae**).

1 legion = 10 cohorts = 60 centuries = 6000 men

| *Legion drawn up in 10 cohorts* | | | |
|---|---|---|---|
| IV | III | II | I |
| | VII | VI | V |
| | X | IX | VIII |

| *Cohort drawn up in 6 centuries* | | |
|---|---|---|
| III | II | I |
| VI | V | IV |

In practice, the legion seldom numbered more than 5000 and a legion in Caesar's army was about 4000, with about 60 men in each so-called century.

A centurion (**centurio**), an experienced veteran, or his deputy (**optio**), commanded each century and each centurion carried a vine-staff (**vitis**) as a symbol of his authority. Some centurions even used their vine-staffs to mete out punishment, and one such was known to his men as **Cedo Alteram** ("Give me another staff") because he was always breaking them in anger over the backs of his victims.

Senior centurions (**primi ordines**) served in the First Cohort, and at their head was the chief centurion (**primipilus**).

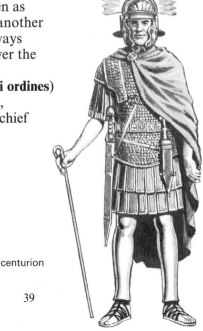

centurion

39

signifer

aquilifer

Every century had its own standard (**signum**) and standard-bearer (**signifer**).

Each legion had a number and usually a name as well, derived from a god (e.g. **Minervia**) or from its insignia (e.g. **Alauda**, "the lark") or from its reputation (e.g. **Victrix**, "victorious"). It had a silver or gold standard in the form of a pole surmounted by an eagle with outstretched wings (**aquila**) and a standard-bearer (**aquilifer**). The loss of a standard was considered so serious that it could lead to the disbandment of a legion.

The regular troops in the legion were mostly heavy-armed infantry (**pedites**). There were 300 cavalry (**equites**). The extra-legionary troops included the **cohors praetoria** (a special bodyguard of the general, picked from veterans), **fabri** (engineers) and the **auxilia** (auxiliary forces). The **auxilia** were composed of light-armed troops (**milites levis armaturae**), including **funditores** who slung stones (**lapides missiles**) or lead bullets (**glandes**), **sagittarii** (archers) and **calones** (servants who looked after the baggage).

The commander of a legion was usually a **legatus**, a word which means basically a deputy chosen by the general. Caesar had ten **legati** in Gaul, many of whom not only commanded legions but were often sent on independent missions with full powers.

Below the **legatus** were six **tribuni militum** in each legion.

legatus

These were usually young men who were serving with the army to gain administrative experience before returning to civilian life; but during campaigns they sometimes took command, occasionally with outstanding success.

Cavalry and auxiliary troops were generally recruited from Rome's provincial allies, infantry being organised in cohorts and cavalry in squadrons (**alae**, literally "wings"). These troops were commanded by a **praefectus** who was normally, but not invariably, a Roman. On discharge, these auxiliaries received Roman citizenship.

Battle tactics varied, but generally the **vexillum**, a red flag, was displayed as a signal for attack, a bugle or trumpet (**tuba**) called the troops to fall in beside their standards (**signa**) which acted as reference points for all manoeuvres, e.g. **signa inferre**, "to attack"; **signa convertere**, "to wheel". First contact with the enemy would be made by cavalry and light troops. Legionaries began their attack by throwing the javelin (**pilum**) before making hand-to-hand contact with the enemy with the short stabbing-sword (**gladius**).

# The Soldier's Equipment

In the early empire, the Roman soldier could expect reasonable conditions and prospects in the army. Pay was adequate and allowed for some savings, even after deductions for food rations, clothing, armour, the annual dinner and the burial fund. There was the further prospect of a money payment with every new emperor, and a money grant with discharge after twenty-five years' service.

The soldier's defensive equipment consisted of bronze and iron helmet (**galea**) and body armour (**lorica**), made up either of a form of chain-mail or of overlapping metal strips to allow the maximum freedom of movement—in either case this was worn over a woollen **tunica**. Boots (**caligae**) with stout leather soles and hobnails were always worn and, in cold climates, leather trousers (**bracae**) often formed part of the general attire. To complete his body protection, the soldier carried a large, semi-cylindrical shield (**scutum**) of leather and wood with a central boss and metal binding.

His weapons were the two-edged stabbing-sword (**gladius**) carried on the right side and slung on a separate belt (**balteus**), a dagger (**pugio**) and two throwing-spears or javelins (**pila**).

On a normal march the soldier was heavily laden (**impeditus**). His kit-load has been assessed at eighteen kilograms (60 Roman pounds) and as much again in weapons and armour. It is therefore not surprising that ancient writers have likened the soldier to a pack-animal. He carried a pack with three days' rations (about three kilograms of wholemeal flour, vegetables and low quality wine), cooking utensils (**vasa**), entrenching tools—including hatchet, spade and basket—and stakes for the camp palisade (**vallum**). Heavy equipment (**impedimenta**), such as leather tents and corn grinders, was carried by the pack animals (**iumenta**).

A normal day's march was thirty-two kilometres covered in about five hours: at the end of this, a camp would be built. In emergencies, the army might make a forced march (**magnum iter**). At all times great stress was laid on strict drill and arduous training.

Centurions and officers had a more decorative uniform, especially a moulded bronze breast-plate to protect the body. Senior officers wore a special scarlet cloak (**paludamentum**).

A Roman legionary soldier of the early first century AD. Painting by P. Compton. (*Reproduced by courtesy of the Trustees of the British Museum*)

In the years 58 BC and 57 BC Caesar, having halted the Helvetii and forced them to return to their homeland, penetrated even farther into Gaul, dealt with the Germans under Ariovistus and then found himself facing the formidable Belgians. The following extracts from Book II of the *Gallic War* describe his encounter with the most warlike of the Belgian tribes – the Nervii.

In the battle described in the first passage the Nervii put up very fierce resistance and would have defeated the Romans if Caesar had not intervened personally.

*line*

2 **equitum:** This refers to the cavalry of the Nervii.

3 **altitudo:** Note how this word governs two genitives—*the depth of the river* and *a depth of about three feet.*

4 **subsequebatur:** The force of the prefix **sub-** is *right up under,* i.e. *very close to.*

5 **consuetudine sua:** *according to his habit,* i.e. *as usual.*

6 **expeditas:** The derivation of this word is **ex** and **pedes,** suggesting that obstacles have been removed from among the feet. When this happens, people are able to move more quickly. The term is then extended to the removal of any impediment and so, in the case of soldiers, it came to mean *without their baggage.* The opposite is **impeditus,** *hindered,* i.e. *with their baggage.*

7 **inde:** This word may refer to time or place, i.e. *from there* or *from that time (after that).*

8 **agmen claudebant:** *brought up the rear.*

**praesidio erant:** Latin uses a number of nouns in the dative case along with a part of **esse** in such a way that they are best translated by a verb. For example, this phrase means literally *they were for a guard to* ..., i.e. *they guarded.* Compare **auxilio erant omnibus,** *they helped everyone.* This construction is called Predicative Dative.

13 **cedentes:** The participle is used as a noun, *the retreating Gauls.*

15 **opere dimenso:** Before the camp was made, surveyors measured out the outer limits of the camp. This procedure was followed wherever the army was, so that each soldier knew exactly what he had to do.

16 **prima impedimenta:** *the head of the baggage train.*

17 **quod tempus . . . convenerat:** *the time which had been agreed.*

# 57

# The War against the Nervii

**First contact with the enemy**

intra silvas hostes in occulto sese continebant. in aperto loco secundum flumen paucae stationes equitum videbantur. fluminis erat altitudo pedum circiter trium.

Caesar, equitatu praemisso, subsequebatur omnibus
5  copiis. quod hostibus appropinquabat, consuetudine sua sex legiones expeditas ducebat; post eas totius exercitus impedimenta collocaverat; inde duae legiones, quae proxime conscriptae erant, totum agmen claudebant praesidioque impedimentis erant. equites nostri cum fun-
10  ditoribus sagittariisque flumen transgressi cum hostium equitatu proelium commiserunt. cum se illi identidem in silvas ad suos reciperent ac rursus ex silva in nostros impetum facerent neque nostri cedentes longius insequi auderent, interim legiones sex, quae primae venerant,
15  opere dimenso, castra munire coeperunt.

**A desperate situation**

ubi prima impedimenta nostri exercitus ab iis, qui in silvis abditi latebant, visa sunt (quod tempus inter eos commit-

occultus, -a, -um, hidden
secundum flumen, along the river
statio, -onis (*f*), outpost
circiter, about
equitatus, -us (*m*), cavalry
consuetudo, -inis (*f*), custom
expeditus, -a, -um, without baggage
impedimenta, -orum (*n.pl*), baggage

colloco (1), to place
proxime, most recently
agmen, -inis (*n*), (army) column
identidem, repeatedly
sui, suorum (*m.pl*), his men
interim, meanwhile
dimensus, -a, -um, measured
castra, -orum (*n.pl*), camp
munio (4), to fortify
abditus, -a, -um, hidden

conscribo, -ere (3), -scripsi, -scriptum, to recruit
insequor, -i (3), -secutus sum, to pursue closely

*line*

19 **his** refers to the cavalry.

22 **in manibus nostris:** *locked in hand to hand fighting with our troops.*

Note how the repeated use of **et** reinforces the phrase **paene uno tempore**.

24 **eos:** accusative after **ad**.

**opere** refers to the task of fortifying the camp.

26 **proponendum:** Supply **erat**. (Compare **dandum** in line 27.) Similarly, supply **erant** with **revocandi**.

28 **aggeris:** *material for the rampart.*

29 **quarum rerum:** an example of "Linking Relative". This phrase summarises all the actions just mentioned. Note how fond Caesar is of **res**.

31 **impediebat:** Although there are two subjects (**brevitas** and **incursus**), this verb agrees with the nearer one.

**erant subsidio:** Predicative Dative. Compare line 8.

*Map 4* The thrust through Gaul, 57–56 BC

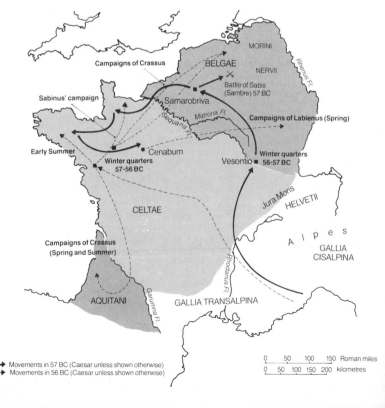

tendi proelii convenerat) subito omnibus copiis provol-
averunt impetumque in nostros equites fecerunt. his
20 facile pulsis ac proturbatis, incredibili celeritate ad flumen
decucurrerunt ut paene uno tempore et ad silvas et in
flumine et iam in manibus nostris hostes viderentur.
eadem autem celeritate adverso colle ad nostra castra
atque eos qui in opere occupati erant contenderunt.

25 Caesari omnia uno tempore erant agenda: vexillum
proponendum (quod erat signum proelii); signum tuba
dandum; ab opere revocandi milites; ei qui paulo longius
aggeris petendi causa processerant, arcessendi; acies
instruenda; milites cohortandi; signum dandum. quarum
30 rerum magnam partem temporis brevitas et incursus
hostium impediebat. his difficultatibus duae res erant
subsidio—scientia atque usus militum.

| | |
|---|---|
| **provolo** (1), to dart forward | **aciem instruere,** to draw up a |
| **proturbo** (1), to throw into |   line of battle |
|   confusion | **brevitas, -atis** (*f*), shortness |
| **adverso colle,** uphill | **incursus, -us** (*m*), attack |
| **vexillum, -i** (*n*), standard | **impedio** (4), to hinder |
| **tuba, -ae** (*f*), trumpet | **subsidium, -i** (*n*), help |
| **agger, -eris** (*m*), rampart | **scientia, -ae** (*f*), knowledge |
| **acies, -iei** (*f*), line of battle | **usus, -us** (*m*), experience |

**propono, -ere** (3), **-posui, -positum,** to display

A Roman sarcophagus depicting a battle between Romans and Gauls. The
Gauls are armed with swords and shields but have no armour to protect them.
(*Photo: The Mansell Collection*)

33 **necessariis rebus imperatis:** Note again the use of **res** (cf. line 30).

35 **non longa:** literally *not long*. Translate *short*.

37 **pugnantibus occurrit:** *he came upon (them) already fighting.*

38 Supply **fuit** with **tam paratus**.

39 **insignia:** These were decorations or feathered crests which had been taken off while the army was marching but which they normally fitted to their helmets before entering battle.

40 **tegimenta:** These were leather cases used to cover the shields when they were not in use.

41 **quae prima signa quisque conspexit, ad haec constitit:** *each man took up position near the standard he saw first.* The relative clause introduced by **quae** comes before its antecedent **haec**, a device commonly used by Latin authors to create more emphasis and dramatic effect.

43 **in tanta rerum iniquitate:** *in such inequality of circumstance,* i.e. some of the troops faced far greater difficulties than others and this affected how different groups of soldiers fared.

44 **fortunae:** genitive with **eventus varii**.

46 **exanimatos:** agrees with **Atrebates**. Expand the participle into a relative clause: *who were out of breath.* The Atrebates were neighbours and allies of the Nervii.

48 **conantes** refers to the Atrebates.

49 **impeditam:** Compare line 6. They were **impediti** since they were not able to move around easily in the water. The adjective agrees with **partem** even though it refers to the men.

50 **in locum iniquum:** either *on to uneven ground* or *on to the steep bank*.

51 **regressos ac resistentes:** a good example of the difference between the meanings of the perfect and present participles.

## Caesar intervenes

Caesar, necessariis rebus imperatis, ad cohortandos milites decucurrit et ad legionem decimam devenit.

35 milites non longa oratione cohortatus, proelii committendi signum dedit. atque in alteram partem item cohortandi causa profectus, pugnantibus occurrit. temporis tanta fuit exiguitas hostiumque tam paratus ad dimicandum animus ut non modo ad insignia accommod-

40 anda sed etiam ad galeas induendas scutisque tegimenta detrahenda tempus defuerit. quae prima signa quisque conspexit, ad haec constitit ne in quaerendis suis pugnandi tempus dimitteret. itaque in tanta rerum iniquitate fortunae quoque eventus varii sequebantur.

45 legionis nonae et decimae milites, pilis emissis, cursu ac lassitudine exanimatos vulneribusque confectos Atrebates celeriter ex loco superiore in flumen compulerunt; et transire conantes insecuti, gladiis magnam partem eorum impeditam interfecerunt. ipsi transire

50 flumen non dubitaverunt et, in locum iniquum progressi, rursus regressos ac resistentes hostes in fugam dederunt.

| | |
|---|---|
| **cohortor** (1), to encourage, exhort | **eventus, -us** (*m*), outcome, result |
| **oratio, -onis** (*f*), speech | **pilum, -i** (*n*), javelin |
| **item,** in the same manner | **cursus, -us** (*m*), running |
| **exiguitas, -atis** (*f*), shortness | **lassitudo, -inis** (*f*), weariness |
| **dimico** (1), to fight | **exanimatus, -a, -um,** breathless |
| **insigne, -is** (*n*), decoration | |
| **accommodo** (1), to fit | **confectus, -a, -um,** exhausted |
| **tegimentum, -i** (*n*), cover | **superior, -oris,** higher |
| **quisque, quaeque, quidque,** each | **dubito** (1), to hesitate |
| **iniquitas, -atis** (*f*), inequality | **iniquus, -a, -um,** uneven |
| | **in fugam dare,** to put to flight |

**detraho, -ere** (3), **-traxi, -tractum,** to pull off
**desum, deesse, defui,** to be lacking, wanting
**consisto, -ere** (3), **constiti,** to halt, stand
**compello, -ere** (3), **-puli, -pulsum,** to drive

49

52 **diversae:** *facing in different directions*, i.e. they had caught them in a kind of pincer-movement.

54 **ex loco superiore:** Take with the Ablative Absolute (**profligatis Veromanduis**).

55 **totis fere:** As usual, **fere** follows the word it qualifies—*almost the whole*.
**a fronte:** not *from the front* but *on the front*, i.e. *in front*.
**totis . . . nudatis castris:** By separating off **totis** from **nudatis castris**, Caesar ties all the intervening words into the Ablative Absolute.

56 **non magno intervallo:** *at no great distance* (compare **non longa** in line 35).

57 **septima:** Supply **legio**. Note that **constitisset** has two subjects: **legio duodecima et (legio) septima**.

58 **agmine:** Both **acies** and **agmen** may be translated as *line*, but they indicate different types of line. **acies** describes the army drawn up for battle, i.e. with the broad side facing the enemy; **agmen**, on the other hand, describes the army in marching column—long and narrow. The latter is used here since they were running in a kind of column, some faster than others, all converging on the same spot.

59 **quorum pars . . . pars . . .:** Caesar is fond of using **pars . . . pars . . .** (where other authors might have used **alii . . . alii . . .**), even following the plural **quorum**. Note that the verb **coepit** is singular; it has to be taken with both **circumvenire** and **petere**.
**aperto latere:** *on their exposed flank*, i.e. *on their left* (caused by the advance of the 8th and 11th legions which had been stationed on their left).
**legiones:** i.e. the 7th and 12th legions.

60 **summum castrorum locum:** This does not mean *the highest point of the camp* but *the high ground of the camp*, i.e. *the high ground on which the camp was situated*.

62 **primo hostium impetu:** Again the genitive appears between the adjective and the noun. (Cf. **in ipsis fluminis ripis** in line 54.)
**cum se in castra reciperent:** Note how the phrase **in castra** is tied in between **se** and **reciperent**. The imperfect denotes that the action was going on when they encountered the enemy.

63 **adversis:** *head on*.
**occurrebant:** The imperfect is used because one after the other *they kept on running into them* as they retreated in disorder. (Compare **petebant**.)

64 **aliam in partem:** The accusative of motion is used as if **fugam petebant** were the verb **fugiebant**.
**calones:** These were slaves or servants attached to the troops. Translate *camp followers*.

## Crisis at the camp

item alia in parte diversae duae legiones, undecima et octava, profligatis Veromanduis (quibuscum erant congressi) ex loco superiore, in ipsis fluminis ripis proeliaban-
55  tur. at tum, totis fere a fronte et ab sinistra parte nudatis castris, cum in dextro cornu legio duodecima et non magno ab ea intervallo septima constitisset, omnes Nervii confertissimo agmine ad eum locum contenderunt; quorum pars aperto latere legiones circumvenire, pars
60  summum locum castrorum petere coepit.

eodem tempore equites nostri levisque armaturae pedites, qui primo hostium impetu pulsi erant, cum se in castra reciperent, adversis hostibus occurrebant ac rursus aliam in partem fugam petebant. et calones, qui ab
65  decumana porta ac summo iugo collis nostros victores flumen transiisse conspexerant, praedandi causa egressi,

| | |
|---|---|
| **diversus, -a, -um,** facing in opposite directions | **levis, -is, -e,** light |
| **profligo** (1), to rout, dislodge | **armatura, -ae** (*f*), armour, equipment |
| **proelior** (1), to fight | **pedites, -um** (*m.pl*), infantry |
| **a fronte,** in front | **se recipere,** to retreat, withdraw |
| **nudo** (1) to lay bare, expose | **collis, -is** (*m*), hill |
| **cornu, -us** (*n*), wing (of army) | **praedor** (1), to pillage, plunder |
| **confertus, -a, -um,** closely packed | |
| **latus, lateris** (*n*), side | |

---

**ab decumana porta:** *from the gate at the rear of the camp,* i.e. the one furthest removed from the enemy, which in this case was at the top of the hill.

65  **nostros victores:** The adjective **nostri** is used as a noun meaning *our troops* and the noun **victores** is used in apposition. Translate *our victorious troops* (literally *our men being victors*).

68 **fugae sese mandabant:** Note how many different ways Caesar has found to express *fleeing* in this section of the text: compare **hostes in fugam dederunt** (line 51); **se in castra reciperent** (line 62); **fugam petebant** (line 64); **aliam in partem ferebantur** (line 70).

69 **eorum:** Take this genitive with **clamor fremitusque**.

70 **alii aliam in partem:** Strictly speaking, this phrase should have been written twice: *some in one direction, others in another direction*; but Latin does not require this when two parts of **alius** occur together.

71 **quibus rebus:** Again, the word **res** sums up well all the action that has taken place. It is used similarly in line 75.

**equites Treveri:** The Romans always relied on their allies to provide their cavalry.

72 **ab civitate:** The preposition is used because Caesar is thinking of the people who made up the state. Translate *by their people*.

73 **compleri:** The present infinitive indicates *was being occupied*. Compare **teneri**. To arrive at the correct order of events, it is important to tackle the sentence as it unfolds: **permoti . . . Treveri qui . . . missi . . . venerant, cum vidissent, desperatis . . . rebus, . . . contenderunt**.

74 **circumventas teneri:** *had been surrounded and were being pinned down.*

75 **contenderunt.** Note the sudden switch to the perfect tense after a long series of imperfects. The latter has indicated the intermittent nature of the action, the initiative swinging to one side and then the other. Up to that point it was not clear which way the pendulum would finally swing. The use of the perfect **contenderunt** indicates a decisive action taken by the Treveri.

**pulsos superatosque:** Supply **esse**.

76 **civitati:** Compare line 72. Translate *to their people*.

cum respexissent et hostes in nostris castris versari
vidissent, praecipites fugae sese mandabant. simul
eorum, qui cum impedimentis veniebant, clamor fremi-
70   tusque oriebatur; aliique aliam in partem perterriti ferebantur. quibus omnibus rebus permoti, equites Treveri,
qui auxilii causa ab civitate missi ad Caesarem venerant,
cum multitudine hostium castra nostra compleri et
legiones paene circumventas teneri vidissent, desperatis
75   nostris rebus, domum contenderunt. Romanos pulsos
superatosque civitati renuntiaverunt.

**praeceps, praecipitis,**
  headlong
**se mandare** (1), to entrust
  oneself

**fremitus, -us** (*m*), uproar,
  commotion

**versor, -ari** (1), **versatus sum,** to move about

*Map 5* The Battle of the Sambre

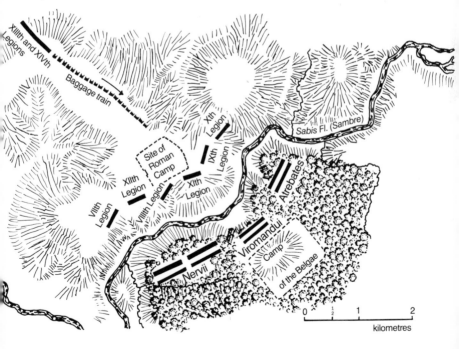

77 Although the sentence beginning in line 77 is a very long one, the meaning will be clear provided it is tackled clause by clause in the order in which the ideas appear. In the final translation, each ablative absolute should probably be translated as a main clause so that the 12 lines of Latin text might become five or six separate sentences in English.

78 **ubi:** *where.*

80 **fere:** As usual, **fere** follows the word it qualifies. (Cf. line 55.)

81 **in his:** *among these.*

83 **se sustinere:** *to stand up.*

**reliquos esse tardiores:** An Accusative and Infinitive depending on **vidit** (line 85). Translate the comparative **tardiores** as *somewhat slow.*

84 **nonnullos . . . vitare:** Both **excedere** and **vitare** are to be taken with **nonnullos** to form Accusative and Infinitive clauses depending on **vidit** (line 85). They were trying to keep out of range of the weapons.

85 **vidit:** The subject of this verb is **Caesar** in line 77.

**uni militi:** *from one soldier.* With certain verbs of "taking away" the person from whom something is taken is put in the dative. (Cf. **adimere** and **abripere**.)

87 **nominatim:** The adverbial ending **-tim** has the basic meaning *something by something*, e.g. **paulatim**, little by little; **gradatim**, step by step; **viritim**, man by man. Caesar knew his men so well that he was able to name each centurion as he met him.

88 **manipulos laxare:** The Romans usually relied on their well-drilled close formations in both defence and attack. Each man relied on the men on either side of him for protection, and the main weapon used was the javelin (**pilum**). On this occasion, however, there was so much confusion that it was impossible to get men from different sections to form up in the normal way, and so Caesar decided that they would have to fight their way out of trouble by using their swords. Because they required more room for arm movements he ordered them *to open up their ranks.*

**quo:** As usual, **quo** replaces **ut** when the Purpose clause contains a comparative.

---

| | |
|---|---|
| **dexter, -tra, -trum,** right | **eo,** to that place, there |
| **reliqui, -ae, -a,** remaining | **nominatim,** by name |
| **vulnus, -eris** (*n*), wound | **signa inferre,** to advance |
| **tardus, -a, -um,** slow | **laxo** (1), to loosen, open up |

**urgeo, -ere** (2), **ursi,** to press hard, put under pressure
**interficio, -ere** (3), **-feci, -fectum,** to kill
**amitto, -ere** (3), **amisi, amissum,** to lose

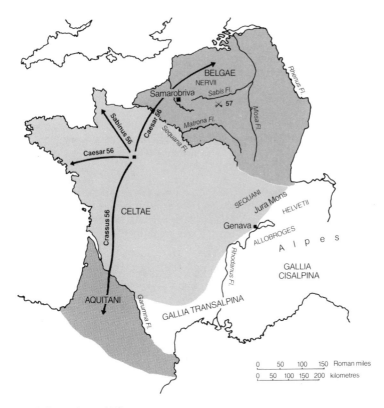

*Map 6* Campaigns of 56 BC

## Caesar rallies his troops

Caesar ab decimae legionis cohortatione ad dextrum
cornu profectus, ubi suos urgeri vidit, quartae cohortis
omnibus centurionibus occisis signiferoque interfecto,
80  signo amisso, reliquarum cohortium omnibus fere centurionibus aut vulneratis aut occisis (in his primipilo P.
Sextio Baculo, fortissimo viro, multis gravibusque vulneribus confecto ut iam se sustinere non posset), reliquos
esse tardiores et nonnullos proelio excedere ac tela vitare
85  vidit, scuto uni militi detracto (quod ipse eo sine scuto
venerat), in primam aciem processit, centurionibusque
nominatim appellatis, reliquos milites signa inferre et
manipulos laxare iussit quo facilius gladiis uti possent.

89 **cuius** refers to Caesar. Translate *by his arrival.*
  **spe illata militibus:** *the soldiers were filled with hope.* The dative case
  (**militibus**) is normal when the preposition **in** is used to produce a
  compound verb and is not repeated with the noun.

90 **pro se quisque:** *each man for his own part.*

93 **monuit:** *instructed.* This is a less strong word than **iussit.** Caesar would
  issue general instructions to the individual commanders and would rely
  on them to issue specific orders to their troops, working within the
  broad strategy that he had laid down.

94 **coniungerent:** The subject of this verb is **legiones** not the tribunes.
  Translate *that the legions should join together.*
  **conversa signa inferrent:** This is a very neat way of saying **signa
  converterent et signa inferrent.** There were three steps in the operation:
  link up, wheel round, advance.

95 **alius alii subsidium ferret:** As in line 70, this phrase has to be translated
  twice to arrive at the meaning: (literally) *one man helped one man,
  another helped another,* i.e. *they helped one another.* Note that **alii** here
  is dative.

96 **neque timerent ne:** *and they were not afraid that . . ..* Note that **timerent**
  is plural, picking up the plural idea contained in **alius . . . ferret.**

99 **praesidio fuerant: praesidio** is a Predicative Dative. Translate *had been
  guarding.* (Cf. line 8.)
  **proelio nuntiato:** *on hearing news of the battle,* i.e. a report came to
  them that the battle was swinging in favour of the Romans.

100 **cursu incitato:** literally *their running having been quickened.* Translate
  *(they) quickened their pace.*
  **conspiciebantur:** *began to be seen.*

101 **castris potitus: potior** governs the ablative case.
  **et,** as usual, links two similar ideas. In this case, they are the two
  perfect participles **potitus** and **conspicatus.**

102 **quae res . . . gererentur:** an Indirect Question depending on
  **conspicatus.**

103 **subsidio misit:** Predicative Datives may be used with verbs of motion
  as well as with **esse.** Translate *(he) sent . . . to help.*
  **qui:** *they,* referring to **decima legio.**

104 **et . . . et . . . et . . .:** Here, **et** links three similar words, all of them
  being the subject of **versaretur**; the verb is singular, agreeing with the
  nearest subject **imperator.**

cuius adventu spe illata militibus ac redintegrato animo,
90   cum pro se quisque in conspectu imperatoris operam
navare cuperet, paulum hostium impetus tardatus est.

## Victory

Caesar, cum septimam legionem (quae iuxta constiterat)
item urgeri ab hoste vidisset, tribunos militum monuit ut
paulatim legiones sese coniungerent et conversa signa in
95   hostes inferrent. quo facto, cum alius alii subsidium ferret
neque timerent ne ab hoste circumvenirentur, audacius
resistere ac fortius pugnare coeperunt.

interim milites legionum duarum quae in novissimo
agmine praesidio impedimentis fuerant, proelio nuntiato,
100  cursu incitato, in summo colle ab hostibus conspiciebantur; et Titus Labienus, castris hostium potitus et ex loco
superiore quae res in nostris castris gererentur conspicatus, decimam legionem subsidio nostris misit. qui, cum
cognovissent quanto in periculo et castra et legiones et
105  imperator    versaretur,    summa    celeritate    advenire
contenderunt.

redintegro (1), to renew
animus, -i (*m*), spirit
conspectus, -us (*m*), sight
operam navare, to do one's
   best
tardo (1), to slow down

iuxta, near by
subsidium, -i (*n*), help
novissimum agmen, the
   rearguard
praesidio esse (+ *dat*.), to
   protect

coniungo, -ere (3), -iunxi, -iunctum, to join
circumvenio, -ire (4), -veni, -ventum, to surround
conspicor, -ari (1), conspicatus sum, to notice
cognosco, -ere (3), cognovi, cognitum, to find out, learn

57

107 **tanta rerum commutatio:** Note again the effective use of **res** to
summarise all the complicated incidents which have preceded.
**est facta:** *was brought about.*

108 **etiam qui:** *even those who.*
**scutis innixi:** *supporting themselves on their shields.*

110 **etiam inermes armatis occurrerunt:** *(though they were) unarmed they
attacked (the enemy who were) armed.* Caesar emphasises the
contrast by placing **inermes** and **armatis** side by side.

112 **pugnant:** The historic present is used here to indicate in a vivid way
the continuous battle; contrast with this the use of the perfect
**occurrerunt** (line 110) which indicates the sudden charge.
**quo** is used for **ut** here because the verb **praeferrent** contains the idea
of comparison. (Cf. line 88.)

115 **proximi iacentibus insisterent:** *the next rows stood on them (where)
they lay.*

116 **ex eorum corporibus:** literally *from their bodies,* i.e. standing on top of
them.

117 **his** refers to **proximi**: *when these were knocked down.*
**qui superessent:** Supply **ei**—*(those) who survived.*

118 **ut ex tumulo:** *as if from a mound.*
**conicerent . . . remitterent:** These subjunctives also express Result after
**tantam virtutem praestiterunt ut.**

123 **omnium:** Take with **consensu**.

horum adventu tanta rerum commutatio est facta ut nostri, etiam qui vulneribus confecti procubuissent, scutis innixi, proelium redintegrarent. tum calones, perterritos
110 hostes conspicati, etiam inermes armatis occurrerunt. equites vero, ut turpitudinem fugae virtute delerent, omnibus in locis pugnant quo se legionariis militibus praeferrent.

at hostes etiam in extrema spe salutis tantam virtutem
115 praestiterunt ut, cum primi eorum cecidissent, proximi iacentibus insisterent atque ex eorum corporibus pugnarent; his deiectis et coacervatis cadaveribus, qui superessent, ut ex tumulo, tela in nostros conicerent et pila intercepta remitterent.

120 hoc proelio facto et prope ad internecionem gente ac nomine Nerviorum redacto, maiores natu, una cum pueris mulieribusque in aestuaria ac paludes collecti, omnium qui supererant consensu, legatos ad Caesarem miserunt seque ei dediderunt.

---

**commutatio, -onis** (*f*), change
**inermis, -is, -e,** unarmed
**vero,** even
**turpitudo, -inis** (*f*), disgrace
**se praeferre** ( + *dat.*), to surpass
**coacervo** (1), to pile up
**tumulus, -i** (*m*), mound

**ad internecionem redigere,** to destroy utterly, annihilate
**maiores natu,** the elders
**pueri, -orum** (*m.pl*), children
**aestuarium, -i** (*n*), a creek
**palus, paludis** (*f*), swamp, marsh
**consensus, -us** (*m*), agreement
**se dedere,** to surrender

**procumbo, -ere** (3), **-cubui, -cubitum,** to fall
**innitor, -i** (3), **innixus sum** ( + *dat.*), to lean upon
**occurro, -ere** (3), **occurri, occursum** ( + *dat.*), to attack
**insisto, -ere** (3), **institi** ( + *dat.*), to stand (upon)
**supersum, superesse, superfui,** to survive
**intercipio, -ere** (3), **-cepi, -ceptum,** to intercept
**redigo, -ere** (3), **redegi, redactum,** to reduce

## Predicative Dative

Look at the following sentences:

hanc pupam filiae Davi **dono** dabo.
*I shall give this doll* **as a gift** *to Davus' daughter.*

leones spectatoribus **admirationi** fuerunt.
*The lions were* **objects of amazement** *to the spectators.*

duae legiones **praesidio** impedimentis erant.
*Two legions* **protected** *the baggage.*

id erat Corneliae **admirationi** et **curae**.
*That was* **a cause of wonder** *and* **anxiety** *to Cornelia.*

The datives in bold type are Predicative Datives. The other datives indicate the person(s) or thing(s) affected by the Predicative Dative.

When used with **esse** (the verb with which they are most commonly associated) Predicative Datives are usually best translated either by a verb or by such expressions as "objects of amazement", "cause of wonder", "source of protection", etc., e.g.

**bono esse,** to be of advantage to, to benefit
**auxilio esse,** to be of assistance to, to help
**exitio esse,** to be a cause of destruction to, to destroy
**periculo esse,** to be a source of danger to, to endanger
**saluti esse,** to be a means of safety to, to save
**odio esse,** to be an object of hate to, to be hated by
**praesidio esse,** to be a means of protection to, to protect
**usui esse,** to be of use to
**laudi esse,** to be a reason for praise
**dedecori esse,** to be a cause for disgrace, to bring shame upon

When used with other verbs (e.g. **mittere, ire, venire, relinquere**), the meaning of the Predicative Dative is often best expressed by the English infinitive, e.g.

decimam legionem **subsidio** nostris misit.
*He sent the Tenth Legion* **to help** *our men.*

# Exercise 57a

*Translate:*

1 vallum saepe praesidio est castris.
2 scimus latrones odio esse viatoribus.
3 illae bestiae periculo erunt adstantibus.
4 Caesar ad dextrum cornu progressus suis saluti fuit.
5 tempestates saepe exitio sunt navibus.
6 miles ille fortissimus auxilio salutique fuit omnibus.
7 speramus te nobis subsidio venturum esse.
8 hae statuae erant civibus admirationi.
9 Caesar duas cohortes navibus praesidio reliquit.
10 maximae laudi erat consulibus rempublicam contra hostes
   defendisse.
11 maximo erat dedecori nostris a Belgis vinci.
12 Graeci odio erant Troianis.

## res

The basic meaning of the noun **res** is *thing*, but it must be
translated in a variety of ways to suit the context, e.g.

> rem explicare      *to explain the situation*
> totam rem narravit. *He told the whole story.*
> ad eam rem parati   *ready for that undertaking*

Like the word *things* in English, the plural **res** can mean
*possessions, property, circumstances, affairs, considerations,*
etc., e.g.

> his rebus adducti      *influenced by these thoughts*
> ad eas res conficiendas   *to complete those preparations*
> omnibus rebus ad profectionem comparatis
> *when everything was ready for the departure*

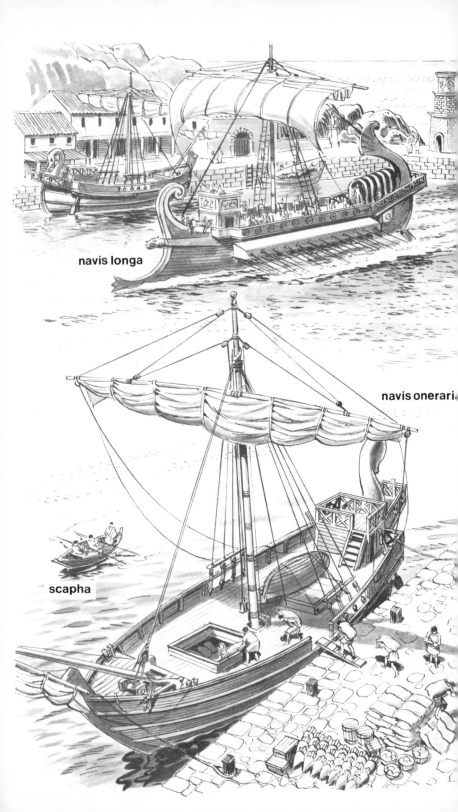

navis longa

navis onerari

scapha

# Roman Ships

Unlike the Greeks and Phoenicians, the Romans were not a seafaring people. Admittedly, travel by sea in good weather was much quicker and a good deal less laborious, in many cases, than travel overland. In four days, a Roman could sail from Italy to Spain, whereas the same journey by land would have taken a month.

These advantages were, however, much outweighed by the disadvantages—a sailing season which extended only from May to October, possible attacks by pirates (Caesar himself as a young man was captured by them), no passenger services aboard apart from a supply of water. Indeed, travellers took everything with them—tents, bedding, food and wine, and servants to look after them.

Navigation also posed problems. Quite apart from the difficulty of steering by only the sun during the day and by the stars at night, the ships had to cope with the Mediterranean's prevailing north winds which allowed a vessel to reach Alexandria from Rome in about ten days but might lengthen the return journey to a couple of months. Most Roman travellers by sea preferred to hug the coast and make a nightly landfall with its promise of a meal and a bed ashore.

Seneca certainly did not enjoy his brief experience of travel by sea, i.e. crossing the Bay of Naples!:

"I must be fool enough for anything! I allowed myself to be talked into going by sea. It was flat calm when we started. Certainly, the sky was heavy with black clouds; and these almost always lead to wind and rain. Still, I imagined that I could dash across the few miles from Naples to Puteoli, no matter what the sky looked like. Therefore, to finish the trip quickly, I headed straight across the open sea for Nisida, meaning to cut out the bays.

When I reached the point of no return, first of all the inviting calm vanished. There was no storm as yet, but a swell was running and the sea was becoming increasingly choppy. I began asking the helmsman to put me ashore on some beach. He replied that the coast was rugged with no place for landing; anyway, he said, land was the last place to head for in a storm.

I was too upset, however, to think of the danger. I was already terribly sea-sick. I insisted and forced him to make for the shore, whether he liked it or not. When we got near the land, I didn't wait for the ship to heave to but plunged in fully clothed. You can imagine my feelings as I crawled over the jagged rocks, looking for a clear passage. It was all the worse because I could not stand on my feet. No wonder sailors fear land!"

Seneca, Epistolae Morales 53

Many types of vessel were in use in ancient times, but only two figure in Caesar's invasion of Britain—the **navis longa** and the **navis oneraria**. The **navis longa** was essentially a speedy war-galley powered by banks of oars and used in naval warfare to ram enemy ships. The **navis oneraria** was a sailing vessel, cargo-carrying, flat-bottomed and broad in the beam.

Larger ships would have **scaphae**, a term which includes a wide variety of small craft ranging from dinghies to longboats. These were generally towed astern and used as harbour boats. No ship would ever have sufficient of these to provide a lifeboat service for all on board.

The illustration on page 62 shows a typical galley driven by three banks of oars, hence the name "trireme". The names "quadrireme" and "quinquereme" do not, however, seem to indicate four or five banks of oars, but four or five oarsmen allotted to three oars, thus allowing for one or two of the three banks of oars to be operated by two men to an oar. No one

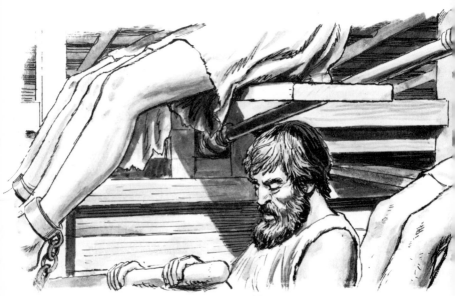

nowadays is really quite sure how these men were seated, despite the investigation of ancient wrecks by under-water archaeology, but the illustration below shows one possible arrangement.

Warships fitted with a ram would also often have a prow with a curved figurehead or scroll. Other ships generally had a goose-headed stern (as in the sailing-ships shown on page 62).

The single rudder was not known in ancient times, and steering was invariably provided by a pair of steering-oars joined by a tiller bar so that they could be operated by one steersman standing on the poop-deck.

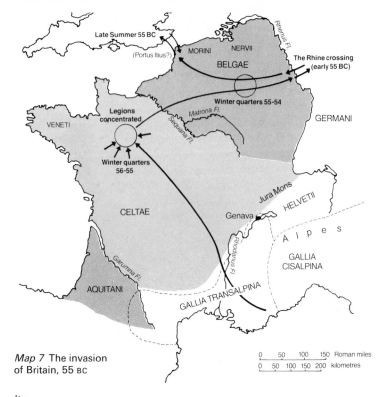

*Map 7* The invasion of Britain, 55 BC

*line*

1 **exigua parte reliqua:** an Ablative Absolute—literally *a small part being left*. The verb **esse** has no present participle. The time was August 55 BC. In ancient times military operations usually ended with the coming of winter.

3 **fere:** *almost*. As usual, **fere** follows the word it qualifies.

   **omnibus bellis:** Ablative of Time, and so no need for the preposition **in**.

4 **subministrata:** Supply **esse** to form an Accusative and Infinitive with **auxilia**. In fact, very little help seems to have been sent from Britain, and Caesar is merely using this as a pretext for invading the island.

   **magno sibi usui fore: usui** is a Predicative Dative, strengthened here by the adjective **magno**. **fore** is one form of the future infinitive of **esse** (=**futurum esse**): *it would be*.

6 **loca portus aditus:** All three words are objects of **cognovisset** and, as is often the case, there is no **et** or **-que** linking them.

7 **quae:** "Linking Relative" (*all these things*) referring to the details mentioned in the previous sentence.

   **neque enim** is to be taken with **quisquam**: *for no one*. (Cf. **neque quicquam** in the next line: *and nothing*.)

# 58
# Caesar invades Britain

While Caesar himself was mastering the Belgae, other tribes to the west were being conquered by his lieutenant, Publius Crassus. In 56 BC Caesar overcame the Veneti in Brittany and Crassus penetrated Aquitania. By 55 BC Caesar had bridged the Rhine and made a display of force among the German tribes. Confident of his hold over Gaul, he prepared to invade Britain, giving as his motive his desire to cut off British military help to their fellow Gauls on the continent and to harness British economic potential (including hides, slaves, woollen cloaks, pearls, tin and good hunting-dogs); but probably there was also the motive of sheer curiosity about Britain as "earth's remotest bound".

## Investigations

exigua parte aestatis reliqua, Caesar, etsi in his locis
maturae sunt hiemes, tamen in Britanniam proficisci
contendit; nam omnibus fere Gallicis bellis hostibus
nostris inde subministrata auxilia intellegebat; et magno
5    sibi usui fore arbitrabatur si modo insulam adiisset et
genus hominum perspexisset, loca portus aditus cognovisset; quae omnia fere Gallis erant incognita. neque enim
temere praeter mercatores illo adit quisquam, neque

**exiguus, -a, -um,** small
**aestas, -atis** (*f*), summer
**etsi,** although
**maturus, -a, -um,** early, earlier
**hiems, hiemis** (*f*), winter
**subministro** (1), to supply
**auxilia, -orum** (*n.pl*), reinforcements

**si modo,** if only
**genus, generis** (*n*), kind, nature
**portus, -us** (*m*), harbour
**aditus, -us** (*m*), landing place
**incognitus, -a, -um,** unknown
**temere,** without good reason
**illo,** (to) there

**perspicio, -ere** (3), **-spexi, -spectum,** to examine, observe

9 **eis ipsis** refers to the merchants.

10 Why did Caesar write **Gallias** and not **Galliam**?

12 **quanta esset...:** This Indirect Question and the five others which follow all depend on **reperire poterat**. In each case, **neque** provides the link between the clauses, and each clause is introduced by a question word.

13 **usum belli:** *experience in war.*

14 **qui:** *which*—an adjective agreeing with **portus**.

   **ad multitudinem idonei:** *suitable for a large number*, i.e. *able to cope with a large number.*

   **maiorum:** Caesar's galleys would be bigger than the ships which would normally use these harbours.

16 **idoneum esse arbitratus: Gaium Volusenum** acts as the accusative for this Accusative and Infinitive and also as the object of **praemittit**.

17 **navi:** Caesar is more fond of this form of the ablative than **nave**.

19 **in Morinos:** *into the territory of the Morini*; they were a Belgian tribe near the northern coast where the modern Calais and Boulogne are. He had beaten them earlier in battle but had not been able to subdue them completely because they withdrew into the forests. It was important for him to deal with them before he left for Britain so that they did not threaten his supply lines.

24 **qui polliceantur:** a Purpose clause in which **ut** is replaced by **qui**, referring to **legati**.

   **obsides dare:** This was Caesar's normal way of securing a guarantee from tribes that they would not revolt in his absence. The hostages would, of course, be executed if the promise was broken.

25 **liberaliter pollicitus:** literally *having promised generously*; where Latin tends to rely on verbs, English often prefers nouns, e.g. *having made generous promises.*

26 **pollicitus hortatusque:** -**que**, like **et**, joins words of the same type.
   **ut in ea sententia permanerent:** *to stick to that policy.*

28 **quantum ei facultatis dari potuit qui:** *as far as was possible for him since he.* **qui** with the subjunctive **auderet** explains why Volusenus did not carry out a full reconnaissance. **quantum facultatis** means literally *how much of an opportunity* (Partitive Genitive). He could not have reconnoitred more than a very small part of the Kent coast because he was absent only four days. A crucial point was the fact that he failed to find a suitable harbour, although one did exist eastwards along the coast from Dover, near Sandwich—used roughly 100 years later by the Emperor Claudius' invading troops.

29 **navi egredi:** It is not necessary to use **ex** with **navi** because of the force of the prefix in the verb **egredi**.

eis ipsis quicquam praeter oram maritimam atque eas
10   regiones quae sunt contra Gallias notum est.

itaque vocatis ad se undique mercatoribus, neque
quanta esset insulae magnitudo, neque quae aut quantae
nationes incolerent, neque quem usum belli haberent aut
quibus institutis uterentur, neque qui essent ad maiorum
15   navium multitudinem idonei portus, reperire poterat.
ad haec cognoscenda idoneum esse arbitratus Gaium
Volusenum cum navi longa praemittit. huic mandat ut,
exploratis omnibus rebus, ad se quam primum revertatur.
ipse cum omnibus copiis in Morinos proficiscitur quod
20   inde erat brevissimus in Britanniam traiectus. huc naves
undique ex finitimis regionibus iubet convenire.

interim, consilio eius cognito et per mercatores perlato
ad Britannos, a compluribus insulae civitatibus ad eum
legati veniunt qui polliceantur obsides dare atque imperio
25   populi Romani obtemperare. quibus auditis, liberaliter
pollicitus hortatusque ut in ea sententia permanerent, eos
domum remittit.

Volusenus, perspectis regionibus omnibus quantum ei
facultatis dari potuit qui navi egredi ac se barbaris
30   committere non auderet, quinto die ad Caesarem rever-
titur, quaeque ibi perspexisset renuntiat.

---

**ora maritima,** the sea-coast
**contra** ($+ acc.$), opposite
**notus, -a, -um,** known
**idoneus, -a, -um,** suitable
**mando** (1), to instruct
**exploro** (1), to reconnoitre
**quam primum,** as soon as
    possible

**traiectus, -us** ($m$), crossing
**obses, obsidis** ($m$), hostage
**obtempero** (1) ($+ dat.$), to
    obey
**sententia, -ae** ($f$), opinion

**reperio, -ire** (4), **repperi, repertum,** to find out, discover
**perfero, -ferre, pertuli, perlatum,** to convey
**polliceor, -eri** (2), **pollicitus sum,** to promise
**committo, -ere** (3), **-misi, -missum,** to entrust
**audeo, -ere** (2), **ausus sum,** to dare

A Roman anchor

69

34  **qui:** Compare line 24 for **qui** used to introduce a Purpose clause.

   **quod bellum . . . fecissent:** The subjunctive is used because it forms part of what they said (subordinate clause in indirect speech).

35  **seque:** It is important to see which two things **-que** is joining. In fact, it is two whole clauses:

   **qui se excusarent    quod bellum . . . fecissent**
   **(qui) pollicerentur    se . . . facturos (esse)**

   **imperasset** is a contracted form of **imperavisset**.

36  **hoc . . . accidisse:** an Accusative and Infinitive depending on **arbitratus**.

37  **neque . . . neque . . .:** These words provide markers for two balanced clauses—

   **neque post . . . volebat**
   and  **neque belli . . . habebat.**

   **belli gerendi:** genitive with **facultatem**.

38  **propter anni tempus:** As he often does, Caesar here puts the genitive between the preposition and the noun, thus tying the whole phrase together.

39  **imperat:** Note that, besides its more common use with **ut** + subjunctive, **imperare** may also be used with a direct object. (Compare page 31, line 70 and page 33, line 84.)

41  **coactis contractisque:** These verbs are not quite identical in meaning: **coactis** is the word that would normally be used for *assembling a fleet*, i.e. requisitioning the ships; **contractis** adds the notion of *concentrating* them in one place.

42  **quod:** *which*, referring to the number of ships.

43  **quod navium longarum:** Partitive Genitive—literally *what he had of warships*, i.e. *all the warships he had*. This phrase is the object of **distribuit**.

44  **quaestori:** Although the quaestor's main job was looking after the financial matters of the army, he would frequently be used also in a military capacity. Looking after a small contingent of troops was the main way in which a young Roman nobleman would acquire his first experience of command.

   **legatis:** The **legatus**, on the other hand, would hold the command of a large body of troops such as a legion.

   **praefectis:** These were the officers of auxiliary forces such as the cavalry and the engineers.

   **huc accedebant:** *there were in addition to these.* **accedere** is often used in this sense, equivalent to the passive of **addere**. **huc = ad has**.

dum in his locis Caesar navium parandarum causa
moratur, ex magna parte Morinorum ad eum legati
venerunt qui se excusarent quod bellum populo Romano
35 fecissent, seque ea quae imperasset facturos pollicerentur.
hoc sibi Caesar satis opportune accidisse arbitratus, quod
neque post tergum hostes relinquere volebat neque belli
gerendi propter anni tempus facultatem habebat, magnum eis numerum obsidum imperat. quibus adductis, eos
40 in fidem recepit.

## Caesar begins his preparations

navibus circiter LXXX onerariis coactis contractisque
(quod satis esse ad duas transportandas legiones existimabat), quod praeterea navium longarum habebat
quaestori legatis praefectisque distribuit. huc accedebant
45 XVIII onerariae naves, quae ex eo loco ab milibus
passuum octo vento tenebantur quominus in eundem
portum venire possent. has equitibus distribuit. P. Sul-

**se excusare,** to apologise
**opportune,** conveniently
**tergum, -i** (*n*), back
**in fidem recipere,** to accept
   into submission (i.e. under
   his protection)

**circiter,** about, around
**praeterea,** besides

**distribuo, -ere** (3), **-ui, -utum,** to distribute
**accedo, -ere** (3), **accessi, accessum,** to be added

45 **ex eo loco:** This refers to the main harbour of embarkation.

   **ab milibus passuum octo:** An idiomatic use of **ab** meaning *at a distance
   of*.

46 **quominus ... possent:** *so that they were not able.*

   **in eundem portum:** Caesar does not name the port from which he sailed,
   although in his second invasion of Britain he called the harbour **Portus
   Itius** (probably the modern Boulogne).

48 **eo praesidio quod:** literally *with that garrison which,* i.e. *with the size of garrison which.*

50 **idoneam ad navigandum tempestatem:** Notice that **ad navigandum** is placed between the adjective and noun so that there is no doubt that it has to be taken with **idoneam.**

51 **tertia fere vigilia:** The period between sunset and sunrise was divided into four watches (**vigiliae**). The length of the watches therefore varied according to the time of year. At this time of year, the third watch would begin about midnight and end about 2.30 a.m. The use of **fere** presumably does not mean that Caesar was uncertain whether it was the first, second or third watch, but that the sailings of the various ships took place at various times within that watch.

**in ulteriorem portum:** This refers to the port eight miles along the coast where the eighteen merchant ships were moored (see line 45).

52 **se** refers to Caesar.

53 **a quibus:** This refers to the cavalry.
**cum:** *although, whereas.*
**paulo tardius:** *a little too slowly.*
**esset administratum:** literally *it was carried out (by them),* i.e. *they carried out their instructions.*

54 **ipse:** i.e. Caesar.
**hora circiter diei quarta:** The period of daylight between sunrise and sunset was divided into twelve equal hours (**horae**) which, of course, varied in length according to the time of year. In August, the fourth hour would fall some time between 9 a.m. and 10 a.m. (Compare the note on line 51.) Caesar's troops were transported in warships which were propelled by oars and therefore not affected greatly by adverse winds. The merchant ships, on the other hand, relied on sails and, because the cavalry took too long to travel the eight miles and embark, they missed the favourable winds and had to turn back to port.

55 **in omnibus collibus:** i.e. on the cliffs of Dover.

**expositas:** not so much *drawn up* for battle as *displayed,* i.e. spread out along the cliffs to suggest massive numbers and so try to intimidate the Romans.

57 **ita montibus angustis mare continebatur:** The *narrow mountains* are, of course, the "cliffs" of Dover. The adjective **angustus** probably means *rising steeply.* Caesar was looking for a landing place where the climb from the sea was much more gradual. The use of **continebatur** is also interesting; the cliffs were like the banks of a river, but in this case they were holding back the sea.

59 **hunc** agrees with **locum.**

picium Rufum legatum cum eo praesidio, quod satis esse
arbitrabatur, portum tenere iussit.

## Caesar sets sail for Britain

50   his constitutis rebus, nactus idoneam ad navigandum
tempestatem, tertia fere vigilia solvit equitesque in ulteriorem portum progredi et naves conscendere et se sequi
iussit. a quibus cum paulo tardius esset administratum,
ipse hora circiter diei quarta cum primis navibus Britan-
55   niam attigit, atque ibi in omnibus collibus expositas
hostium copias armatas conspexit.

    cuius loci haec erat natura: ita montibus angustis mare
continebatur ut ex locis superioribus in litus telum adigi
posset. hunc ad egrediendum nequaquam idoneum

**portum tenere,** to reach
  harbour
**tempestas, -atis** (*f*), weather
**navem conscendere,** to
  embark, go on board ship
**administro** (1), to carry out,
  perform

**copiae, -arum** (*f.pl*), forces
**litus, -oris** (*n*), shore
**nequaquam,** by no means

**nanciscor, -i** (3), **nactus sum,** to obtain
**solvo, -ere** (3), **solvi, solutum,** to set sail
**attingo, -ere** (3), **attigi, attactum,** to touch, reach
**adigo, -ere** (3), **adegi, adactum,** to hurl

The cliffs of Dover. (*Photo: The Photo Source*)

60 **dum . . . convenirent: dum** used with the subjunctive means *until* and
denotes Purpose—*until they might assemble, to give them time to
assemble.*

**ad horam nonam:** a little after 3 p.m. at this time of year. He therefore
lay *at anchor* (**in ancoris**) for about six hours.

61 **legatis . . . convocatis** is dative, not Ablative Absolute.

62 **et quae . . . et quae . . .: et . . . et . . .** shows that the two clauses (both
Indirect Questions) are balanced and depend on **ostendit**.

63 **ad nutum:** literally *at the nod*, i.e. *immediately and without question.* The
whole operation would depend on split-second timing.

66 **secundum** agrees with both **ventum** and **aestum**.

67 **aperto ac plano litore:** There have been many theories about Caesar's
actual landing place. Most people believe that it was near Deal, about
10 kilometres north-east of Dover. Others claim that a study of the
tides in the English Channel would indicate that at this time the tide
would have been flowing down channel towards the west, in which case
his landing would have been near Lympne in Romney Marsh. The
coastline is so changed since Caesar's day that we cannot be completely
certain.

69 **barbari:** *the natives.* As far as the Romans were concerned, anyone
who was not Roman or Greek was **barbarus**.

**consilio:** i.e. the plan to sail farther along the coast to find a more
suitable landing place.

70 **essedariis:** The Romans had not encountered this method of fighting
before. The **essedum** was a two-wheeled chariot pulled by two horses.
The Britons had little in the way of cavalry. The chariot was used to
carry the warriors into the battle area, where they dismounted to fight
on foot; it remained available if they wished to make a quick retreat.
They thus combined the mobility of cavalry with the solid reliability of
the infantryman. Their ability to bring in reinforcements quickly could
be disconcerting.

72 **in alto:** *in deep (water).*

73 **militibus:** This is dative case (Dative of Agent) and has to be taken with
the gerundives **desiliendum, consistendum** and **pugnandum**. Translate
*the soldiers had to . . .* The participle **oppressis** agrees with **militibus**,
and the three phrases between **militibus** and **oppressis** indicate the ways
in which the soldiers were put under pressure.

75 **et . . . et . . . et . . .:** The *balancing* words preceded by **simul** help the
reader to identify more easily the various things that the soldiers had
to do at the same time. Note that **erat** has to be supplied with
**desiliendum** and **consistendum**.

60 locum arbitratus, dum reliquae naves eo convenirent, ad
horam nonam in ancoris exspectavit. interim legatis
tribunisque militum convocatis et quae ex Voluseno
cognovisset et quae fieri vellet ostendit; monuitque ut ad
nutum et ad tempus omnes res ab eis administrarentur.
65 his dimissis, et ventum et aestum uno tempore nactus
secundum, dato signo et sublatis ancoris, circiter milia
passuum septem ab eo loco progressus, aperto ac plano
litore naves constituit.

## Strong resistance by the Britons

at barbari, consilio Romanorum cognito, praemisso
70 equitatu et essedariis, reliquis copiis subsecuti, nostros
navibus egredi prohibebant. erat ob has causas summa
difficultas quod naves propter magnitudinem nisi in alto
constitui non poterant; militibus autem ignotis locis,
impeditis manibus, magno et gravi onere armorum
75 oppressis simul et de navibus desiliendum et in fluctibus

| | |
|---|---|
| **nutus, -us** (*m*), nod | **essedarius, -i** (*m*), chariot |
| **aestus, -us** (*m*), tide | soldier |
| **secundus, -a, -um,** favourable | **ob** ( + *acc.*), on account of |
| **apertus, -a, -um,** open | **nisi,** except |
| **planus, -a, -um,** flat | **fluctus, -us** (*m*), wave |

**constituo, -ere** (3), **-ui, -utum,** to draw up, anchor
**prohibeo, -ere** (2), **-ui, -itum** ( + *infin.*), to prevent (from)

*Map 8* The coast of France and southern England

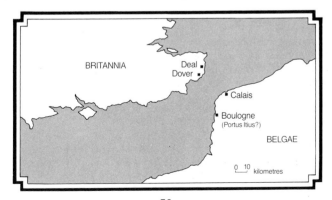

75

76 **consistendum:** They *had to get a footing.*

   **cum:** *on the other hand*—or *whereas.* The subjunctives **conicerent** and **incitarent** depend on **cum.**     **illi:** the Britons.

77 **ex arido:** *from dry (land).*

79 **insuefactos:** literally *accustomed,* i.e. *trained for this sort of work.*

81 **non eadem alacritate . . . utebantur:** *did not display* (literally *use*) *the same keenness.* The relative pronoun **quo** agrees with the nearer antecedent **studio,** although it refers to both **alacritate** and **studio. quo** is ablative because it is governed by **uti.**

82 **consuerant:** The verb **consuescere** means *to grow accustomed.* The perfect tense, therefore, means literally *I have grown accustomed,* i.e. *I am accustomed,* and the pluperfect tense means *I was accustomed.*

83–86 In this sentence the five passive infinitives all depend on **iussit.** Three of the infinitives are to be taken with **naves,** and two with **hostes.**

84 **remis incitari:** This suggests more than merely *being removed.* The oarsmen would row at double-quick time to manoeuvre the ships quickly.

   **ad latus apertum:** *on the open side,* i.e. on the enemy's right. The shield was carried on the left arm and thus protected the left side more than the right. In the Roman army, each soldier relied very much on the soldier to his right for protection from attacks on the right flank.

85 **fundis sagittis tormentis:** a list without any connecting "and". (Cf. line 6.)

86 **quae res:** *this manoeuvre.*

87 **et . . . et . . . et . . .:** These again are very helpful in showing that the phrases all go with **permoti.**

89 **paulum modo:** *but only a little.*

90 **cunctantibus:** The use of the present participle shows that the standard-bearer acted while they were still delaying, i.e. the action of the present participle coincided with that of the main verb.

91 **qui:** Supply **is** as the antecedent—*the soldier who.*

92 **contestatus deos ut . . .:** *having called on the gods to see to it that . . .* **ea res:** *this action* or *what he was about to do.*

93 **aquilam prodere:** The greatest disgrace that could befall a legion was to have its standard captured by the enemy.

95 **officium praestitero:** To understand this use of the future perfect tense one must supply something like *(whatever the outcome), I shall have done my duty.*

consistendum et cum hostibus erat pugnandum; cum illi aut ex arido aut paulum in aquam progressi, omnibus membris expeditis, notissimis locis audacter tela conicerent et equos insuefactos incitarent.

80 quibus rebus nostri perterriti atque huius generis pugnae imperiti non eadem alacritate ac studio, quo in pedestribus uti proeliis consuerant, utebantur.

quod ubi Caesar animadvertit, naves longas paulum removeri ab onerariis navibus et remis incitari et ad latus

85 apertum hostium constitui, atque inde fundis sagittis tormentis hostes propelli ac submoveri iussit. quae res magno usui nostris fuit. nam et navium figura et remorum motu et inusitato genere tormentorum permoti, barbari constiterunt ac paulum modo pedem rettulerunt.

## Heroism saves the day

90 atque nostris militibus cunctantibus, maxime propter altitudinem maris, qui decimae legionis aquilam ferebat, contestatus deos ut ea res legioni feliciter eveniret, "desilite," inquit "milites, nisi vultis aquilam hostibus prodere; ego certe meum reipublicae atque imperatori

95 officium praestitero."

| | |
|---|---|
| **aridus, -a, -um,** dry | **inusitatus, -a, -um,** unaccustomed |
| **insuefactus, -a, -um,** trained | |
| **pugna, -ae** (*f*), battle, fight | **pedem referre,** to retreat |
| **imperitus, -a, -um** ( + *gen.*), inexperienced (in) | **cunctor** (1), to delay, hesitate |
| **alacritas, -atis** (*f*), keenness | **contestor** (1), to call to witness |
| **studium, -i** (*n*), eagerness, zeal | **feliciter evenire,** to turn out well |
| **pedestris, -is, -e,** on foot | |
| **funda, -ae** (*f*), sling | **respublica, reipublicae** (*f*), the state |
| **sagitta, -ae** (*f*), arrow | |
| **tormentum, -i** (*n*), catapult | **officium praestare,** to do one's duty |
| **figura, -ae** (*f*), shape | |
| **motus, -us** (*m*), movement | |

**consuesco, -ere** (3), **consuevi, consuetum,** to grow accustomed
**animadverto, -ere** (3), **-verti, -versum,** to notice
**propello, -ere** (3), **-puli, -pulsum,** to drive away
**submoveo, -ere** (2), **-movi, -motum,** to dislodge
**prodo, -ere** (3), **prodidi, proditum,** to betray

97 **inter se:** *one another.*

98 **ne tantum dedecus admitteretur:** *not to allow such a disgrace to happen.*
**universi:** This word suggests not only that they all reacted, but that they did it *en masse* or *with one accord.*

99 **hos** refers to the men who had been on the same ship as the standard-bearer. The subject of **conspexissent** is *those on the nearest ships who had seen what had happened.* Caesar has used a kind of shorthand here, combining the two notions of *being* **on** *the nearest ships* and *seeing it* **from** *the nearest ships.*

101 **pugnatum est acriter:** This impersonal use of the verb in the passive is common where the writer wishes to emphasise the action rather than identify the actual people who were involved. The literal translation is *it was fought fiercely* but English would prefer *there was fierce fighting.*

102 **neque . . . neque . . . neque . . .:** The repeated use of **neque** helps us to identify the phrases which depend on **poterant.**

104 **notis omnibus vadis:** Ablative Absolute.
**ubi . . . conspexerant:** When used with the pluperfect, **ubi** means *whenever.* Note that the main verb is imperfect tense, indicating that they attacked repeatedly.

hoc cum voce magna dixisset, se ex navi proiecit atque in hostes aquilam ferre coepit. tum nostri, cohortati inter se ne tantum dedecus admitteretur, universi ex navi desiluerunt. hos item ex proximis navibus cum conspexissent, subsecuti hostibus appropinquaverunt.

100

pugnatum est ab utrisque acriter. nostri tamen, quod neque ordines servare neque firmiter insistere neque signa subsequi poterant, magnopere perturbabantur. hostes vero, notis omnibus vadis, ubi ex litore aliquos singulares

**dedecus, dedecoris** (*n*), disgrace
**universi, -ae, -a,** all together
**utrique,** both sides
**acriter,** fiercely

**ordo, -inis** (*m*), rank
**firmiter insistere,** to get a firm foothold
**singularis, -is, -e,** singly, one by one

**admitto, -ere** (3), **-misi, -missum,** to commit

105 **impeditos** has almost the effect of a noun here: either *those who were in difficulties* or *them when they were in difficulties.*

106 **plures paucos: plures** refers to the Britons, **paucos** to the Romans whom the Britons picked off one by one.

**alii:** *some of them,* referring to one group of the **hostes** (line 103).

107 **in universos:** This refers to those Romans who had managed to keep their ranks intact: *whole groups* rather than **singulares.** (Cf. line 98.)

109 **quos . . .conspexerat:** Compare line 105 for this use of the pluperfect tense (what is called the "frequentative" use). It means literally *whomsoever he had seen,* i.e. *whenever he saw any soldiers.* As with the previous example, the main verb (**submittebat**) is in the imperfect tense.

**laborantes:** *in difficulties,* a common use of **laborare.**

110 **his** (*them*) refers to those mentioned in the **quos** clause.

**simul = simulac.**

111 **constiterunt . . . fecerunt . . . dederunt:** Note how the three verbs in the perfect tense, used in quick succession, emphasise the rapidity and decisiveness of their action.

112 **longius:** *for any great distance.*

113 **cursum tenere:** See lines 46 and 53. The ships which were carrying the cavalry were late in sailing and were then forced by adverse winds to turn back to port.

114 **hoc unum:** *this one thing.*

**ad:** *in relation to.*

**Caesari defuit:** literally *was missing for Caesar.* The inability of the cavalry to carry out their instructions was the one part of the plan which went wrong and, in Caesar's estimation, prevented him from winning complete victory. Translate *This was the one thing Caesar lacked to maintain his previous success.*

118 **quaeque:** As usual, you must decide which two similar things are linked by **-que.** It cannot be two relative clauses since there is only one. In this case, it is two Accusative and Infinitive clauses, which appear in abbreviated form. The Britons made two promises:

> **(sese) obsides daturos (esse)**
> **sese facturos (esse)**

**quae imperasset** is the object of **facturos.** The clause is in the subjunctive because it is part of what they said to Caesar.

**imperasset** is a contracted form of **imperavisset.**

105    ex navi egredientes conspexerant, incitatis equis, impeditos adoriebantur, plures paucos circumsistebant, alii
ab latere aperto in universos tela coniciebant.

     quod cum animadvertisset Caesar, scaphas longarum
navium militibus compleri iussit et, quos laborantes
110   conspexerat, his subsidia submittebat. nostri simul in
arido constiterunt, in hostes impetum fecerunt atque eos
in fugam dederunt. neque longius prosequi potuerunt,
quod equites cursum tenere atque insulam capere non
potuerant. hoc unum ad pristinam fortunam Caesari
115   defuit.

     hostes proelio superati, simulatque se ex fuga re-
ceperunt, statim ad Caesarem legatos de pace miserunt.
obsides daturos quaeque imperasset sese facturos polliciti
sunt.

| | |
|---|---|
| **in fugam dare,** to put to flight | **pristinus, -a, -um,** previous |
| **insulam capere,** to reach the island | **se recipere,** to recover |
| | **pax, pacis** (*f*), peace |

**adorior, -iri** (4), **adortus sum,** to attack
**circumsisto, -ere** (3), **-steti,** to surround
**submitto, -ere** (3), **-misi, -missum,** to send up
**prosequor, -i** (3), **-secutus sum,** to pursue

# The Army in Camp

To avoid being surprised, the Roman army was careful to make a well-fortified camp whenever it stopped in enemy territory. Every camp followed an exact pattern so that each man knew exactly the job he had to do and where he had to do it. If two legions used a single camp, they were quartered separately.

In choosing a site, scouts (**exploratores**) looked especially for good supplies of water and wood, and preferably also a position on a slight slope. If necessary, the ground was levelled and then it was pegged out in square or rectangular form by surveyors, starting from the general's tent (**praetorium**) at the centre. The ditch (**fossa**) was then dug by the soldiers and the earth was thrown up to form an earth rampart (**vallum, agger**), usually topped by battlements and parapets (**pinnae, loricae**).

The men's leather tents were then set up in fixed positions leaving a space sixty metres wide between tents and rampart (**intervallum**). The **praetorium** housed the general and his staff as well as standards, treasury and a place for taking the auspices. Beside this was the paymaster's tent (**quaestorium**) and the **forum** where the men could be addressed or disciplined and booty distributed.

The camp was guarded day and night, the night being divided into four watches (**vigiliae**), each of about three hours. The guards were relieved at the end of each watch. Pickets of horse and foot guarded the gates and outposts (**stationes**), while sentinels patrolled the rampart and **praetorium**.

In camp, as in battle, there was perfect discipline. For breaking camp, a trumpet signalled the taking down of tents; a second trumpet meant the gathering of equipment and preparation for the march. At this point, the remnants of the camp would be destroyed. The third trumpet rounded up stragglers and then in answer to the herald's enquiry, made three times, the men raised their right hands and cried that they were ready to march. The advance then began in silence and perfect order.

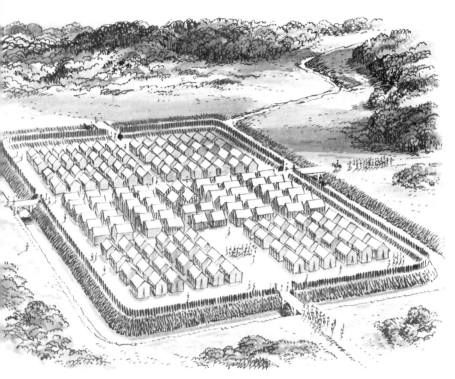

A temporary camp

A permanent camp was similar to the temporary camp described above, but the outer wall was of turf or stone. Corner towers were also added and the interior buildings were wooden or stone. These buildings included granaries, hospital, administrative block and the commander's house. A bath building or annexe might stand outside the camp.

Josephus, a historian of the 1st century AD, comments that the finished camp had the appearance of a miniature city: inside, the tents were divided up by symmetrical streets; from the outside, one was faced by a wall with towers at regular intervals, raised platforms to support various artillery engines, and a broad gate in each of the four walls. The main gate (**porta decumana**, so called because the Tenth Cohort of the legion was camped there) was on the side farthest from the enemy. Thanks to the skill and the numbers of the workers, the whole construction was completed "swifter than thought".

# Siege Warfare

When attacking a walled town or camp, the Romans blockaded it by encircling it with a rampart (**vallum**) and a ditch (**fossa**) to stop reinforcements of men or food entering. In this way, they also prevented the besieged men from sending out appeals for help to their allies.

The walls of the town were attacked with a battering-ram (**aries**) and bombarded by various devices. The **onager**, a large catapult on wheels, hurled stones at the walls and the defenders. The largest **onager** could hurl a 30 kg missile a distance of half a mile. Smaller catapults (**catapultae** or **ballistae**) were used to shoot arrows at the defenders and flaming darts (**fervefacta iacula**) to set fire to the buildings.

The attacking soldiers advanced under cover of specially constructed shelters (**vineae**) with grappling hooks (**falces**) and scaling ladders (**scalae**); or a group might lock their shields together over their heads to form a protective roof. This

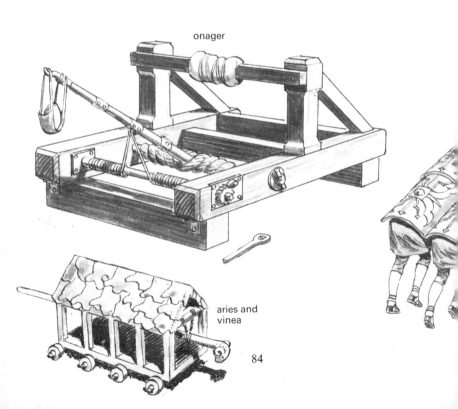

onager

aries and
vinea

84

formation was called a "tortoise" (**testudo**). Assault towers (**turres**) were built in storeys to the height of the wall and were wheeled up an earth ramp (**agger**) to the base of the wall. After climbing up to the top by means of ladders (**scalae**) set inside the towers, the soldiers would let down a drawbridge, rush on to the wall and fight the defenders hand-to-hand.

Meanwhile, the defenders would also gather missiles and hurl them from the walls at the advancing soldiers. Sometimes, they even built their own towers inside the town for this purpose.

In the passage which follows, the Nervii turn the tables on the Romans and use Roman methods to attack the camp of Quintus Cicero.

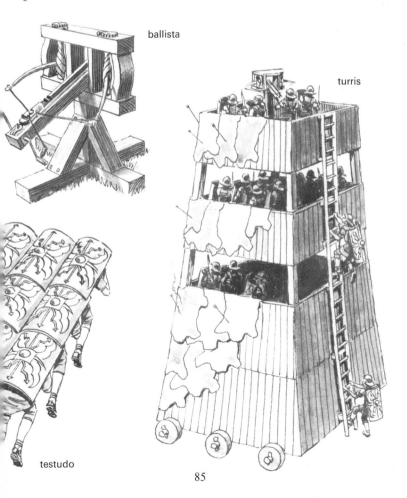

ballista

turris

testudo

# 59

# The Romans under Siege

Caesar's invasion of Britain in 55 BC had been nothing more than a reconnaissance in force. He invaded the island again in late July 54 BC, this time with much larger forces (a convoy of 800 ships) and with more success. He defeated the British tribes under Cassivellaunus and crossed the River Thames.

But the menace of revolt in Gaul was never far away and by 22nd September Caesar was back on the continent. In previous years, he had been able to concentrate his forces in one area during the winter months when there was traditionally no fighting. That year, however, the harvest had been poor and food shortages forced him to disperse his forces in winter camps (**hiberna**) throughout northern Gaul, as indicated in Map 9.

This was the opportunity that Ambiorix had been waiting for. He was an astute politician and a resourceful general. His tribal area (he was a king of the Eburones) was close to the camp of Sabinus and Cotta; so, posing as a friend of Caesar and a supporter of the Romans, he told the Roman commanders that a huge force of Germans had crossed the Rhine and was bearing down on their camp. He offered the Romans safe-conduct through his territory to the security of the camp of either Cicero or Labienus. After much heart-searching and debate, the Romans accepted this offer but, once out of the protection of their camp, they were an easy prey to ambush and treachery, and nearly the whole force together with its officers was annihilated.

Ambiorix could now turn his attention to Cicero's camp.

MENAPII
EBURONES
Rhenus Fl.
MORINI
Sabinus **Ambiorix**
BELGAE and Cotta
**Cicero** TREVERI
Samarobriva NERVII **Labienus**
**Crassus** ADUATUCI
**Plancus**
Matrona Fl.
Sequana Fl.
VENETI

CELTAE

Jura Mons HELVETII
A l p e s
Rhodanus Fl. GALLIA
CISALPINA
Garumna Fl.
AQUITANI GALLIA TRANSALPINA

■  Winter quarters
→  March of Caesar
- - →  March of Ambiorix

| 0 | 50 | 100 | 150 | Roman miles |
|---|----|-----|-----|-------------|
| 0 | 50 | 100 150 | 200 | kilometres |

*Map 9* Ambiorix attacks, 54 BC

*line*

1 **hac victoria:** This refers to the ambush of Sabinus and Cotta in 54 BC.

4 **re demonstrata:** *having told them the result of the battle.*

5 **sui liberandi occasionem:** *the opportunity of setting themselves free.* **sui** is the genitive of the reflexive pronoun **se.** By putting **in perpetuum** in between **sui** and **liberandi** Caesar shows that the whole phrase is to be taken together. (Compare page 50, line 55.)

7–8 **interfectos esse . . . interiisse:** Note how Caesar arranges the two Accusative and Infinitive clauses so that the first and last words are the infinitives, thus adding considerable emphasis to the disaster which had taken place.

8 **nihil esse:** The Accusative and Infinitive construction continues without any introductory word of speaking.

9 **oppressam legionem interfici:** Accusative and Infinitive—*for the legion to be overwhelmed and killed.* English would more naturally translate *to overwhelm and wipe out the legion.*

**cum Cicerone:** This was Quintus Cicero, the brother of the orator. He became a **legatus** to Caesar in Gaul in 55 BC.

12 **quam maximas manus possunt:** Compare line 68 on page 30 for this expanded expression. Most Latin authors would have omitted **possunt.**

15 **is dies sustentatur:** literally *that day was endured,* i.e. *they held out during that day.*

16 **hanc adepti victoriam:** literally *having won this victory;* translate *if they won this victory.*

17 **fore = futuros esse.**

19 **magnis propositis praemiis:** With this Ablative Absolute we must supply some expression such as *to the messengers,* understood from the verb **pertulissent** which follows. The force of **per-** is *through the enemy lines.*

20 **missi:** *those who were sent.*

## An uprising

hac victoria sublatus, Ambiorix statim cum equitatu in Aduatucos, qui erant eius regno finitimi, proficiscitur; neque noctem neque diem intermittit peditatumque sese subsequi iubet. re demonstrata Aduatucisque concitatis,
5 postero die in Nervios pervenit hortaturque ne sui in perpetuum liberandi atque ulciscendi Romanos occasionem dimittant. interfectos esse legatos duos magnamque partem exercitus interiisse demonstrat: nihil esse negotii subito oppressam legionem, quae cum Cicerone
10 hiemet, interfici; se ad eam rem profitetur adiutorem. facile hac oratione Nerviis persuadet.

itaque confestim quam maximas manus possunt cogunt et de improviso ad Ciceronis hiberna advolant. nostri celeriter ad arma concurrunt, vallum conscendunt.
15 aegre is dies sustentatur quod omnem spem hostes in celeritate ponebant atque, hanc adepti victoriam, in perpetuum se fore victores confidebant.

mittuntur ad Caesarem confestim ab Cicerone litterae, magnis propositis praemiis si pertulissent. obsessis omni-
20 bus viis, missi intercipiuntur. noctu ex materia, quam

**demonstro** (1), to show, point out
**concito** (1), to rouse, stir up
**postero die,** on the following day
**in perpetuum,** for ever
**occasionem dimittere,** to let slip the opportunity
**nihil negotii est,** it is no great task
**hiemo** (1), to spend the winter
**adiutor, -oris** (*m*), helper

**confestim,** immediately
**manus, -us** (*f*), company, band
**de improviso,** unexpectedly
**hiberna, -orum** (*n.pl*), winter camp (quarters)
**advolo** (1), to swoop upon
**aegre,** with difficulty
**sustento** (1), to sustain, maintain
**litterae, -arum** (*f.pl*), dispatches
**praemium, -i,** (*n*), reward
**materia, -ae** (*f*), materials, timber

**intermitto, -ere** (3), **-misi, -missum,** to pause, let pass
**ulciscor, ulcisci** (3), **ultus sum,** to take revenge on, avenge oneself on
**intereo, -ire, -ii, -itum,** to perish
**profiteor, -eri** (2), **professus sum,** to offer
**adipiscor, -i** (3), **adeptus sum,** to obtain
**confido, -ere** (3), **-fisus sum,** to be confident

*line*

21 **comportaverant:** The subject is the Romans. See the notes on Roman camps (page 82) for details of how the Romans used natural materials gathered locally to fortify their camp.

22 **excitantur:** *were erected, were built up.*

24 **fossam complent:** This refers to the ditch round the Roman camp, outside the rampart. The rampart itself was not very high, but the combined height/depth of rampart/ditch produced a formidable obstacle for the enemy.

   **eadem ratione qua:** *using* (literally *with*) *the same tactics as.*

25 **resistitur:** Again, the statement is made in the passive form to describe general resistance by all the troops rather than specific resistance by certain individuals. Compare the use of **intermittitur** in line 26. In line 3, on the other hand, **intermittit** is active since it indicates action by a certain individual.

26 **ad laborem:** Normally, the preposition **ad** has a "physical" meaning (e.g. movement "towards" or position "near"), but it is also used to express other relationships. For example, **ad laborem** here means *as far as work was concerned*, and in line 28 **ad oppugnationem** means *to deal with the attack*.

27 **non aegris, non vulneratis:** Caesar creates a dramatic effect by using **non . . . non . . .** instead of the more usual **neque . . . neque . . .** and by putting these phrases at the beginning.

28 **opus sunt:** *were needed.*

29 **comparantur:** The subject of this verb is the whole clause **quaecunque . . . opus sunt**. Note that, again, the verb is passive indicating activities carried out generally (cf. line 25).

30 **instituitur:** There are two subjects—**multae sudes** and **magnus numerus**. The verb agrees with the nearer subject, **numerus**.

32 **cum tenuissima valetudine esset:** *although he was in very poor health.* (Ablative of Description)

33 **ad quietem:** Compare **ad laborem** in line 26.

34 **aliquam causam amicitiae:** *some claim to friendship* (**amicitiae** is genitive).

38 **reliquorum:** This refers to the other Roman commanders in different parts of Gaul.

   **errare eos dicunt:** *They* (the Nervii) *said that they* (Cicero's men) *were mistaken.*

munitionis causa comportaverant, turres admodum CXX
excitantur incredibili celeritate.

### The second day

    hostes postero die, multo maioribus coactis copiis, castra
oppugnant, fossam complent. eadem ratione, qua pridie,
25  ab nostris resistitur. hoc idem reliquis deinceps fit diebus.
nulla pars nocturni temporis ad laborem intermittitur;
non aegris, non vulneratis facultas quietis datur.
quaecunque ad proximi diei oppugnationem opus sunt
noctu comparantur: multae praeustae sudes, magnus
30  muralium pilorum numerus instituitur; turres contabul-
antur, pinnae loricaeque ex cratibus attexuntur. ipse
Cicero, cum tenuissima valetudine esset, ne nocturnum
quidem sibi tempus ad quietem relinquebat.

    tunc duces principesque Nerviorum, qui aliquam
35  causam amicitiae cum Cicerone habebant, colloqui sese
velle dicunt. facta potestate, commemorant omnem esse
in armis Galliam; Germanos Rhenum transiisse; Caesaris
reliquorumque hiberna oppugnari. errare eos dicunt, si

**admodum,** about
**ratio, -onis** (*f*), method, way
**pridie,** on the previous day
**deinceps,** one after another,
  in turn
**quies, quietis** (*f*), rest
**quicunque, quaecunque,**
  **quodcunque,** whoever,
  whatever
**praeustus, -a, -um,** burned at
  the end
**sudis, -is** (*f*), stake
**muralis, -is, -e,** used in
  fighting from walls

**contabulo** (1), to cover with
  boards
**pinna, -ae** (*f*), battlement
**lorica, -ae** (*f*), breast-work,
  parapet
**cratis, -is** (*f*), wickerwork
**valetudo, -inis** (*f*), health,
  state of health
**tunc,** then, at that point
**potestas, -atis** (*f*), power,
  opportunity
**commemoro** (1), to relate

**instituo, -ere, -ui, -utum,** to erect, set up
**attexo, -ere** (3), **-texui, -textum,** to weave on, add by weaving

39 **quicquam praesidii:** *any support* (Partitive Genitive).

**ab eis qui suis rebus diffidant:** This refers to Caesar and his generals who, according to the Nervii, had enough problems of their own without thinking of tackling Cicero's problem too.

40 **licere illis:** Again, there is no verb of speaking to introduce this indirect statement (Accusative and Infinitive).

**illis** refers to the Romans, and **per se** to the Nervii, who are speaking.

40–41 The infinitives **discedere** and **proficisci** depend on **licere**.

42 **unum:** *one thing.*

44 **ab hac spe repulsi:** literally *driven back from this hope*, i.e. *after this disappointment.*

45 **haec** is the object of **cognoverant** and of **docebantur**, the Nervii being the subject of both verbs. It may seem unusual to have a direct object (**haec**) with a passive verb. In the active, **docere** may take two objects, e.g. **me multa docet**, *he teaches me many things.* In the passive, that becomes **multa doceor**, *I am taught many things.* Note also the interesting change of tense: *they had learned* from previous experience, and *they were also being taught* how to do it by prisoners on the spot. The use of **et . . . et . . .** links the two ideas together.

47 **nulla copia** is ablative: literally *with no supply*, i.e. *since they did not have a supply.*

48 **ad hunc usum idonea:** The use of **ad** here is similar to its use in **ad laborem** in line 26. Translate *suitable for this purpose.*

49 **qua ex re:** *from this fact, by observing this.*

50 **multitudo:** *the huge number.*

51 **minus horis tribus:** *in less than three hours.*

**milium pedum XV:** "15 000 feet" = 3000 paces, i.e. *three miles.*

54 **parare ac facere:** These infinitives have three objects—**turres, falces testudinesque**.

56 **more Gallico:** *in the way normally used by the Gauls.* Just as the Nervii were using Roman methods, so the Romans had built in the style of the Nervii.

57 **hae** refers to **casas** in the previous sentence.

**ignem:** This is the object of both **comprehenderunt** and **distulerunt**.

quicquam ab eis praesidii sperent qui suis rebus diffidant;
40  licere tamen illis incolumibus per se ex hibernis discedere
et quascunque in partes velint sine metu proficisci. Cicero
ad haec unum modo respondit: non esse consuetudinem
populi Romani accipere ab hoste armato condicionem.

## The siege intensified

ab hac spe repulsi Nervii vallo pedum IX et fossa pedum
45  XV hiberna cingunt. haec et superiorum annorum consuetudine ab nobis cognoverant et a captivis quibusdam
docebantur. sed nulla ferramentorum copia quae esset
ad hunc usum idonea, gladiis caespites circumcidere,
manibus sagulisque terram exhaurire nitebantur. qua
50  quidem ex re hominum multitudo cognosci potuit: nam
minus horis tribus munitionem milium pedum XV· in
circuitu perfecerunt; reliquisque diebus turres ad altitudinem valli, falces testudinesque, quas idem captivi
docuerant, parare ac facere coeperunt.
55  septimo oppugnationis die, maximo coorto vento,
fervefacta iacula in casas (quae more Gallico stramentis
erant tectae) iacere coeperunt. hae celeriter ignem comprehenderunt et venti magnitudine in omnem locum
castrorum distulerunt. hostes maximo clamore turres

**incolumis, -is, -e,** safe, unharmed
**per se,** as far as they were concerned
**consuetudo, -inis** (*f*), custom, experience
**condicio, -onis** (*f*), condition, terms
**ferramentum, -i** (*n*), metal tool
**caespes, -itis** (*m*), a turf
**sagulum, -i** (*n*), cloak
**circuitus, -us** (*m*), circumference
**falx, falcis** (*f*), grappling-hook
**testudo, -inis** (*f*), shelter
**fervefactus, -a, -um,** blazing
**iaculum, -i** (*n*), dart, javelin
**casa, -ae** (*f*), hut
**stramentum, -i** (*n*), straw

**diffido, -ere** (3), **diffisus sum** ( + *dat.*), to distrust, lack confidence (in)
**cingo, -ere** (3), **cinxi, cinctum,** to surround
**circumcido, -ere** (3), **-cidi, -cisum,** to cut round
**exhaurio, -ire** (4), **-hausi, -haustum,** to take away, remove
**nitor, -i** (3), **nisus sum,** to strive, labour
**tego, -ere** (3), **texi, tectum,** to cover
**differo, -ferre, distuli, dilatum,** to spread, carry in different directions

61 **cum torrerentur:** *although they were being scorched.*

63 **nemo:** By putting **nemo** after its verb at the end of the clause Caesar gives it tremendous emphasis. Compare the position of **quisquam** at the end of its clause.

64 **ac tum:** These two words bring the sentence to a climax: *in fact that was the moment when.*

66 **hunc eventum:** This is explained by the **ut** clause which follows.

68 **atque:** *or.* (The Latin means literally *a great number was wounded and a great number was killed.*)

**intermissa flamma:** English would tend to use a plural expression *when the flames had abated* (or translate **flamma** by *fire*).

69 **turri adacta et contingente:** *when a tower had been brought up and was touching.* Note the change in the tenses of the participles.

70 **ex eo quo stabant loco:** *from the point where they were stationed.*

71 **nutu vocibusque:** *by gestures and taunts.*

72 **si introire vellent:** (*to come in*) *if they wished to come in.*

73 **quorum:** refers back to **hostes.** Is **hostes** nominative or accusative?

**nemo:** Again, Caesar strongly emphasises this word by postponing it to the end of the sentence.

74 **deturbati:** Supply **sunt.** This refers to the Nervii.

75 **quanto gravior, tanto crebriores:** *the more serious . . ., the more frequent.* . . . **quanto . . . tanto . . .** is frequently used in this way (each followed by a comparative) to draw a comparison (literally *by how much the more . . ., by so much the more . . .*)

77 **quorum pars:** *some of them.*

**quorum** refers to **nuntii** in the previous sentence.

78 **intus:** *in the camp.*

79 **a prima obsidione:** literally *from the first (part of the) siege,* i.e. *at the beginning of the siege.*

80 **suam ei fidem praestiterat:** *had proved his loyalty to him.*

**hic:** *this man.*

**servo:** *a slave.*

60  testudinesque agere et scalis vallum ascendere coeperunt.
    at tanta militum virtus fuit ut, cum ubique flamma
    torrerentur maximaque telorum multitudine premeren-
    tur, non modo de vallo decederet nemo sed paene ne
    respiceret quidem quisquam, ac tum omnes acerrime
65  fortissimeque pugnarent.

    hic dies nostris longe gravissimus fuit, sed tamen hunc
    habuit eventum ut eo die maximus numerus hostium
    vulneraretur atque interficeretur. paulum quidem inter-
    missa flamma et quodam loco turri adacta et contingente
70  vallum, tertiae cohortis centuriones ex eo quo stabant
    loco recesserunt suosque omnes removerunt. nutu voci-
    busque hostes, si introire vellent, vocare coeperunt.
    quorum progredi ausus est nemo. tum ex omni parte
    lapidibus coniectis deturbati, turrisque succensa est.

## A messenger gets through

75  quanto erat in dies gravior atque asperior oppugnatio,
    tanto crebriores litterae nuntiique ad Caesarem mitteban-
    tur. quorum pars deprehensa in conspectu nostrorum
    militum cum cruciatu necabatur. erat unus intus Nervius,
    nomine Vertico, qui a prima obsidione ad Ciceronem
80  perfugerat suamque ei fidem praestiterat. hic servo spe

ubique, everywhere
gravis, -is, -e, serious
eventus, -us (*m*), outcome
deturbo (1), to dislodge
quanto . . . tanto . . ., the
    (more) . . ., the (more) . . .
in dies, daily

asper, -era, -erum, rough, desperate
creber, -bra, -brum, frequent
cruciatus, -us (*m*), torture
intus, inside
obsidio, -onis (*f*), siege
fidem praestare, to maintain
    good faith, serve loyally

torreo, -ere (2), **torrui, tostum,** to roast, scorch
premo, -ere (3), **pressi, pressum,** to press, put under pressure
decedo, -ere (3), **-cessi, -cessum,** to withdraw, retreat
contingo, -ere (3), **contigi, contactum,** to touch
recedo, -ere (3), **-cessi, -cessum,** to retreat
introeo, -ire, -ii, -itum, to enter
conicio, -ere (3), **-ieci, -iectum,** to hurl
succendo, -ere (3), **-endi, -ensum,** to set on fire
deprehendo, -ere (3), **-endi, -ensum,** to seize
perfugio, -ere (3), **-fugi,** to flee for refuge

82 **has:** *the letter.*

   **effert:** *carried (it) out of the camp.*

83 **Gallus inter Gallos:** *as a Gaul among Gauls.*

84 **ab eo cognoscitur:** literally *it was learned from him* (i.e. the messenger).
   Translate *information was gained from him.*

86 **unum communis salutis auxilium:** *the only means* (**auxilium**) *to achieve
   safety for everyone.*

92 **nostra:** Use the context to decide whether this agrees with **epistola** or
   **consilia**.

94 **ad amentum:** An **amentum** was a thong or strap attached to a javelin
   so that it could be thrown with greater force. On this occasion, the
   strap was used to tie on the message.

96 **profectum:** literally *having set out*; translate *he had set out and.*

   **adfore** = **adfuturum esse:** *(he) would be there*, i.e. *he would arrive.*

98 **tragulam mittit:** *threw the spear.*

99 **neque** must be taken with **animadversa**, not with **conspicitur**. Again, it
   is easier to treat **animadversa** as a main verb followed by *and*
   (compare line 96) or, in this case, *but*. Translate *it was not noticed...,
   but it was seen . . ..*

101 **perlectam . . . recitat:** He first read it himself and then read it out to
    the soldiers.

103 **fumi incendiorum:** Caesar would burn Gallic villages and settlements
    as he reached them, partly to punish them for the uprising, partly to
    boost the morale of the troops who were under siege.

libertatis magnisque persuadet praemiis ut litteras ad Caesarem deferat. has ille in iaculo inligatas effert et, Gallus inter Gallos sine ulla suspicione versatus, ad Caesarem pervenit. ab eo de periculis Ciceronis legion-
85 isque cognoscitur.

Caesar, acceptis litteris, unum communis salutis auxilium in celeritate ponebat. venit magnis itineribus in Nerviorum fines. ibi ex captivis cognoscit quae apud Ciceronem gerantur quantoque in periculo res sit. tum
90 cuidam ex militibus Gallis magnis praemiis persuadet ut ad Ciceronem epistolam deferat. hanc Graecis conscriptam litteris mittit ne intercepta epistola nostra ab hostibus consilia cognoscantur. si adire non possit, monet ut tragulam cum epistola ad amentum deligata intra munit-
95 ionem castrorum abiciat. in litteris scribit se cum legionibus profectum celeriter adfore. hortatur ut pristinam virtutem retineat.

Gallus periculum veritus, ut erat praeceptum, tragulam mittit. haec casu ad turrim adhaesit neque ab nostris
100 biduo animadversa tertio die a quodam milite conspicitur, dempta ad Ciceronem defertur. ille perlectam in conventu militum recitat, maximaque omnes laetitia afficit. tum fumi incendiorum procul videbantur, quae res omnem dubitationem adventus legionum expulit.

---

**inligo** (1), to tie on, fasten
**suspicio, -onis** (*f*), suspicion
**magnum iter,** a forced march
**tragula, -ae** (*f*), javelin, spear (with a throwing strap)
**amentum, -i** (*n*), thong
**deligo** (1), to bind, tie

**casu,** by chance
**biduum, -i** (*n*), (a period of) two days
**conventus, -us** (*m*), gathering, assembly
**laetitia, -ae** (*f*), joy, happiness
**dubitatio, -onis** (*f*), doubt

**defero, -ferre, -tuli, -latum,** to carry (something) away from a place, to carry
**vereor, -eri** (2), **veritus sum,** to be afraid, fear
**praecipio, -ere** (3), **-cepi, -ceptum,** to instruct
**adhaereo, -ere** (2), **-haesi, -haesum,** to stick to
**demo, -ere** (3), **dempsi, demptum,** to take down
**perlego, -ere** (3), **-legi, -lectum,** to read through

# Impersonal Verbs

(a) The following are examples of impersonal verbs which you have met:

| | |
|---|---|
| **Marco** non **licet** exire. | **Marcus is** *not* **allowed** *to go out.* (literally "it is not allowed to Marcus") |
| **mihi placet** manere. | **I decide** *to remain.* (literally "it pleases me") |
| **me taedet** solitudinis. | **I am tired** *of being alone.* (literally "it wearies me") |

The noun (or pronoun) used in the accusative or dative with these verbs becomes the subject in English. With these verbs there is also normally a noun in the genitive or an infinitive.

Further examples of impersonals are:

| | |
|---|---|
| **eum pudet** facinoris. | **He is ashamed** *of his deed.* |
| **me miseret** eius. | **I pity** *her.* |
| festinare **te oportet**. | **You must** *hurry.* |
| **eum decet** captivos liberare. | **It is right for him** *to free the captives.* **He is right** *to free the captives.* |

(b) The following sentences illustrate another impersonal use:

| | |
|---|---|
| acriter **pugnatum est.** | **There was** *keen* **fighting.** (literally "it was fought keenly") |
| ferociter **clamabatur.** | **There was** *fierce* **shouting.** (literally "it was shouted fiercely") |

The passive of the verb is used in the 3rd person singular (neuter) where the writer wishes to emphasise the action rather than the actual person or persons involved.

English tends to express the same idea either by using a noun or by changing the verb to the active voice, e.g.

complures horas **pugnabatur.**
**The battle continued** *for several hours.*
**They fought** *for several hours.*

ad mediam urbem **concursum est.**
**There was a rush** *to the city centre.*
**They rushed** *to the city centre.*

mox ad forum **ventum est.**
*Soon* **they came** *to the forum.*
*Soon the forum* **was reached.**

**nuntiatum est** hostes adesse.
**It was announced** *that the enemy were near.*
**News came** *that the enemy were near.*

a nostris **resistebatur.**
**Resistance was offered** *by our men.*
*Our men* **resisted.**

sic **vivitur.** *Such* **is life.**

# Exercise 59a

*Translate:*
1  Pyramo non licebat Thisben videre.
2  Helvetiis placuit Rhodanum transire.
3  furem non puduit furti.
4  regem filii miserebat.
5  non decet patrem filiam inscia matre despondere.
6  huius libri me taedet.
7  senatui placuit consulem revocare.
8  senatui placuit ne quis eam rem nuntiaret.

# Exercise 59b

*Translate:*
1  eis responsum est non licere per provinciam ire.
2  Rauracis et Tulingis persuasum est ut vicos et oppida exurerent.
3  mox audacius resistebatur et acrius pugnabatur.
4  simul ab eis qui cum impedimentis veniebant clamatum est.
5  patribus Romanis semper parebatur; patri enim licebat filium necare.
6  cum ad mediam urbem perventum esset, ferociter conclamatum est.
7  equitibus imperatum erat ut quarta hora proficiscerentur.
8  adverso colle ad castra nostra contendebatur.
9  cum ante imperatoris oculos pugnaretur, milites Romani occasionem probandae virtutis semper petebant.
10  macte nova virtute, puer! sic itur ad astra.

   **macte** ( + *abl.*), blessings on!   **astra, -orum** (*n.pl*), stars
   The last sentence was addressed to a young man who had proved his courage for the first time.

# Marcus Tullius Cicero

(*Photo: The Mansell Collection*)

In the Roman Republic of the 1st century BC, high public office was more or less the monopoly of a few noble families. Cicero was born the son of a Roman knight in 106 BC at Arpinum, a town about 100 km from Rome. When he stood for public office, he was labelled a **novus homo** ("a new man"), a term which indicated that no one in his family had ever held such an appointment. He seemed, therefore, to have little chance of making his mark as a politician, but such was his ability as an orator that he held in turn all the offices of state, attaining the consulship in 63 BC, the first **novus homo** in thirty years to do so.

He had burst into prominence in 70 BC with his brilliant prosecution of the provincial governor, Verres, and he reached the climax of his political career during his consulship by his detection and suppression of the conspiracy of Catiline.

In the Civil War, Cicero, though a contemporary and personal friend of Caesar, threw in his lot—after much heart-searching—with Pompey, but he was pardoned by Caesar after Pompey's defeat at Pharsalus in 48 BC.

After Caesar's assassination in 44 BC, Cicero emerged again into public life with a series of speeches called "Philippics" in which he denounced Mark Antony for his seizure of power. This act of courage cost him his life, for Antony had him outlawed and murdered in 43 BC.

Despite these notable forays into politics, Cicero is remembered not as a statesman (as he would have wished), but as a writer. Many famous works of Greek and Latin literature have vanished without trace (ancient hand-written manuscripts have a low survival rate), but such was Cicero's fame and popularity that fifty-eight of his speeches made in the law-courts or delivered to the Senate or to the citizen body have come down to us in their written form, together with essays, dialogues and works on philosophy and oratory. Over 800 of his letters are extant and these, like his speeches, reveal not only the dramatic events of the era in which he lived, but also the flaws in his character—vanity, indecisiveness, complacency, self-pity—as well as his great virtues of patriotism, humanity and intelligence.

Above all, he was the greatest master of Latin prose, the one who more than anyone else developed the range and subtlety of the Latin language as a means of expression, and who was to become the model for all later writers and orators.

### The Speeches against Verres

It was not uncommon for ambitious politicians, when standing for office in Rome, to spend large sums of their own money to win votes in the election. At the end of their year as magistrates in Rome, consuls and praetors were usually appointed as governors of provinces in different parts of the empire. The former tended to be given the more important provinces and acted as **proconsul**, the latter the less important provinces with the rank of **propraetor**. As governors, they had total power over the local population, and some used this as an opportunity to recoup the money they had lavished on their elections. One such corrupt governor was Gaius Verres, who was propraetor in Sicily from 73 to 71 BC. On his return to Rome in 70 BC, the Sicilians brought an accusation against him to the senate for misgovernment and oppression.

Cicero had won high praise and respect for his honesty and fair-mindedness when he was **quaestor** in Sicily in 75 BC and, although he was at that time a young and comparatively unknown orator, he was chosen by the Sicilians to act as prosecutor.

After Cicero's first speech for the prosecution, in which the evidence against Verres was utterly overwhelming, Verres abandoned his defence and went into exile. The further speeches for the prosecution, in which Cicero goes into details of the charges against Verres, were never delivered but were published later as a political pamphlet.

Passage 60 gives a general statement of the crimes committed by Verres, while passages 61 and 62 give some illustration of Verres' cruelty, rapacity and greed.

1  **iste** ("that man") is much stronger than **is** or **ille**. In a court case, it refers to the defendant. It is therefore often used (as here) as an expression of contempt which relies very much on sound for its effect. It would also be accompanied by an aggressive pointing gesture.

2  **hoc praetore:** Ablative Absolute—*while this man was governor.*

4  **tenuerunt:** literally *held*, i.e. *were protected by.*

   **tantum quisque habet, quantum . . .,** *each man possesses (only) as much as . . .*

5  **hominis avarissimi satietati superfuit:** *was left over after the greedy scoundrel had taken his fill* (literally *survived the satisfying of . . .*). The word **homo** is used here in a derogatory sense, *fellow*, as it frequently is.

7  **nulla res iudicata est:** *no court judgment was made.*

9  **coactae:** Supply **sunt**—*were extorted.*    **in hostium numero:** *as enemies.*

10  **servilem in modum:** literally *in the manner of slaves*, i.e. *like slaves.*

12  **indicta causa:** literally *their case not having been spoken*, i.e. *without trial* (Ablative Absolute).

15  **cum magna ignominia:** *to the great discredit.*

18  **victores:** *as victors, in their hour of victory.* Cicero is implying that, even after winning victories against the Sicilians, other Roman generals had restored valuable treasures to them, whereas Verres plundered them even though they were not at war. The Marcelli, in particular, were patrons and friends of the Sicilians.

20  **in:** *in the case of.*

22  **religionibus:** To a Roman, the word **religio** meant much more than the word "religion" means to us. The basic meaning is "fear of the gods", and from that meaning other ideas develop such as "religious scruples", "religious rites", "reverence", "religious beliefs", and "conscience".

23  **denique:** This word is used to sum up a catalogue of examples.

   **qui ei antiquo artificio factus videretur:** *which seemed to him to be an antique* (literally *made with ancient craft*).

---

**triennium, -i** (*n*), (period of) three years
**restituo** (3), to restore
**status, -us** (*m*), position, condition
**Siculi, -orum** (*m.pl*), Sicilians
**senatus consultum,** decree of the senate
**ius, iuris** (*n*), law, a right

**avarus, -a, -um,** greedy
**satietas, -atis** (*f*), sufficiency, glut
**iudico** (1), to judge, think
**arator, -oris** (*m*), farmer
**bona, -orum** (*n.pl*), property, possessions
**nefarius, -a, -um,** abominable, wretched
**crucio** (1), to torture

# 60

# The Crimes committed by Verres

Siciliam iste per triennium ita vexavit ac perdidit ut ea
restitui in antiquum statum nullo modo possit. hoc
praetore, Siculi neque suas leges neque nostra senatus
consulta neque communia iura tenuerunt. tantum
5   quisque habet in Sicilia quantum hominis avarissimi
satietati superfuit.

    nulla res per triennium nisi ad nutum istius iudicata est:
innumerabiles pecuniae ex aratorum bonis novo
nefarioque instituto coactae; socii fidelissimi in hostium
10  numero existimati; cives Romani servilem in modum
cruciati et necati; homines nocentissimi propter pecunias
iudicio liberati, honestissimi atque integerrimi indicta
causa damnati et eiecti; portus munitissimi, maximae
tutissimaeque urbes piratis praedonibusque patefactae;
15  classes optimae cum magna ignominia populi Romani
amissae et perditae.

    idem iste praetor monumenta antiquissima partim
regum, partim etiam nostrorum imperatorum, quae victores civitatibus Siculis aut dederunt aut reddiderunt,
20  spoliavit nudavitque omnia. neque hoc solum in statuis
ornamentisque publicis fecit, sed etiam delubra omnia
sanctissimis religionibus consecrata depeculatus est.
deum denique nullum Siculis, qui ei antiquo artificio
factus videretur, reliquit.

| | |
|---|---|
| **nocens, -entis,** guilty | **classis, -is** (*f*), fleet |
| **iudicium, -i** (*n*), judgment | **ignominia, -ae** (*f*), disgrace |
| **honestus, -a, -um,** honourable | **partim,** partly |
| **integer, -tegra, -tegrum,** | **spolio** (1), to loot, pillage |
|   honest, blameless | **delubrum, -i** (*n*), shrine, sanctuary |
| **damno** (1), to condemn | **sanctus, -a, -um,** holy, sacred |
| **tutus, -a, -um,** safe | **depeculor** (1), to plunder |
| **patefacio** (3), to lay open, | **denique,** in short, in fact |
|   expose | **artificium, -i** (*n*), workmanship |

2 **apud illos:** *in their eyes.*

**religiosum:** Compare Chapter 60, line 22.

**ex aere simulacrum:** *a statue (made) from bronze.*

4 **solent.** The subject of this verb is the people of Agrigentum.

5 **duce Timarchide:** an Ablative Absolute, meaning literally *Timarchides being the leader*, i.e. *led by Timarchides.* Timarchides was a notorious agent of Verres.

7 **concursus atque impetus:** These two nouns are used to express a single idea— *a massed attack.* (Compare **vigilibus fanique custodibus** (line 7), **obsistere ac defendere** (line 8), **revulsis effractisque** (line 10), **demoliri ac labefactare** (line 11), **ex domo atque ex cohorte** (line 14), **instructam armatamque** (line 15) where Cicero uses two words to create greater impact, mainly through sound effect.

8 **cum:** *although.*

9 **clavis ac fustibus:** Note again how much more effective the two words are than either word would be on its own.

12 **fama percrebruit:** *the story spread.* On these words depend two Accusative and Infinitive clauses:

    (a) **expugnari deos patrios**
    (b) **manum . . . venisse.**

There is a further balance between the phrases

    **non hostium adventu . . . impetu**
and **sed ex domo . . . praetoria.**

Instead of finishing the sentence there, as he might have, he adds the second Accusative and Infinitive **manum . . . venisse**, which tends to make the balance of the sentence slightly awkward since **sed** is used to link both the ablatives and the accusative clauses.

14 **ex domo atque ex cohorte praetoria:** The adjective **praetoria** has to be taken with both **domo** and **cohorte**. The praetor was, of course, the governor, Verres.

# 61
# Verres foiled by the People of Agrigentum

Herculis templum est apud Agrigentinos non longe a
foro, sane sanctum apud illos et religiosum. ibi est ex aere
simulacrum ipsius Herculis, quod in precibus et gratulat-
ionibus non solum venerari verum etiam osculari solent.

5    ad hoc templum, cum esset iste Agrigenti, duce
Timarchide repente nocte intempesta servorum arma-
torum fit concursus atque impetus. clamor a vigilibus
fanique custodibus tollitur; qui primo cum obsistere ac
defendere conarentur, male mulcati clavis ac fustibus

10    repelluntur. postea, revulsis repagulis effractisque valvis,
demoliri signum ac vectibus labefactare conantur.

interea fama tota urbe percrebruit expugnari deos
patrios non hostium adventu necopinato neque repentino
praedonum impetu, sed ex domo atque ex cohorte

15    praetoria manum fugitivorum instructam armatamque

**apud** ( + *acc.*), among
**sane,** very
**preces, -um** (*f.pl*), prayers
**gratulatio, -onis** (*f*),
   thanksgiving
**veneror** (1), to worship
**osculor** (1), to kiss
**repente,** suddenly
**nocte intempesta,** at dead of night
**vigil, -ilis** (*m*), watchman
**fanum, -i** (*n*), shrine
**obsisto** (3), to resist, bar the way
**mulco** (1), to beat
**clava, -ae** (*f*), club, cudgel
**fustis, -is** (*m*), club, stick
**revulsus, -a, -um,** wrenched off

**repagula, -orum** (*n.pl*), bolts, bars
**effractus, -a, -um,** broken open
**valvae, -arum** (*f.pl*), folding doors
**demolior** (4), to pull down,
   dislodge
**signum, -i** (*n*), statue
**vectis, -is** (*m*), lever, crowbar
**labefacto** (1), to loosen
**expugno** (1), to storm, assault
**patrius, -a, -um,** of one's
   native land
**necopinatus, -a, -um,** unexpected
**repentinus, -a, -um,** sudden
**cohors praetoria,** the
   governor's staff
**fugitivus, -i** (*m*), runaway slave

16 **nemo . . . neque . . . neque . . .:** Normally, a double negative produces a
positive (e.g. **non nemo**, *someone*); in this case, **neque . . . neque . . .**
reinforces **nemo**, i.e. the ablative phrases give us more information
about **nemo**.

    **aetate affecta** and **viribus infirmis** are ablatives of description: *enfeebled
by age* and *physically weak* (literally *with failing age* and *with shaky
strength*).

20 **horam amplius iam:** *already for more than an hour.*

21 **moliebantur:** The imperfect tense used with **iam** is translated *had been
struggling* (and still were struggling).

22 **cum** again means *although*.

    **vectibus subiectis:** not Ablative Absolute, **vectibus** being the normal
ablative used to indicate the instrument used.

23 **deligatum** agrees with **simulacrum** understood.

    **rapere:** Supply **conarentur**.

25 **istius praeclari imperatoris** and **nocturni milites** are both sarcastic gibes
against Verres.

26 **sigilla perparvula: sigillum** is the diminutive of **signum**; **parvulus** is the
diminutive of **parvus**, and the prefix **per-** intensifies the smallness.
Cicero could hardly make the items they stole any smaller or more
insignificant, contrasting them with the massive efforts made in the
attempt to carry off the statue—a very successful attempt to pour
ridicule on Verres.

*Map 10* Sicily and the toe of Italy

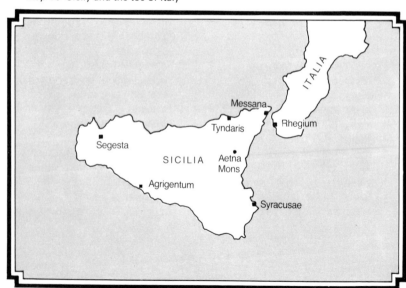

venisse. nemo Agrigenti neque aetate tam affecta neque
viribus tam infirmis fuit qui non illa nocte eo nuntio
excitatus surrexerit telumque arripuerit. itaque brevi
tempore ad fanum ex urbe tota concurritur.

20　　horam amplius iam in demoliendo signo permulti
homines moliebantur; illud interea nulla lababat ex parte,
cum alii vectibus subiectis conarentur commovere, alii
deligatum omnibus membris rapere ad se funibus. ac
repente Agrigentini concurrunt; fit magna lapidatio; dant
25　sese in fugam istius praeclari imperatoris nocturni milites.

　　duo tamen sigilla perparvula tollunt, ne omnino inanes
ad istum praedonem religionum revertantur.

**aetas, aetatis** (*f*), age
**vires, -ium** (*f.pl*), strength
**amplius,** more (than)
**molior** (4), to struggle, toil
**labo** (1), to move, totter
**subicio** (3), to place under
**lapidatio, -onis** (*f*), stone-
　throwing

**praeclarus, -a, -um,**
　distinguished
**sigillum, -i** (*n*), statuette
**perparvulus, -a, -um,** very
　small, diminutive
**inanis, -is, -e,** empty-handed

1 **audistis = audivistis.** Cicero is addressing the jury.
**Tyndaritanos:** Tyndaris was a town on the north coast of Sicily.

2 **Mercurium:** *the statue of Mercury.* This word is to be taken with **esse sublatum** (line 4)—an Accusative and Infinitive depending on **dicere.**

3 **Publius Africanus:** There were two Roman generals of this name who were involved in the capture of Carthage. First, there was Publius Cornelius Scipio who received the title Africanus after defeating the Carthaginians at Zama in 202 BC and thus ending the Second Punic War. Then, in 147 BC, his grandson destroyed Carthage to end the Third Punic War. It is not clear which of these two is referred to here but it is likely to be the latter since the city was destroyed then and treasures would have been removed first. Either way, this statue was obviously an historical gift made by a Roman for whom the jury would have great respect.
**dedisset:** The use of the subjunctive in this relative clause shows that this was part of what the ambassadors had said to the court.

4 **huius:** *of this man.* Cicero would point to Verres as he said this.
**vi scelere imperioque:** This is not so much a list; **-que** is often used to explain what has gone before rather than meaning *and.* The ablatives **vi scelere** also go closely together in a figure of speech called Hendiadys where one idea is conveyed through two words. Translate *by violent crime, abusing his power.*

**qui:** *he,* i.e. Verres.

1–4 It is worth studying the structure of this sentence since it illustrates well how Cicero builds up his sentences. Remember that he was speaking these words to the court.
    Depending on **audistis** is the Accusative and Infinitive **nuper dicere legatos Tyndaritanos.** This is followed by **homines honestissimos ac principes civitatis** which, in true Ciceronian style, lavishly boosts the credentials of the ambassadors.
    Depending on **dicere** is another Accusative and Infinitive: **Mercurium huius vi scelere imperioque esse sublatum.** Cicero must leave the jury in no doubt that this was no ordinary statue; and so he adds the relative clause (**quem . . . dedisset**) in which he plays on the Romans' admiration for the past.

5 **signum** is the object of both **demolirentur** and **deportarent**; for this reason, and also to concentrate the attention of the audience, it is put very early in the sentence. The word on which the two Indirect Commands depend (**imperavit**) is kept to the end. There can be no doubt that it all happened on the specific instructions of Verres; he cannot put the blame on a subordinate.

6 **Messanam:** Messina was a port on the Straits between Italy and Sicily.
**quod** is a Linking Relative: *this instruction* or *the thought of this.*

7 **ab isto:** In line 4, Cicero used **huius** to refer to Verres. Here, he uses the more usual pronoun of contempt—**iste** (the accused), the sound of which enables him almost to spit out his scorn.

# 62

# The Sopater Incident

audistis nuper dicere legatos Tyndaritanos, homines
honestissimos ac principes civitatis, Mercurium, quem
Publius Africanus Carthagine capta Tyndaritanis dedisset, huius vi scelere imperioque esse sublatum. qui ut
5   primum in illud oppidum venit, statim signum ut demolirentur et Messanam deportarent imperavit. quod
cum illis qui aderant indignum videretur, non est ab isto
primo illo adventu perseveratum. discedens mandat
proagoro Sopatro, cuius verba audistis, ut demoliatur.
10  cum recusaret, vehementer minatur et statim ex illo
oppido proficiscitur.

     refert rem ille ad senatum; vehementer undique re-
clamatur. ne multa, iterum iste ad illos aliquanto post

| | |
|---|---|
| **nuper,** recently | **mando** (1), to instruct |
| **legatus, -i** (*m*), ambassador | **proagorus, -i** (*m*), mayor, |
| **princeps, -ipis** (*m*), leader, |   chief magistrate |
|   leading citizen | **recuso** (1), to refuse |
| **ut primum,** as soon as | **minor** (1), to threaten |
| **indignus, -a, -um,** unworthy, | **aliquanto post,** some time |
|   intolerable, shameful |   later |
| **persevero** (1), to persist, | |
|   persevere | |

---

8  **primo illo adventu:** *on that first visit* (an Ablative of Time).

    **discedens:** present participle indicates that he gave the instructions *as
he was leaving.*

9  **cuius verba audistis:** Sopater had already given his evidence to the court.

10  **recusaret:** The subject of this verb is Sopater; the subject of **minatur** is Verres.

12  **ille:** Sopater.

13  **ne multa** (supply **dicam**): one of Cicero's favourite expressions. It
means literally *let me not say many words (when a few will suffice),* i.e.
*to cut a long story short* or *in short.*

14 **senatum non permittere:** This Accusative and Infinitive is followed by another **poenam capitis constitutam (esse)** which also depends on **respondetur**. In this chapter, the senate is the local (town) council, not the senate in Rome.

15 **capitis:** This word is often used as the equivalent of *life*. The genitive denotes the extent of the penalty imposed.
**si quisquam attigisset:** *if anyone laid hands on it.*

16 **religio:** See Chapter 60, line 22. Here it probably means *religious scruples.*

17 **quam mihi religionem narras?:** literally *What religious scruples are you telling* **me** *about?* (Note the emphasis on **mihi** from its position so early in the sentence.) This is a colloquial expression meaning *What's all this nonsense about religious scruples?*
**quam poenam, quem senatum:** With each of these supply **mihi narras**.

18 **vivum:** By giving this word its very emphatic position at the start of the sentence Verres suggests "Let us not talk about niceties like scruples; if you don't do what I say, I'll have no scruples about killing you."

19 **moriere = morieris:** *you will die.*

20–24 Note that the verbs are all historic presents, used here to illustrate the speed with which it all happened.

23 **discedit:** *adjourned, broke up.*     **ille:** Sopater. The praetor is Verres.

24 **negat ullo modo fieri posse:** *he said that that was quite impossible* (literally *he denies that it is able to be done in any way*). The verb **negare** means *to say that . . . not.*

25 **in conventu . . . superiore:** One of the governor's duties was that of a circuit judge. He would periodically visit the main towns and hold the court in the open air (**palam**), seated on his official chair (**sella**) on a raised platform (**de loco superiore**). Cases would be brought from the surrounding districts—which explains the term **conventus**.

26 **hiems summa:** *the depths of winter.*

28 **de porticu:** Verres himself was under cover in the portico, which was slightly raised above the forum; hence the use of **deiciant**.

30 **lictoribus:** *by the lictors.*
**videres:** *you might have seen, you could see.*

31 **id fore = id futurum esse:** an Accusative and Infinitive meaning *that that would happen.* The **id** is taken up and explained by the **ut** clause which follows: *namely that . . ..*

venit, quaerit continuo de signo. respondetur ei senatum
15   non permittere: poenam capitis constitutam, si iniussu
senatus quisquam attigisset. simul religio commemo-
ratur. tum iste "quam mihi religionem narras, quam
poenam, quem senatum? vivum te non relinquam.
moriere virgis nisi mihi signum traditur".

20   Sopater iterum flens ad senatum rem defert, istius
cupiditatem minasque demonstrat. senatus Sopatro responsum nullum dat, sed commotus perturbatusque
discedit. ille, praetoris arcessitus nuntio, rem demonstrat,
negat ullo modo fieri posse.

25   atque haec agebantur in conventu palam de sella ac de
loco superiore. erat hiems summa, tempestas perfrigida,
imber maximus, cum iste imperat lictoribus ut Sopatrum
de porticu in qua ipse sedebat praecipitem in forum
deiciant nudumque constituant. vix erat hoc plane imper-
30   atum cum illum spoliatum stipatumque lictoribus videres.
omnes id fore putabant ut miser atque innocens virgis
caederetur; fefellit hic homines opinio. virgis iste caederet

| | |
|---|---|
| **continuo,** immediately | **minae, -arum** (*f.pl*), threats |
| **permitto** (3), to allow | **conventus, -us** (*m*), assembly, |
| **poena capitis,** death penalty |   court of justice |
| **constituo** (3), to decide, fix | **palam,** openly, in public |
| **iniussu** (+ *gen.*), without the | **hiems, hiemis** (*f*), winter |
|   orders (of) | **perfrigidus, -a, -um,** very cold |
| **attingo** (3), to touch | **praeceps, praecipitis,** head- |
| **commemoro** (1), to mention |   long, head first |
| **vivus, -a, -um,** alive | **plane,** openly, clearly |
| **virga, -ae** (*f*), stick, rod | **spolio** (1), to strip |
| **rem deferre,** to report the | **stipo** (1), to surround, hem in |
|   matter | **caedo** (3), to kill, beat |
| **cupiditas, -atis** (*f*), desire, | **fallo** (3), to deceive |
|   greed | |

32  **hic:** literally *here*, i.e. *on this point.*
    **fefellit hic homines opinio:** literally *on this point, supposition deceived*
    *people*, i.e. *this is just where they were wrong in their expectations.*

    **caederet:** *would he go so far as to flog?*

111

34 **usque eo:** *as far as that.* **eo** is the adverb meaning *to there.* The whole sentence means *his wickedness does not go that far.* This sentence and the next are full of sarcasm.

**non omnia:** By attaching **non** to **omnia** Cicero cleverly suggests *not all, but almost all.*

35 **hominem:** Sopater. In contrast with Chapter 60, line 5, where it is used in a derogatory sense, **homo** here means *poor fellow.*

36 **Marcellorum:** The family of the Marcelli had been friends and patrons of the people of Sicily since the capture of Syracuse by M. Marcellus in 211 BC, during the Second Punic War. C. Marcellus was the governor of Sicily in 79 BC and was one of the jurors in the trial of Verres. He was the grandson of M. Marcellus.

37 **ex quibus** refers to **statuae.**

39 **cum ... tum ...:** a very emphatic way of saying *both ... and ...,* or *not only ... but also ....*

41 **quo cruciatu sit affectus:** literally *with what torture he was affected,* i.e. *how much physical pain he suffered.* Here, as he frequently does, Cicero places the Indirect Question in front of the main clause on which it depends—**venire in mentem necesse est omnibus** (*(it) must be obvious to everyone*), thus giving maximum importance and effect to the words in the Indirect Question.

46 **clamabant fore ut:** literally *they cried that it would be the case that.* Translate *they cried that the immortal gods would ....*

47 **se ulciscerentur:** *would take their own vengeance.*

48 **non oportere:** an impersonal Accusative and Infinitive depending on **clamabant.** Translate *it was not right* or *it was wrong.*

**hominem ... non oportere:** Although **clamabant** is not repeated, its force is continued beyond **ulciscerentur.** The verb **oportere** is normally impersonal (*it is fitting*), but in this sentence it has a subject, namely, the Accusative and Infinitive **hominem perire innocentem.** Translate *it was wrong that an innocent man should die.*

sine causa socium populi Romani atque amicum? non
usque eo est improbus; non omnia sunt in uno vitia;
35   numquam fuit crudelis. leniter hominem clementerque
accepit. equestres sunt medio in foro Marcellorum
statuae, sicut fere ceteris in oppidis Siciliae; ex quibus iste
C. Marcelli statuam delegit; in ea Sopatrum, hominem
cum domi nobilem tum summo magistratu praeditum,
40   divaricari ac deligari iubet.

     quo cruciatu sit affectus venire in mentem necesse est
omnibus, cum esset vinctus nudus in aere, in imbri, in
frigore. neque tamen finis huic iniuriae crudelitatique
fiebat donec populus atque universa multitudo, atrocitate
45   rei misericordiaque commota, senatum clamore coegit ut
isti simulacrum illud Mercurii polliceretur. clamabant
fore ut ipsi se di immortales ulciscerentur: hominem
interea perire innocentem non oportere. tum frequens
senatus ad istum venit, pollicetur signum. ita Sopater de
50   statua C. Marcelli, cum iam paene obriguisset, vix vivus
aufertur.

**improbus, -a, -um,** wicked,
   depraved
**vitium, -i** (*n*), fault, vice
**equester, -tris, -tre,**
   equestrian, on horseback
**deligo** (3), to choose, select
**domi,** at home, in his own
   community
**praeditus, -a, -um** ( + *abl.*),
   endowed (with), honoured
   (with)
**divarico** (1), to set astride
**afficio** (3), to treat
**mens, mentis** (*f*), mind

**vincio** (4), to bind
**aes, aeris** (*n*), bronze
**frigus, -oris** (*n*), cold
**iniuria, -ae** (*f*), an act of
   injustice
**donec,** until
**universus, -a, -um,** entire, all
**atrocitas, -atis** (*f*), brutality
**misericordia, -ae** (*f*), pity
**simulacrum, -i** (*n*), statue
**frequens, -entis,** packed, in
   full force, en masse
**obrigesco** (3), to grow stiff

# Roman Administration

Public officials at Rome in the time of the Republic were elected every year by the citizens—each to hold office for one year. These public appointments, held in a recognised sequence, formed a ladder of advancement (**cursus honorum**) for career politicians. There was a lower age-limit for holding each office: usually 31 for **quaestor**, 37 for **aedile**, 40 for **praetor** and 43 for **consul**. The number of these officials varied at different historical periods, but there were at least two at each level. The tyranny which the Romans had experienced under the last of the kings, Tarquinius Superbus, led them to the conclusion that no one man should have supreme power in the city.

The **quaestors** were in charge of finance, often assisting more senior officials such as governors of provinces.

The **aediles** directed city services such as maintenance of public buildings, street-cleaning, policing, weights and measures, but their most eye-catching activity was the presentation of the public games which they were expected to subsidise from their own resources. Obviously, this could be used as a means of exploiting public support, and Julius Caesar was one of those who used it to great effect.

The **praetors** were law officials, responsible for the proclamation of the laws and the running of the courts in which they often acted as judges. After their year of office, they were eligible under the Republic to serve as provincial governors, with the rank of **propraetor**.

The **consuls**, always two in number, held jointly an office resembling that of a president or prime minister. They chaired meetings of the senate, initiated business there and acted as commanders of the army in war. At the end of their year of office, they were eligible for important provincial governorships as **proconsuls**.

Exceptionally, when there was a serious crisis, a **dictator** was appointed to take over from the consuls as sole commander of the army. The maximum period for which he could hold this post was six months.

Various citizen assemblies, in theory, passed the laws, but in practice the day-to-day administration of government and law was carried out by the **senate**, in origin merely an advisory body which was made up of the original landowners and others who had held high office in the state. The quaestorship was the lowest level of magistrate qualifying for entry to the senate. Having become a senator, one remained a senator for life.

Every five years, two **censors** were appointed to carry out a census of the people and to discover such information as the age of citizens and the amount of property each held. They also supervised the roll of the senate and had the power to remove the names of senators who were guilty of misconduct.

During the Empire, while these officials continued to be elected and to hold office, effective power over the state passed into the hands of the emperor.

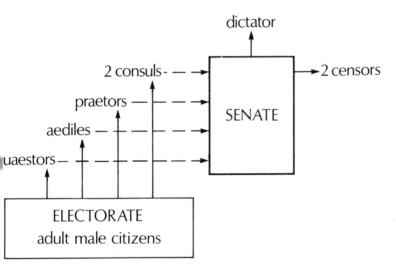

The **cursus honorum**

# 63

# Cicero speaks against Catiline

Cicero's speeches against Catiline, four in all, mark the climax of his career as an orator.

L. Sergius Catilina was a member of a noble family which had fallen on hard times. In a bid to restore his family fortunes, he had aimed at the consulship several times, but for a variety of reasons was unsuccessful. In desperation, he began to plan a revolution in which the consuls would be murdered and he would seize power himself.

One of the consuls in 63 BC was Cicero. In the following shortened version of his first speech against Catiline, we read Cicero's powerful denunciation of Catiline, who has even had the effrontery to appear in person in the Senate although details of his revolutionary plans are already common knowledge.

*line*

1 **quo usque tandem?** *How long, pray tell me?* **tandem** is used in questions to express the speaker's impatience or indignation.

**abutere = abuteris** (future tense).

2 **furor iste tuus:** The adjective **iste,** as usual, indicates contempt; when combined also with **tuus,** the point is really hammered home.

2–4 **nihilne ... nihil ... nihil ... nihil ... nihil ...:** Cicero is fond of this powerful rhetorical technique of starting a series of clauses with the same word (Anaphora). This also provides you with a useful clue towards tackling the translation. Since you know that each of the clauses must have a similar grammatical pattern, you can decide which words must be regarded as common to all the clauses. In this case, you must understand with each clause **-ne, te** and **moverunt** (or **movit**):

| | |
|---|---|
| nihilne te nocturnum praesidium Palati | (movit)? |
| nihilne (te) urbis vigiliae | (moverunt)? |
| nihilne (te) timor populi | (movit)? |
| nihilne (te) concursus bonorum omnium | (movit)? |
| nihilne (te) horum ora vultusque | moverunt? |

By reading over the above expanded version you should appreciate how much more effective the condensed Latin version is.

# M. TULLI CICERONIS
## ORATIO IN CATILINAM PRIMA
## IN SENATU HABITA

*How long will this intolerable situation be allowed to continue? We
know all about your plans even though we have not done anything to
combat them so far.*

quo usque tandem abutere, Catilina, patientia nostra?
quamdiu etiam furor iste tuus nos eludet? nihilne te nocturnum praesidium Palati, nihil urbis vigiliae, nihil timor
populi, nihil concursus bonorum omnium, nihil horum
5  ora vultusque moverunt? patere tua consilia non sentis?

---

**in** (+ *acc.*), against
**orationem habere,** to
  deliver a speech
**abutor** (3) (+ *abl.*), to
  abuse, take advantage
  (of), exhaust
**patientia, -ae** (*f*),
  patience
**quamdiu?** how long?

**furor, -oris** (*m*),
  madness, frenzy
**eludo** (3), to mock,
  make sport (of)
**nihil movere,** to make
  no impression on
**concursus, -us** (*m*),
  rallying
**pateo** (2), to be
  exposed, lie open

---

3 **praesidium Palati:** The Palatine Hill was the site of the original
  settlement of Rome and, when any danger threatened the city, a
  garrison was placed on it since it was one of the more easily defended
  sites. By this time, it had become one of the most fashionable places to
  live in the city.

  **vigiliae:** "watches" would normally be necessary only when an enemy
  was near the city. There had not been an armed enemy threatening
  Rome since the time of Hannibal, about 150 years earlier.

4 **bonorum:** *of good men,* i.e. *patriots.*
  **horum** refers to the senators before whom Cicero is making the speech.

6 **quid ... quid ...:** Compare lines 2–4. The expanded version would be:

> **quid proxima (nocte egeris)?**
> **quid superiore nocte egeris?**

These two clauses are followed by three other Indirect Questions introduced by **ubi, quos, quid.** All five depend on the direct question **quem nostrum ignorare arbitraris,** which comes at the end of the sentence. Cicero often uses this technique of introducing an Indirect Question before the main clause. In this way, he gives prominence to the information contained in the Indirect Question and also heightens the suspense.

**proxima (nocte):** This was the night before the speech, i.e. 6–7th November: **superiore nocte** was the night before that.

7 **quem nostrum:** *which of us.* **nostrum** is the genitive of **nos.**

**quem nostrum ignorare arbitraris?** is what is called a Rhetorical Question, i.e the speaker is really indicating that the question does not require an answer because it should be so clear to everyone. Here he means *All of us know.*

8 **o tempora! o mores!** *What an age we live in!* As we say, "How times have changed!" Cicero suggests that the honourable traditions and customs of Ancient Rome have been abandoned.

9 **hic:** *this man.*

**vivit? immo vero: immo** corrects the previous statement **(vivit)** by indicating that he has stated it far too mildly.

11 **designat ad caedem:** *he marks down for assassination.*

**unum quemque nostrum:** *each one of us.*

12 **viri fortes:** *brave men that we are,* said sarcastically.

13 **videmur:** literally *seem.* Translate *we convince ourselves that we.*

**istius:** Again, Cicero uses this word as an expression of contempt. It relies very much on sound for its effect.

14 **te duci oportebat:** *you ought to have been led.*

15 **pestem conferri:** Supply **oportebat.**

16 **iamdiu machinaris:** *you have long been plotting.* Latin uses the present tense with **iam diu** to express the idea *you have been plotting and still are plotting.*

The repetition of **te ... te ... tu ...** in lines 14–15 is an oratorical technique used to produce dramatic effect and emphasis.

17 **in Etruriae faucibus:** *in a mountain pass in Etruria.* Etruria was the area immediately to the north of Rome, but the actual site of the camp (Faesulae) was about 140 miles north of Rome (not far from Florence).

**castra sunt ... collocata:** Note how Cicero uses each successive phrase to shock his audience more and more: (*a*) **castra sunt in Italia** – possibly nothing alarming in that provided it is a Roman army preparing to set off against foreign enemies; but (*b*) **contra populum Romanum;** (*c*) not

quid proxima, quid superiore nocte egeris, ubi fueris, quos convocaveris, quid consilii ceperis, quem nostrum ignorare arbitraris? o tempora! o mores! senatus haec intellegit, consul videt. hic tamen vivit. vivit? immo
10 vero, etiam in senatum venit, fit publici consilii particeps, notat et designat oculis ad caedem unum quemque nostrum. nos autem, viri fortes, satisfacere reipublicae videmur, si istius furorem ac tela vitemus.

*The evidence against you is already very strong, but as consul I am reluctant to execute you till everyone is convinced. Your every move, however, will be watched.*

ad mortem te, Catilina, duci iussu consulis iampridem
15 oportebat, in te conferri pestem quam tu in nos omnes iamdiu machinaris.

castra sunt in Italia contra populum Romanum in Etruriae faucibus collocata. crescit in dies singulos hostium numerus. eorum autem castrorum imperatorem
20 ducemque hostium intra moenia atque adeo in senatu

**consilium capere,** to
  adopt a plan
**particeps, -ipis** ( + *gen.*),
  sharing (in), taking part (in)
**noto** (1), to note, mark
**designo** (1), to mark
  out, designate
**caedes, -is** (*f*),
  slaughter, death
**satisfacio** (3) ( + *dat.*),
  to do one's duty (to)

**iampridem,** long ago
**confero, -ferre,** to bestow
**pestis, -is** (*f*), destruction
**machinor** (1), to devise, plot
**fauces, -ium** (*f.pl*), jaws, throat,
  mountain-pass
**cresco** (3), to increase
**moenia, -ium** (*n.pl*),
  (city) walls

---

just in Italy but **in Etruriae faucibus,** with the emphasis on **Etruriae;** and
(*d*) the final word **collocata** confirms that it is a firmly established camp
and not simply a disorganised gathering of a few malcontents.

18 **crescit:** The position of the verb at the start of the sentence gives it
  considerable emphasis. This is followed by the equally emphatic **in dies
  singulos,** rather than simply **in dies,** which would convey the meaning
  but not the effect.

20 **atque adeo:** *yes, and actually* or *and what is more.*

21 **cotidie:** The unusual position of this adverb within the phrase **intestinam aliquam perniciem** gives it great emphasis. Whereas **in dies** (line 18) implies a cumulative effect, one day building on the other, **cotidie** suggests repetition of the same thing each day.

22 **molientem:** *devising.* The participle agrees with **imperatorem ducemque.**

23 **factum esse oportuit:** *ought to have been done* (cf. line 14).

   **certa de causa:** *for a particular reason.*

24 **interficiere** = **interficieris.**

24–25 **tam ... tam ... tam ...:** Cicero is fond of this build-up of "triples", with the last one tending to be slightly longer. (Anaphora)

25 **tam tui similis:** *so like you;* **tui** is the genitive of **tu.**

   **id** refers to **interficiere.**

26 **quamdiu:** *as long as.*

27 **ut nunc vivis:** *as you now live.*

28 **multis meis et firmis: et** is regularly used to link the adjective **multi** with another adjective.

   **ne possis:** *so that you cannot* – Purpose Clause depending on **obsessus** which means *surrounded* or *hemmed in.*

29 **multorum:** Take with **oculi et aures.**

30 **non sentientem:** *though you do not realise it,* agreeing with **te.**

32 **mihi crede:** literally *trust me,* i.e. *take my advice.*

   **obliviscere** is imperative.

33–34 **luce ... omnia:** Cicero again reverses the normal order of the sentence to give the maximum impact to **luce clariora** and **omnia.** **luce** is Ablative of Comparison – *(clearer) than light.*

34 **quae iam mecum licet recognoscas:** literally *you may now recall these with me,* i.e. *let me remind you of these.*

36 **inter falcarios:** *into the street of the sickle-makers.* In ancient Rome, those who practised a particular trade tended to be concentrated in a particular street.

   **non agam obscure:** literally *I shall not discuss (it) vaguely,* i.e. *I shall not be vague* or *To be precise.*

37 **convenisse ... socios:** As frequently happens, **dico** is not repeated before this Accusative and Infinitive.

39 **quid taces?** Cicero has paused after saying **num negare audes** to give Catiline an opportunity to deny the charges, but he has not reacted.

40 **quosdam:** By not naming the senators involved, Cicero creates far more tension and apprehension among his audience. The most successful orators aim at a blend of fact and hints of other unspecified allegations, thus almost certainly convincing the audience that things are even worse than they actually are.

videmus, intestinam aliquam cotidie perniciem reipublicae molientem.  verum ego hoc, quod iampridem
factum esse oportuit, certa de causa nondum adducor ut
faciam.  tum denique interficiere, cum iam nemo tam im-
25  probus, tam perditus, tam tui similis inveniri poterit qui id
non iure factum esse fateatur.  quamdiu quisquam erit
qui te defendere audeat, vives;  et vives ita, ut nunc vivis,
multis meis et firmis praesidiis obsessus ne commovere te
contra rempublicam possis.  multorum te etiam oculi et
30  aures non sentientem, sicut adhuc fecerunt, speculabun-
tur atque custodient.

*Why don't you give up? I knew everything that happened at Laeca's*
*house the moment your meeting ended. What are things coming to*
*that conspirators can plan death and destruction within Rome?*

muta iam istam mentem, mihi crede, obliviscere caedis
atque incendiorum.  teneris undique.  luce sunt clariora
nobis tua consilia omnia.  quae iam mecum licet
35  recognoscas.
dico te priore nocte venisse inter falcarios, (non agam
obscure) in M. Laecae domum:  convenisse eodem complures eiusdem amentiae scelerisque socios.  num negare
audes?  quid taces?  convincam, si negas.  video enim
40  esse hic in senatu quosdam qui tecum una fuerunt.

| | |
|---|---|
| **intestinus, -a, -um,** <br> internal, from within | **muto** (1), to change |
| **pernicies, -ei** (*f*), <br> destruction, disaster | **obliviscor** (3) ( + *gen*), <br> to forget |
| **certus, -a, -um,** definite, certain | **clarus, -a, -um,** clear |
| **perditus, -a, -um,** corrupt | **recognosco** (3), to recall <br> to mind, review |
| **iure,** rightly, justly | **falcarius, -i** (*m*), sickle-maker |
| **fateor** (2), to confess, claim | **ago** (3), to discuss |
| **firmus, -a, -um,** strong, <br> reliable | **obscure,** obscurely, vaguely |
| **auris, -is** (*f*), ear | **amentia, -ae** (*f*), <br> madness |
| **sicut,** just as | **nego** (1), to deny |
| **speculor** (1), to watch, <br> observe | **quid?** why? |
| | **convinco** (3), to prove |

41 **ubinam gentium sumus?** *Where in the world are we?* A nice rhetorical touch. He suggests he must be dreaming since it is unbelievable that these things could be happening in Rome.

44 **de huius urbis:** Supply **exitio.**

**atque adeo:** See line 20.

45 **ego video consul:** The word order is again important. Note how he finishes with the word **consul** in case the point has escaped the notice of his audience.

46 **sententiam:** *their views.* How ridiculous to be asking those senators who are part of the conspiracy for advice on how to deal with the conspiracy!

**quos trucidari oportebat:** *who ought to have been slaughtered.* The antecedent of **quos** is **eos.** Cicero frequently puts the relative clause first for emphasis.

47 **nondum voce vulnero:** As was noted in line 40, he has not named them and has not brought specific charges against them.

48 **igitur:** *then,* used not in the temporal sense, but to pick up an argument after a digression. Here, he returns to the accusations he has made in lines 36–38.

49 **quo placeret:** literally *where it pleased (you),* i.e. *where you wanted.*

50 **quos relinqueres:** *(the men) whom you intended to leave.*

51 **ad incendia:** *for burning* or *to be burned.* Compare note in line 26 on page 90.

**confirmasti:** contracted form of **confirmavisti,** used here, presumably, because it is closer to the rhythm of the other verbs in this section: **fuisti, statuisti, delegisti, discripsisti, dixisti.**

52 **iam:** There had obviously been some doubt previously about whether he would be more useful to the conspirators if he remained in the city or if he joined the army outside the city; but now Cicero's accusations have left him no option.

**paulum tibi esse morae:** *you had to delay a little.*

53 **reperti sunt:** *there were found.*

54 **equites:** Use the term **equites** in your translation since there is no equivalent in English. The **equites** formed the middle rank in Roman society, between the senators and the plebeians.

**qui liberarent:** a Purpose clause – *to free (you).*

**et** links **liberarent** and **pollicerentur.**

55 **interfecturos:** Supply **esse.**

57 **etiam** emphasises **vixdum** and need not be translated in English.

58 **munivi atque firmavi:** Cicero frequently uses two verbs with similar meanings to add force to the sound of what he is saying rather than to add anything to the meaning.

o di immortales! ubinam gentium sumus? in qua urbe
vivimus? quam rempublicam habemus? hic, hic in
nostro numero, patres conscripti, sunt qui de nostro omnium interitu, qui de huius urbis atque adeo de orbis ter-
45  rarum exitio cogitent. hos ego video consul et de republica sententiam rogo. et quos ferro trucidari oportebat,
eos nondum voce vulnero.

fuisti igitur apud Laecam illa nocte, Catilina. distribu-
isti partes Italiae. statuisti quo quemque proficisci
50  placeret. delegisti quos Romae relinqueres, quos tecum
educeres. discripsisti urbis partes ad incendia. confirmasti te ipsum iam esse exiturum. dixisti paulum tibi esse
etiam nunc morae, quod ego viverem. reperti sunt duo
equites Romani qui te ista cura liberarent et sese illa ipsa
55  nocte paulo ante lucem me in meo lectulo interfecturos
pollicerentur.

haec ego omnia, vixdum etiam coetu vestro dimisso,
comperi. domum meam maioribus praesidiis munivi
atque firmavi, exclusi eos quos tu ad me salutatum mane
60  miseras.

| | |
|---|---|
| **patres conscripti,** senators | **trucido** (1), to butcher |
| **sunt qui** ( + *subjunctive*), there are some (men) who | **statuo** (3), to decide |
| | **discribo** (3), to divide, distribute |
| **interitus, -us** (*m*), destruction | **placet,** it pleases, it is decided |
| | **mora, -ae** (*f*), delay |
| **orbis terrarum,** the world | **cura, -ae** (*f*), anxiety |
| **exitium, -i** (*n*), destruction | **vixdum,** scarcely yet |
| | **coetus, -us** (*m*), meeting |
| **sententia, -ae** (*f*), opinion | **comperio** (4), to find out |
| | **firmo** (1), to strengthen |
| **ferrum, -i** (*n*), iron, sword | **excludo** (3), to shut out |

59 **salutatum:** The supine is used here to express Purpose – *to pay their
respects.* It was customary for clients and other well-wishers to visit the
homes of leading politicians early in the morning to pay their respects
and then to accompany them to the Senate-house or Forum.

*line*

61 **quae cum ita sint:** *since this is so* or *under these circumstances.*

**perge quo coepisti:** literally *go where you have begun (to go),* i.e. *finish the journey you have begun.*

62 **aliquando:** *at long last,* the implication being that it is long overdue.

64 **si minus:** *or if you cannot take all.*

67 **non feram, non patiar, non sinam:** All three verbs have roughly the same meaning but by using all three, each introduced by **non** (Anaphora), Cicero drives the point home.

71 **haec lux:** *this light of day.*

**huius caeli spiritus:** literally *the breath of this sky,* i.e. *the air we breathe.*

72 **iucundus:** Although masculine agreeing with the nearer subject (**spiritus**), this adjective must also be taken with **lux.** We must also supply **esse.**

**horum:** *of these men,* i.e. the senators present.

73 Marcus Aemilius Lepidus and Gaius Volcatius Tullus were consuls in 66 BC. The new consuls, L. Aurelius Cotta and L. Manlius Torquatus, were due to take up office on 1st January 65 BC.

74 **in comitio:** The **comitium** was the part of the Forum where the Assembly of the Roman people was held.

**manum paravisse:** Supply **te** from the previous clause.

**consulum ... interficiendorum causa** expresses Purpose.

76 **illa omitto:** *I make no mention of those crimes.* This is a favourite device of Cicero: he first says he is not going to mention something and then proceeds to tell his audience about it.

**neque sunt ... non multa:** The double negative produces a positive – *they are not not many = they are numerous.*

77 **quotiens ... quotiens ...:** These two words introduce parallel clauses (Anaphora):

> **quotiens tu me (consulem) designatum (interficere conatus es)**
> **quotiens (tu me) consulem          interficere conatus es**

**designatum:** Between the time of the election and the taking over of office the successful candidate was said to be **designatus.** Translate *consul designate* or *consul elect.*

79 **petitiones:** This was the technical term for the cut and thrust used by the gladiators.

**parva quadam declinatione et, ut aiunt, corpore:** Cicero continues the metaphor from the arena: *by a slight swerve, as they say, of the body.*

80 **tibi:** *from you.* The dative case is normal with verbs of *taking away (from).* However, the final two words of the sentence (**de manibus**) produce the real climax: not only was Catiline known to be carrying a weapon within the city, but an even greater indictment was the fact that it was actually in his hands ready to use.

*Why don't you get out of the city and take your fellow rogues with you? There can't be much pleasure living in Rome when you know that everyone knows all about your plans to kill leading citizens, not to mention your attempts on my own life.*

quae cum ita sint, Catilina, perge quo coepisti, egredere aliquando ex urbe! patent portae. proficiscere! nimium diu te imperatorem tua illa castra desiderant. educ tecum etiam omnes tuos, si minus, quam plurimos! purga
65  urbem! magno me metu liberabis, dummodo inter me atque te murus intersit. nobiscum versari iam diutius non potes. non feram, non patiar, non sinam.

quid est, Catilina, quod te iam in hac urbe delectare possit? in qua nemo est extra istam coniurationem per-
70  ditorum hominum qui te non metuat, nemo qui non oderit. potestne tibi haec lux, Catilina, aut huius caeli spiritus iucundus, cum scias esse horum neminem qui nesciat te pridie Kalendas Ianuarias, Lepido et Tullo consulibus, stetisse in comitio cum telo, manum consulum et
75  principum civitatis interficiendorum causa paravisse. ac iam illa omitto (neque enim sunt aut obscura aut non multa) commissa postea: quotiens tu me designatum, quotiens vero consulem interficere conatus es! quot ego tuas petitiones parva quadam declinatione et, ut aiunt,
80  corpore effugi! quotiens tibi iam extorta est ista sica de manibus!

**pergo** (3), to go on, proceed
**aliquando,** at last
**nimium,** too much, too
**desidero** (1), to long for
**purgo** (1), to cleanse
**dummodo** ( + *subjunctive*), provided that
**interesse,** to be between
**versor** (1), to associate with, go about among
**patior** (3), to suffer, endure
**extra** ( + *acc.*), outside
**metuo** (3), to fear
**odi** (*perfect*), **odisse,** to hate

**caelum, -i** (*n*), sky, heaven
**spiritus, -us** (*m*), breath
**iucundus, -a, -um,** pleasant, pleasing, enjoyable
**comitium, -i** (*n*), assembly, public meeting-place
**manus, -us** (*f*), band
**principes, -um** (*m.pl*), leading citizens
**omitto** (3), to say nothing of
**petitio, -onis** (*f*), attack
**extorqueo** (2), to wrest away (from)
**sica, -ae** (*f*), dagger

*line*

82 **quae tua est ista vita?** *What sort of life is it that you are living?*

83 **ex hac tanta frequentia: tantus** is normal in Latin after **hic, haec, hoc,**
whereas English would tend to say *from this great crowd* or *from such a
great crowd as this.* Cicero is referring to the well-attended meeting of
the senate which he is addressing.

84 **quid quod:** *what of the fact that.*
**ista:** Cicero points to the seats close to Catiline.

85 **quod = quid quod.**

86 **nudam atque inanem:** Again, two words of similar meaning are used;
either one would have conveyed the meaning, but together they create
far greater impact.

87 **quo animo:** *with what feelings.*
**tandem:** See line 1.

88 **ferendum:** Supply **esse.**

*Even close friends are shunning you and your country is pleading with you to release her from fear by leaving the city. Surely that is not too much to ask.*

nunc vero quae tua est ista vita? venisti paulo ante in senatum. quis te ex hac tanta frequentia totque tuis amicis ac necessariis salutavit? quid quod adventu tuo ista
85     subsellia vacuefacta sunt? quod omnes consulares, simulatque assedisti, partem istam subselliorum nudam atque inanem reliquerunt? quo tandem animo hoc tibi ferendum putas?

**frequentia, -ae** (*f*), a crowded assembly
**necessarii, -orum** (*m.pl*), relatives
**subsellium, -i** (*n*), bench

**vacuefacio** (3), to empty, vacate
**simulatque,** as soon as
**assido** (3), to sit down beside

89 **servi mehercule mei:** Although they belong to the **si** clause, Cicero brings these words forward to the beginning of the sentence, to make the dramatic contrast between unimportant things like slaves and the citizens and parents mentioned later.

**isto pacto ut:** *in the same way as.*

90 **relinquendam:** Supply **esse.**

91 **putarem:** *I would think.*

**tu tibi urbem:** Several words must be understood from the previous sentence since the two are balanced:

**(ego mihi) domum meam relinquendam (esse) putarem**
**tu tibi       urbem           (relinquendam esse) non arbitraris?**

92 **tui:** Note how this word comes at the end of the clause to emphasise *your own parents.*

94 **nunc:** *as it is.*

**omnium nostrum:** For the form **nostrum** see line 7.

95 **nullum** agrees with **facinus.**

98 **valuisti:** *you have used your strength, you have used every means in your power.*

**evertendas:** Supply **leges.**

**superiora illa:** *those previous crimes.*

99 **ferenda non fuerunt:** *they ought not to have been endured.*

**me totam:** Remember it is the state which is speaking. This phrase therefore refers to every aspect of the life of the city.

100 **propter unum te:** *on account of you alone.*

**unum te:** Begin the translation *The fact that ...*

**non est ferendum:** The subject of this phrase is the whole clause **me totam esse ...**

101 **mihi:** Compare line 80.

103 **si patria loquatur:** *if your country were to say.*

106–7 **si patria ..., si cuncta Italia, si omnis respublica loquatur:** The repetition of **si** tells us that we must understand certain words as common to all three clauses, namely, **mecum** and **loquatur.**

106 **vita** is Ablative of Comparison (cf. line 33).

servi mehercule mei si me isto pacto metuerent, ut te
90 metuunt omnes cives tui, domum meam relinquendam
putarem. tu tibi urbem non arbitraris? si te parentes
timerent atque odissent tui neque eos ulla ratione placare
posses, ut opinor, ab eorum oculis aliquo concederes.
nunc te patria, quae communis est parens omnium nos-
95 trum, odit ac metuit, et tecum, Catilina, sic agit: "nullum
iam aliquot annis facinus exstitit nisi per te, nullum flagitium sine te. tu non solum ad neglegendas leges verum
etiam ad evertendas valuisti. superiora illa, quamquam
ferenda non fuerunt, tamen, ut potui, tuli. nunc vero me
100 totam esse in metu propter unum te, Catilina, non est
ferendum. quam ob rem discede atque hunc mihi
timorem eripe."
haec si tecum, ut dixi, patria loquatur, nonne impetrare
debeat? quae cum ita sint, Catilina, dubitas abire in ali-
105 quas terras et vitam istam fugae solitudinique mandare?

*People are wondering why I have taken no action against you. It is not
as simple as that. Executing you would not remove the total threat to the
state. The only solution is for you to leave and take your wicked supporters with you.*

etenim si mecum patria, quae mihi vita mea multo est
carior, si cuncta Italia, si omnis respublica loquatur: "M.

| | |
|---|---|
| **placo** (1), to appease, pacify | **neglego** (3), to neglect, ignore |
| **opinor** (1), to think | **everto** (3), to overthrow |
| **aliquo,** somewhere, to some place or other | **valeo** (2), to be strong, be able |
| **concedo** (3), to withdraw | **metus, -us** (*m*), fear |
| **patria, -ae** (*f*), native land | **impetro** (1), to have a request granted |
| **facinus, -oris** (*n*), crime | **fuga, -ae** (*f*), flight |
| **exsisto** (3), **-stiti**, to come into being, arise | **solitudo, -inis** (*f*), solitude, exile |
| **flagitium, -i** (*n*), disgraceful deed | **mando** (1), to entrust |
| | **carus, -a, -um,** dear, precious, esteemed |

**108–9** As in lines 106–7, so in these lines certain words must be understood with the three objects (**auctorem, principem, evocatorem**); in this case, they are **tune exire patiere**.

**109** **evocatorem servorum:** The Romans relied very heavily on slaves in the running of their economy and in their daily lives; and the possibility of a revolt among them had always to be treated seriously. Only ten years before this speech was delivered, the slaves had revolted in Italy under Spartacus and had inflicted several defeats on Roman armies. It took two years to put down the revolt. The fear of another revolt therefore would be very much in the minds of the senators if there was even the suggestion of a conspiracy. It was particularly heinous for a Roman to try to mobilise slaves.

**patiere = patieris.**

**110–11** Again, Cicero uses a "triple" expression, in this case cued in by the words **nonne ... non ... non ... (non = nonne)**. With all three sections therefore we must take the words **hunc** and **imperabis**. (Anaphora)

**113** **vocibus:** words.

**115** **Catilinam morte multari** explains **hoc** in more detail.

**116** **non dedissem:** *I would not have given.*

**hoc uno interfecto:** *if this one man is killed,* i.e. Catiline.

**117** **pestem:** *cancer,* a most appropriate description of Catiline's scheming because it was destroying the state from within.

**reprimi ... comprimi:** Both infinitives must be taken with **posse**. These two words are very carefully chosen: **reprimere** means *to hold in check;* **comprimere** means *to choke till it cannot breathe,* i.e. *eliminate.*

**118** **quodsi se eiecerit:** *but if he casts himself out,* i.e. *leaves the city of his own accord.*

**120** **adulta:** *advanced, grown large.*

**121** **stirps ac semen:** The biological metaphor is continued.

**122** **secedant:** *let (them) depart.* The other present subjunctives which follow should be treated in the same way.

**124** **domi suae:** *in his own home.*

**124–127** All the infinitives depend on **desinant**.

**125** **tribunal praetoris urbani:** The **praetor urbanus** had a court in the Forum where he tried civil cases between Roman citizens. Cicero is suggesting that Catiline's supporters are crowding round the praetor's platform to try to intimidate him into passing judgment in favour of their friends.

**128** **hoc** is explained in more detail by the four Accusative and Infinitive clauses which begin with **tantam** (Anaphora). With each of them must be understood **fore,** the future infinitive of **esse**.

**vobis** refers to the senators. For the **equites,** see line 54.

Tulli, quid agis? tune auctorem sceleris, principem
coniurationis, evocatorem servorum exire patiere?
110  nonne hunc in vincla duci, non ad mortem rapi, non
summo supplicio mactari imperabis? quid tandem te
impedit?"

his ego sanctissimis reipublicae vocibus pauca
respondebo. ego si hoc optimum factu iudicarem, patres
115  conscripti, Catilinam morte multari, unius usuram horae
gladiatori isti ad vivendum non dedissem. hoc autem uno
interfecto, intellego hanc reipublicae pestem paulisper reprimi, non in perpetuum comprimi posse. quodsi se
eiecerit secumque suos eduxerit, exstinguetur atque de-
120  lebitur non modo haec adulta reipublicae pestis, verum
etiam stirps ac semen malorum omnium.

quare secedant improbi, secernant se a bonis, unum in
locum congregentur, muro denique (id quod saepe iam
dixi) secernantur a nobis. desinant insidiari domi suae
125  consuli, circumstare tribunal praetoris urbani, obsidere
cum gladiis Curiam, faces ad inflammandam urbem
comparare. sit denique inscriptum in fronte unius
cuiusque, quid de republica sentiat. polliceor hoc vobis,

**quid agis?** what are you
  up to?
**auctor, -oris** (*m*),
  author, instigator
**evocator, -oris** (*m*),
  recruiter
**vinclum = vinculum**
**supplicium, -i** (*n*),
  punishment
**macto** (1), to reward,
  punish
**optimum factu,** the best
  thing to do
**multo** (1), to punish
**usura, -ae** (*f*), use,
  enjoyment
**comprimo** (3), to choke,
  suppress

**exstinguo** (3), to
  eliminate, destroy
**stirps, stirpis** (*f*), stalk,
  root
**semen, -inis** (*n*), seed
**secedo** (3), to go away,
  withdraw
**secerno** (3), to separate
**congregor** (1), to assemble
**desino** (3), to cease, stop
**insidior** (1) ( + *dat*.), to
  lie in ambush (for)
**Curia, -ae** (*f*), Senate-
  house
**fax, facis** (*f*), firebrand
**inflammo** (1), to set on
  fire
**frons, frontis** (*f*), forehead

131 **omnibus bonis** would include ordinary citizens as well as senators and equites.

132 **patefacta, illustrata, oppressa, vindicata** are all to be taken with **esse**. The listing of these without any link between them, such as **et**, is most effective. We must imagine Cicero pausing after each one of them to let the point sink in. They are in pairs – **patefacta** and **illustrata** (*discovered and exposed*) and **oppressa** and **vindicata** *(crushed and punished)*.

133 **videatis:** *you will see.* Latin prefers the present tense in this Result clause since the "seeing" is thought of as occurring at the same time as the verb on which the **ut** clause depends, i.e. **fore.**

134 **hisce ominibus:** *under these omens.*

**hisce:** The **-ce** ending is a relic of the original form of **hic, haec, hoc** (**hice, haece, hoce**). The ending survives as **-c** in several cases (e.g. **hic, haec, hoc, hunc, hanc, huic, hoc, hac**). Cicero frequently uses the original form for sound effect and emphasis.

**cum salute:** literally *along with the safety.* Since **proficiscere** in the next line is an imperative, translate this phrase *and thus bring about the safety of the state.* Similarly, **cum tua peste ac pernicie** may be translated *bring about your own ruin and destruction.*

136 **tu, Iuppiter:** At this point Cicero turns and addresses the statue of Jupiter. The Senate was meeting in the Temple of Iuppiter Stator. i.e. Jupiter the Protector.

137 **hunc:** *this man,* i.e. Catiline.

138 **a tuis aris:** The repetition of **a** tells us that each of these phrases must be taken with **arcebis:** another example of Anaphora.

141 **vivos mortuosque:** Translate **-que** as *or.*

**mactabis:** The future is a polite way of giving an instruction to the god.

patres conscripti, tantam in nobis consulibus fore diligen-
130 tiam, tantam in vobis auctoritatem, tantam in equitibus
Romanis virtutem, tantam in omnibus bonis consen-
sionem ut Catilinae profectione omnia patefacta, illustrata, oppressa, vindicata esse videatis.

*Protect us from these evil men, Jupiter, and punish those who
threaten all we hold dear.*

hisce ominibus, Catilina, cum summa reipublicae
135 salute, cum tua peste ac pernicie proficiscere ad impium
bellum ac nefarium. tum tu, Iuppiter, quem Statorem
huius urbis atque imperii vere nominamus, hunc et huius
socios a tuis aris ceterisque templis, a tectis urbis ac
moenibus, a vitis fortunisque civium omnium arcebis; et
140 homines bonorum inimicos, hostes patriae, latrones
Italiae aeternis suppliciis vivos mortuosque mactabis.

**diligentia, -ae** (*f*),
  alertness,
  attentiveness
**consensio, -onis** (*f*),
  agreement
**illustro** (1), to illumine,
  make clear
**vindico** (1), to punish
**omen, ominis** (*n*), omen, sign

**impius, -a, -um,** wicked
**imperium, -i** (*n*), empire
**vere,** rightly
**nomino** (1), to name
**ara, -ae** (*f*), altar
**tectum, -i** (*n*), building
**arceo** (2), to keep away,
  exclude
**latro, -onis** (*m*), robber

# The Sequel

Cicero's powerful denunciation of Catiline had the desired effect. Catiline immediately left Rome and joined the rest of his followers in Etruria. In the following year (62 BC) his army, now much reduced by desertions, was overwhelmed by senatorial forces and Catiline himself was killed in the battle.

That final outcome still lay in the future, but even after his first speech against Catiline, the tide was beginning to run Cicero's way. Catiline had now shown his hand; Cicero's assertion that Catiline intended to burn down the city won over to his side some of Catiline's supporters, and his fortunate interception of incriminating letters enabled him to arrest five of Catiline's fellow-conspirators before they could leave Rome.

The Senate had already strengthened Cicero's hand by passing the emergency decree: **consules videant ne quid detrimenti respublica capiat,** *Let the consuls ensure that the state suffers no harm.* Since that was a little vague, however, Cicero called an emergency meeting of the Senate, produced the evidence and got the Senate's backing to impose the death penalty on the five prisoners. They were promptly executed the same evening.

Cicero was the hero of the hour, the saviour of his country; but the fact that he had executed citizens without giving them the right of appeal to the whole citizen body left him vulnerable to prosecution himself. When Cicero's bitter enemy, Publius Clodius, became tribune, therefore, he was able to drive Cicero into exile in March 58 BC by introducing a bill outlawing anyone who had put to death a Roman citizen without proper trial in a court of law.

For the unfortunate victim, exile normally implied a move of at least 500 miles from Italy, but Cicero got no farther than Thessalonica in Greece, only a little over 200 miles from Italian soil. He remained there until his recall from exile in September 57 BC.

# Conditional Sentences

1 In previous books you met numerous examples of conditional clauses introduced by **si** or **nisi,** in which the verbs were in the indicative, e.g.

> **si tu vales, ego gaudeo.**
> *If you are well, I am pleased.*
>
> **si id dixit, errabat.**
> *If he said that, he was wrong.*
>
> **nisi diligentius laborabis, verberaberis.**
> *If you do not work harder, you will be beaten.*
>
> **si suos eduxerit, exstinguetur haec pestis.**
> *If he takes his men away, this cancer will be removed.*

It will be noted that, with the exception of the last two examples, the Latin verbs can be translated into the same tense in English. In the two exceptions, **laborabis** and **eduxerit** are future and future perfect (recognising that the action does refer to the future), whereas English uses the present tense.

2 In the present book, you have met several examples of conditional sentences in which the verbs are in the subjunctive mood. This shows that the condition either cannot now be fulfilled (past time) or is unlikely to be (present or future time). In such sentences

> pluperfect subjunctive refers to the past
> imperfect subjunctive refers to the present
> present subjunctive refers to the future.

Examples:

si hostes epistolam **legissent,** consilia eius **cognovissent.**
*If the enemy **had read** the letter, they **would have learned** his plans.*

si te parentes **timerent,** ab eorum oculis **concederes.**
*If your parents **were afraid** of you, you **would withdraw** from their sight.*

haec si tecum patria **loquatur,** nonne impetrare **debeat?**
*If your country **were to speak** to you like this, surely it **would deserve** to gain its request?*

Note the pattern:

pluperfect subjunctive in both clauses: **"had... would have"**
imperfect subjunctive in both clauses: **"were (now)... would (now)"**
present subjunctive in both clauses:   **"were to... would"**

Sometimes, Latin authors use a mixture of these tenses, e.g.

si ego ea in curia **dixissem,** omnes me nunc **spernerent.**
*If I* **had said** *that in the senate (in the past), everyone* **would be despising** *me now (in the present).*

## Exercise 63a

*Translate:*

1 si ianuam diligentius custodivisses, fur non effugisset.
2 si ianuam diligentius custodires, fur non effugeret.
3 si ianuam diligentius custodias, fur non effugiat.
4 sive ianuam custodivisses sive in lecto mansisses, fur facile effugisset.
5 si forte Athenas naviges, multa et mira videas.
6 si Athenas navigabis, multa et mira videbis.
7 si prima luce domo proficiscamur, ad oram eodem die perveniamus.
8 etiamsi vera dixeris, nemo tibi credet.
9 etiamsi vera dixisses, nemo tibi credidisset.
10 si pater meus viveret, nos de periculo viarum moneret.
11 nisi te ipsum vidissem, epistolam scripsissem.
12 si ad forum ambules, Ciceronem orationem habentem audias.

   **sive... sive...,** whether... or...

## Exercise 63b

*Translate:*

1 si his libris usus esses, multa certe didicisses.
2 si vir dives essem, omnes adulescentes filiam meam ducere vellent.
3 si unus ex militibus gladium vel scutum abiecisset, ceteri eum ignaviae accusavissent.
4 sive hostes castra ponerent sive aciem instruerent, nostri se ad proelium pararent.
5 si cives de victoria certiores fecisses, tibi gratias egissent.
6 si consul cives de proelio certiores faciat, ei gratias non agant.

7 etiamsi praedones mihi mortem minentur, pecuniam eis non dem.
8 sive dives esses sive pauper, te amarem.
9 si pecuniam mihi ademisses, ab accusatoribus furti accusatus esses.
10 si quis tyrannum risisset, capitis condemnatus esset.
11 cives, si ex acie fugiatis, vos intra moenia non accipiant.
12 si nuntius celerius advenisset, hostes impetum facere
   prohibuissemus.

   **si quis,** if anyone

# VERBS: Present Subjunctive

The Present subjunctive is found in principal clauses meaning
"let" or "may". The negative is **ne**.

e.g. **gaudeamus!** Let us rejoice!
   **regina leges nostras defendat!** May the queen defend our
   laws!
   **ne discedat!** Let him not leave!
   **sis felix!** May you be lucky!
   **ne falsa dicant!** Let them not tell lies!
   **puella sit beata!** May the girl be happy!

These uses express a wish or command.

# Exercise 63c

*Translate:*

domum redeamus!
sit nomen inscriptum!
vivat rex!
hostes vincas!
ne interficiamini!
ne damneris!
ne castigemini!
nos ipsos virtute defendamus!
deos veneremini!
bene res eveniat!
cantemus!
proficiscamur!
bene dormiatis!
ab urbe secedant!

fiat lux!
secernant se a nobis!
sitis beatissimi!
oremus!
gaudeas!
ne obliviscaris!
ne statua tollatur!
sim felix!
ne obliviscantur!
felix et faustum tibi sit!
ne obliviscamur!
omnia experiamur!
ne urbem deleatis!

### The National Anthem

servet reginam deus!
vivat regina optima!
servet deus!
compos victoriae
plenaque gloriae
sit felix atque floreat!
servet deus!

### A Legal Phrase

**caveat emptor!** This indicates that, in any transaction, responsibility rests with the buyer to ensure that he isn't being cheated (literally, *Let the buyer beware!*).

### The Lord's Prayer

Pater noster, qui es in caelis,
sanctificetur nomen tuum!
adveniat regnum tuum!
fiat voluntas tua, sicut in caelo, ita etiam in terra!
panem nostrum quotidianum da nobis hodie!
et remitte nobis debita nostra, sicut et nos remittimus
    debitoribus nostris!
et ne nos inducas in tentationem,
sed libera nos a malo!
nam tuum est regnum et potentia et gloria per omnia saecula.
                                      Amen.

### R.I.P. = requiescat in pace

# 64
# In Defence of Milo

The conflict between Milo and Clodius was one between rival gangs. Milo was an ally of Cicero and the Senate, Clodius a henchman of Caesar who was keeping a close watch on the political scene in Rome from his HQ in Gaul. The strife between these rival gangs erupted into open violence in the winter of 53 BC, when Milo was standing for the consulship and Clodius for the praetorship. Such was the violence that the elections could not be held and had to be put off until January 52 BC; it was on the 18th of that month that the rivals clashed on the Appian Way, a clash in which Clodius was killed.

There was no doubt about the fact that Clodius was killed by Milo's men. That was not in dispute. What Cicero was trying to do was to defend Milo against the charge of having plotted to murder Clodius.

Cicero had special reasons for coming to Milo's aid: Milo was a close friend and had, as tribune of the plebs, worked hard to bring about Cicero's return from exile; Clodius had for various reasons long been an enemy of Cicero and in 58 BC had proposed the very law that forced him into exile.

Nowadays, we think that a lawyer appearing for a client should be acting purely in a professional capacity. The Romans thought quite differently. A pleader in the law-courts had to convince the jury that he was simply there as a friend to speak for the accused, however professionally skilled in the law he might actually be. Cicero employs all his professional skill to present Milo's rather shady character in the best possible light and he certainly takes a bold line, intimating to the jury that his defence will not rest on Milo's great services to Rome. He will simply demonstrate that, far from Milo's having plotted the death of Clodius, the boot was on the other foot! Clodius was the aggressor; Milo merely acted in self-defence.

*line*

1 **ad eam orationem:** *to that part of my speech.*

**propria vestrae quaestionis:** *properly belonging to your inquiry.*

2 **quaestio** is the regular word for a criminal inquiry i.e. court. (Cf. the verb **quaerere** in line 13.)

**videntur ea refutanda:** literally *those things seem to need to be refuted,* i.e. *I think I must refute.*

3 **saepe** is to be taken with both **in senatu** and **in contione.**

4 **paulo ante:** *a moment ago,* i.e. when they were making the speech for the prosecution.

**rem:** *the issue.*

6 **negant esse fas ei qui:** *They say that a man who ... has no right.*

7 **tandem:** When used in a question, **tandem** suggests impatience and astonishment. Translate *pray tell me.*

**hoc disputant:** *put forward this argument.*

8 **quae primum ... Horatii;** literally *which saw as its first trial (the trial) concerning the head (i.e. life) of Marcus Horatius.* Translate *in which the first capital trial was that of Marcus Horatius.* Prior to that case, according to the historian Livy, sentences imposed by magistrates were carried out without question. Horatius was the first person to appeal to the **comitia** – the full assembly of the people.

10 **cum:** *although.*

12 **hoc** is taken up and explained in the two Accusative and Infinitive clauses introduced by **aut ... aut ...**

13 **quaeratur:** In this sentence, there are several impersonal uses of the verb: **quaeratur** (literally *it is inquired*), *there is an investigation;* **negari solere** (literally *it is usually denied*), *there is usually a denial;* **factum esse** (literally *that it was done*), *that the deed occurred;* **defendi solere** (literally *it is usually defended*), *the defence usually is.* It will be noted that English most naturally uses nouns to translate these impersonal verbs.

**recte et iure:** recte is *morally right;* **iure** is *legally right.*

15 **illud:** Supply **tempus** – *that occasion.*

16 **cum vi vis illata defenditur:** *when violence (is) offered (and) is repelled by violence.*

**insidiatori vero et latroni:** By bringing these datives up to the start of the sentence, Cicero gives them considerable emphasis and also sets the context for the thinking in the rest of the sentence. Equally, by keeping the question to the end of the sentence, he adds force to it.

18 **iudices:** *gentlemen of the jury.*

**nata:** literally *inborn,* i.e. *natural,* referring to the unwritten laws of nature.

# M TULLI CICERONIS
## PRO T. ANNIO MILONE
## AD IUDICES ORATIO

*Let us clear away one difficulty first. Can killing someone ever be justified?*

   sed antequam ad eam orationem venio, quae est propria
vestrae quaestionis, videntur ea refutanda, quae et in senatu ab inimicis saepe iactata sunt et in contione ab impro-
bis et paulo ante ab accusatoribus, ut rem plane videre
5  possitis.
   negant intueri lucem esse fas ei qui a se hominem
occisum esse fateatur.  in qua tandem urbe hoc homines
stultissimi disputant?  nempe in ea quae primum iudicium de capite vidit M. Horatii, fortissimi viri qui populi
10  comitiis liberatus est, cum sua manu sororem esse inter-
fectam fateretur.
   an est quisquam qui hoc ignoret, cum de homine occiso
quaeratur, aut negari solere omnino esse factum aut recte
et iure factum esse defendi?  atqui si tempus est ullum iure
15  hominis necandi, certe illud est non modo iustum verum
etiam necessarium, cum vi vis illata defenditur.  insidiatori vero et latroni quae potest inferri iniusta nex?
   est igitur haec, iudices, non scripta sed nata lex ut, si vita
nostra in aliquas insidias, si in vim et in tela aut latronum

---

**iudex, -icis** (*m*), judge, juror
**antequam,** before
**proprius, -a, -um,**
  special, peculiar
**refuto** (1), to refute, disprove
**inimicus, -i** (*m*),
  personal enemy
**iacto** (1), to bandy
  about, allege
**contio, -onis** (*f*),
  meeting, assembly
**intueor** (2), to look at, see
**occido** (3), to kill

**nempe,** surely, certainly
**iudicium, -i** (*n*),
  judgment, trial
**comitia, -orum** (*n.pl*),
  assembly, elections
**fateor** (2), to confess
**omnino,** altogether
**atqui,** and yet, however
**insidiator, -oris** (*m*), one
  who lies in ambush
**nex, necis** (*f*), death
**aliquis, -quis, -quid,** some
**insidiae, -arum** (*f.pl*), ambush

20 **omnis honesta ratio esset: honesta** is used predicatively – *every method would be justifiable.*

22 **causam crimenque:** *the case and the charge.*

23 **reliquum est ut debeatis:** *all that remains is that you must.*

24 **quod:** Linking Relative – *this.*

**quo** introduces a Purpose Clause – *so that.*

25 **rem gestam:** *what actually happened.*

26 **quaeso,** used parenthetically, means *please.*

27 **in praetura:** *during his praetorship.*

28 **videret** is also governed by **cum.**

**tracta esse comitia:** *that the elections had been delayed.*

29 **anno superiore:** literally *in the previous year.* In fact, however, although the elections should have taken place "last year" (i.e. in 54 BC for the magistrates who were to hold office in 53 BC), the elections were not held until the middle of 53 BC. Since he wanted a full year in office, Clodius withdrew from these elections and decided to stand in 53 BC for office in 52 BC.

30 **posset qui:** The subject of **posset** is the **qui** clause: *anyone who . . .*

31 **annum suum:** *his proper year* for holding office. Clodius had been aedile in 56 BC. According to law, no one could hold office for two years after holding another post. He could not therefore hold office again till 53 BC. Since Romans would normally stand for office in the earliest year possible, people would think of 53 BC as being "his year" for holding the praetorship.

33 **hoc est:** *that is.* (Cf. **id est,** *i.e.*)

35 **occurrebat ei:** literally *it kept occurring to him,* i.e. *he kept thinking.*

36 **summo consensu:** literally *with the greatest agreement,* i.e. *by the unanimous vote.*

**eum consulem fieri:** literally *that he was being elected consul,* i.e. *that he was winning the election for the consulship.* Open canvassing was allowed, which explains the use of the word **sermonibus** (line 40). Several attempts had been made to hold the **comitia,** but on each occasion they had been interrupted. The voting that had been possible had indicated that Milo was likely to be elected.

37 **homo** is used here in a derogatory sense: *the fellow.*

38 **ad omne facinus paratissimus:** *prepared to commit every crime,* i.e. *prepared to stop at nothing.* Note how fond Cicero is of superlatives. His opponents' characters are always blackest of the black, while his friends are always beyond reproach.

39 **certissimum consulem:** Supply **esse** or **futurum esse.**

20   aut inimicorum incidisset, omnis honesta ratio esset ex-
pediendae salutis.  silent enim leges inter arma.

*Now to the charge itself. What are the facts?*

quam ob rem, iudices, ut aliquando ad causam crimenque veniamus, reliquum est ut nihil iam quaerere aliud
debeatis nisi uter utri insidias fecerit.  quod quo facilius
25   perspicere possitis, rem gestam vobis dum breviter
expono, quaeso, diligenter attendite!

*All Clodius' previous activities and statements point to his intention
to murder Milo.*

P. Clodius, cum statuisset omni scelere in praetura
vexare rempublicam videretque ita tracta esse comitia
anno superiore ut non multos menses praeturam gerere
30   posset qui annum integrum ad dilacerandam rempublicam quaereret, subito reliquit annum suum seseque in
annum proximum transtulit ut haberet, quod ipse
dicebat, ad praeturam gerendam, hoc est ad evertendam
rempublicam, plenum annum atque integrum.
35   occurrebat ei mancam ac debilem praeturam futuram
esse suam consule Milone.  eum porro summo consensu
populi Romani consulem fieri videbat.  ubi vidit homo
ad  omne  facinus  paratissimus  fortissimum  virum,
inimicissimum suum, certissimum consulem, idque intel-

---

**incido** (3), to fall into
**ratio, -onis** (*f*), method
**expedio** (4), to make
　　ready, obtain, secure
**sileo** (2), to be silent
**quam ob rem,** therefore
**aliquando,** at last
**crimen, -inis** (*n*),
　　accusation
**uter, utra, utrum,** which
　　(of two)
**breviter,** briefly

**expono** (3), to explain
**statuo** (3), to decide
**praeturam gerere,** to
　　hold the praetorship
**integer, -gra, -grum,** whole
**dilacero** (1), to tear apart
**everto** (3), to overthrow
**mancus, -a, -um,** ineffective
**debilis, -is, -e,** feeble, weakened
**porro,** furthermore
**facinus, -oris** (*n*), crime,
　　disgraceful deed

43 **silvas publicas:** These were large tracts of forest land owned by the
state, which were let out mainly to the **publicani** (private companies of
tax-gatherers who paid a fixed tax to the state and then rented the land
to others at a profit). Clodius had been using his gangs of slaves to
harass those who were paying the rent, since he hoped to take over the
land for his own purposes.

44 **vexarat** = **vexaverat.**

**ex Appennino:** Although singular, this refers to the Apennines
generally. The slaves who acted as herdsmen on the hills had a very
rough life.

**quos videbatis:** *and you have repeatedly seen them yourselves.* This
suggests that Clodius had actually dared to bring them into the city.

45 **res:** *his plan.*

46 **Miloni:** dative indicating the person from whom something is taken.

48 **Favonio:** dative depending on **respondit.**

**qua spe fureret:** literally *with what hope he was acting madly,* i.e. *what he
hoped to gain from such mad acts.*

49 **summum:** *at most.*

50 **esse periturum:** Supply **eum.**      **vocem:** *remark.*

51 **hunc:** As he said this, Cicero would point to Cato who was in court.
Translate *here.*

53 **sollemne legitimum necessarium: sollemne** signifies that it involved the
*annual* performing of sacred rites; **legitimum** suggests that it was
*required by the laws* of the town. Note Cicero's fondness for using
"triple" expressions.

**iter Miloni esse:** literally *there was a journey for Milo,* i.e. *Milo had (to
make) a journey.*

54 **ad flaminem prodendum:** *to nominate a priest.* **prodere** is the technical
word for nominating a priest.

55 **dictator:** Although it sounds grand, this was probably an honorary title
dating back to the days when Lanuvium had been an independent
town. The office was limited now to religious duties.

56 **ante suum fundum:** *in front of his own farm-house.*

**re:** *from what actually happened.*

57 **ita profectus est ut:** literally *he so departed that he (left/failed to attend),*
i.e. *his departure involved (leaving/not attending).* We cannot be sure
from what Cicero says whether **relinqueret** means that *he left* after
attending the earlier part of the meeting or that *he abandoned* the
meeting, i.e. he did not attend it at all. **contionem** is the object of
**relinqueret.**

60 **obire facinoris locum tempusque:** *to meet the time and place for the deed,*
i.e. to be in good time at the place where he planned to attack Milo.

40 lexit non solum sermonibus sed etiam suffragiis populi
Romani saepe esse declaratum, palam agere coepit et
aperte dicere occidendum Milonem. servos agrestes et
barbaros, quibus silvas publicas depopulatus erat
Etruriamque vexarat, ex Appennino deduxerat, quos
45 videbatis. res erat minime obscura. etenim palam dic-
titabat consulatum Miloni eripi non posse, vitam posse.
significavit hoc saepe in senatu, dixit in contione. quin
etiam M. Favonio, fortissimo viro, quaerenti ex eo qua
spe fureret, Milone vivo, respondit triduo illum aut sum-
50 mum quadriduo esse periturum. quam vocem eius ad
hunc M. Catonem statim Favonius detulit.

*The opportunity arises.*

interim cum sciret Clodius (neque erat difficile scire)
iter sollemne legitimum necessarium ante diem XIII
Kalendas Februarias Miloni esse Lanuvium ad flaminem
55 prodendum, quod erat dictator Lanuvii Milo, Roma subito ipse profectus pridie est ut ante suum fundum (quod re
intellectum est) Miloni insidias collocaret; atque ita profectus est ut contionem turbulentam, in qua eius furor
desideratus est, quae illo ipso die habita est, relinqueret,
60 quam nisi obire facinoris locum tempusque voluisset,
numquam reliquisset.

sermo, -onis (*m*),
  conversation
suffragium, -i (*n*), vote
palam, openly, publicly
aperte, openly
agrestis, -is, -e, wild
barbarus, -a, -um,
  uncivilised
depopulor (1), to
  plunder, lay waste
dictito (1), to say
  repeatedly

consulatus, -us (*m*),
  consulship
quin etiam, moreover
furo (3), to be mad
triduum, -i (*n*), (a
  period of) three days
pereo, perire, to die
flamen, -inis (*m*), priest
turbulentus, -a, -um,
  stormy
desidero (1), to feel the
  lack of, miss
obeo, -ire, to meet

63 **calceos et vestimenta:** To attend the Senate, Milo would have been wearing special shoes made of red leather and the **toga praetexta.** For travelling, he changed into less formal footwear and the **paenula,** which was a long sleeveless cape made of wool with a hole for the head – certainly not a suitable garment for fighting.

64 **ut fit:** *as usually happens.* In those days, too, men made jokes about having to wait till their wives were ready!

65 **id temporis:** *at that time.*

**si venturus erat:** *if he was intending to come.*

66 **redire potuisset:** *could have returned,* i.e. could already have been back in Rome.

68 **ut solebat:** *which was usual for him.* It was common to take educated Greeks with one when travelling to help reduce the boredom of the journey. An uncultured fellow like Clodius would never do this, of course!

69 **numquam fere:** *almost never,* i.e. *hardly ever.*     **cum:** *whereas.*

**hic insidiator:** *this (so-called) plotter* – he points to Milo. This expression and the **qui** clause which follows are, of course, used ironically.

70 **apparasset** = **apparavisset.**

71 **paenulatus** is contrasted with **expeditus.**

73 **hora fere undecima:** *about an hour before sunset.* Asconius, a scholar of the 1st century AD, who carried out a careful investigation of the facts, says it happened in the early afternoon. He also contradicts Cicero's account of the unwarlike nature of Milo's companions.

75 **adversi:** *from in front.*

78 **partim ... partim ...:** *some ... others ...* These words subdivide **illi qui erant cum Clodio** into two groups.

79 **hunc:** Again, he points to Milo in the court.

80 **incipiunt** governs both **recurrere** and **caedere.**

81 **ex quibus qui:** *of those who...* **quibus** is a Linking Relative, referring back to **servos.** These slaves are subdivided into two groups by **partim ... partim ...** (cf. line 78).

**animo fideli et praesenti fuerunt:** literally *were with faithful and prompt mind,* i.e. *who were loyal and showed presence of mind* (Ablative of Description).

82 **pugnari:** literally *that it was being fought,* i.e. *that there was fighting.* (Cf. lines 13, 14 for impersonal verbs.)

**cum** governs not only **viderent** but also **prohiberentur, audirent** and **putarent.**

83 **Milonem occisum:** an Accusative and Infinitive depending on both **et ... audirent** and **et ... putarent.**

Milo autem, cum in senatu fuisset eo die quoad senatus
est dimissus, domum venit, calceos et vestimenta mutavit,
paulisper, dum se uxor ut fit comparat, commoratus est,
65 dein profectus id temporis cum iam Clodius, si quidem eo
die Romam venturus erat, redire potuisset.

*Clodius and Milo meet on the Appian Way.*

obviam fit ei Clodius expeditus, in equo, nulla raeda,
nullis impedimentis, nullis Graecis comitibus, ut solebat,
sine uxore, quod numquam fere; cum hic insidiator (qui
70 iter illud ad caedem faciendam apparasset) cum uxore
veheretur in raeda, paenulatus, magno et impedito et
muliebri et delicato ancillarum puerorumque comitatu.
fit obviam Clodio ante fundum eius hora fere undecima
aut non multo secus. statim complures cum telis in hunc
75 faciunt de loco superiore impetum. adversi raedarium
occidunt. cum autem hic de raeda, reiecta paenula, de-
siluisset seque acri animo defenderet, illi qui erant cum
Clodio, gladiis eductis, partim recurrere ad raedam ut a
tergo Milonem adorirentur, partim, quod hunc iam inter-
80 fectum putarent, caedere incipiunt eius servos, qui post
erant: ex quibus qui animo fideli et praesenti fuerunt,
partim occisi sunt, partim (cum ad raedam pugnari viderent, domino succurrere prohiberentur, Milonem occisum

**autem,** on the other hand
**quoad,** until
**commoror** (1), to delay
**expeditus, -a, -um,**
  unencumbered
**apparo** (1), to prepare
**delicatus, -a, -um,**
  gentle, harmless
**comitatus, -us** (*m*),
  retinue
**secus,** otherwise

**acer, acris, acre,**
  spirited
**adorior** (4), to attack
**incipio** (3), to begin
**post,** behind
**praesens, -entis,**
  present, immediate,
  prompt
**succurro** (3), ( + *dat.*),
  to come to the
  assistance (of)

84 **fecerunt servi:** This picks up **partim** in line 82 and balances **partim occisi sunt. servi** is really superfluous but, after such a long parenthesis, it is necessary to remind the listeners what the subject is.

**id ... quod:** *what.*

89 **vi victa vis vel:** The skilful orator makes effective use of this sort of sound effect (alliteration).

90 **est** has to be taken with both **victa** and **oppressa.**

**id:** Clodius' death.

91 **hoc** is the object of **praescripsit.** It is explained in more detail in the **ut** clause in line 93.

**doctis:** *to civilised men.*

92 **praescripsit** has four subjects: **ratio, necessitas, mos** and **natura ipsa.**

93 **quacunque ope possent:** literally *with whatever help they were able,* i.e. *by every means at their disposal.*

94 **propulsarent:** Everything from **sin** to **propulsarent** is part of the Condition beginning with **sin.**

95 **quin iudicetis:** *without judging, unless you judge.*

**omnibus:** dative of agent with **esse pereundum** – *all ought to die.*

96 **vestris sententiis:** literally *by your opinions,* i.e. *by your verdict.*

98 **num quid aliud:** *does any other thing.*

**igitur:** *then,* summing up an argument.

99 **hic** refers to Milo, **illi** to Clodius. Supply **insidias fecit.**

**ut:** Before **ut** in lines 99 and 100, English needs to insert an expression such as *the verdict must be.*

100 **ut scelere solvamur:** *that we be treated as guiltless.*

---

**re vera,** really, in actual fact
**potius,** rather
**sin,** but if
**ratio, -onis** (*f*), reasoning, logic
**ferus, -a, -um,** wild
**belua, -ae** (*f*), beast

**praescribo** (3), to direct, prescribe
**propulso** (1), to repel, ward off
**profecto,** certainly
**impune,** without punishment
**solvo** (3), to loosen, free

et ex ipso Clodio audirent et re vera putarent) fecerunt id
85 servi Milonis, nec imperante nec sciente nec praesente
domino, quod suos quisque servos in tali re facere
voluisset.

*These are the facts. My client simply defended himself. You must*
*acquit him.*

haec, sicut exposui, ita gesta sunt, iudices. insidiator
superatus est, vi victa vis vel potius oppressa virtute aud-
90 acia est. si id iure fieri non potuit, nihil habeo quod
defendam. sin hoc et ratio doctis et necessitas barbaris et
mos gentibus et feris etiam beluis natura ipsa praescripsit,
ut omnem semper vim, quacunque ope possent, a
corpore, a capite, a vita sua propulsarent, non potestis
95 hoc facinus improbum iudicare quin simul iudicetis omnibus qui in latrones inciderint, aut illorum telis aut vestris
sententiis esse pereundum.

num quid igitur aliud in iudicium venit nisi uter utri
insidias fecerit? profecto nihil; si hic illi, ut ne sit
100 impune; si ille huic, ut scelere solvamur.

### Epilogue

Cicero's speech in defence of Milo was taken down in shorthand and
published. It was still in circulation over a century later, but it is from
a much-expanded version, which Cicero produced afterwards, that
the above extracts have been taken.

The first-century AD writer Asconius (in a book which he wrote to
help his children understand Cicero's speeches) describes the circumstances of the speech as follows:

"On the day of the trial, 8th April, all city shops were closed;
Pompey had posted guards in the Forum and in all the approaches to
it. The court itself was ringed with troops but, when Cicero began to
speak, he was greeted with howls and jeers from Clodius' supporters,
who were in no way cowed by the presence of armed men. Because of
this hostile reception, Cicero spoke with far less resolution and bold-
ness than he usually displayed."

Milo was found guilty. In fact, he did not await the verdict but went
into voluntary exile at Massilia (Marseilles).

Cicero, too, soon found himself removed from the political scene at
Rome, because in the following year (51 BC) the Senate decided that

all ex-praetors and ex-consuls who had not governed a province should now do so. This group included Cicero who found himself unexpectedly engaged in drawing lots for a major province. He drew Cilicia, a huge mountainous region of central and southern Asia Minor; and it was well over a year later, in 50 BC, before he returned to Rome, which was by this time on the brink of civil war between Pompey and Caesar.

Cicero, after much heart-searching, threw in his lot with Pompey. After Pompey's defeat and death, Caesar pardoned him but, with Caesar as dictator, Cicero's political career was now at a standstill. Fortunately he was able to turn this period of enforced absence from public life to good account by producing important works on philosophy and oratory.

After Caesar's assassination in 44 BC, Cicero made his final appearance in public life as the champion of the Senate against Antony, ignoring Antony's partner Octavius who, after all, was then only a youth of nineteen.

Concentrating his attention on Antony, whom he saw as the re-embodiment of the Senate's arch-enemy Julius Caesar, he denounced him in a series of fourteen brilliant speeches. He himself, at first jokingly, called them Philippics – the title given to the famous speeches in which the great Greek orator, Demosthenes, had made an attack on King Philip of Macedon in the 4th century BC.

Antony took his revenge on Cicero by having him proscribed and assassinated on 7th December, 43 BC.

The Roman historian Livy describes Cicero's death as follows:

"First, Cicero fled to his Tusculan villa; then he moved by devious routes to his villa at Formiae, intending to board a ship at Caieta. Several times the ship put out from there, but sometimes it was driven ashore by contrary winds, at another time he could not endure the tossing of the ship in the ground-swell. At last, weariness of flight and of life itself came over him and he turned back again towards his villa which was just over a mile from the sea. 'I will die,' he said, 'in the country whose saviour I have often been.'

"There is no doubt his slaves were ready to face Antony's soldiers, but Cicero himself ordered the litter to be set down and no resistance to be offered. He leant out of the litter and held out his neck unflinchingly to the soldiers. They cut off his head, but even this did not satisfy their savagery. They cut off also his hands, saying they were taking vengeance on them for what they had written against Antony.

"His head was brought to Antony and on his orders it was placed between his hands on the very Rostra from which often as consul, often as ex-consul, and in that very year as Antony's opponent, he had poured forth his unsurpassable eloquence."

# The Letters of Pliny

The extracts which form the material of Chapters 65–68 come from the letters of Pliny which the author himself collected and published in nine books between AD 97 and 108. The fact that he collected and published them himself is very significant. Although they are real letters, they were obviously aimed at a wider public right from the start, containing as they do the sort of news stories of general interest exemplified in this book by "A Ghost Story" (Ch.65) and "The Boy and the Dolphin" (Ch.66).

In Chapters 67 and 68, we read parts of Pliny's eye-witness account of the AD 79 eruption of Vesuvius which engulfed Pompeii and Herculaneum; the excavation of these two cities, begun only about two centuries ago and still in progress, has revealed in fascinating detail the life of Roman provincial cities in the first century AD.

Pliny was the nephew and adopted son of Gaius Plinius Secundus whose last hours are graphically described in Chapter 67. It was the custom for an adopted son to take the adoptive father's name; so Pliny's own name, originally Publius Caecilius Secundus, became Gaius Plinius Caecilius Secundus. Not surprisingly, this led to confusion, and in the Middle Ages they were believed to be one person; it was only in the fourteenth century that their separate identities were established by a scholar from Verona, since when they have been known respectively as the Elder and the Younger Pliny.

(*Left*) The Elder Pliny and (*right*) the Younger Pliny. Fifteenth-century statues on the front of the Cathedral at Como. (*Photo: The Mansell Collection*)

2 **si attenderes acrius:** *if you listened more carefully.*

3 **longius reddebatur:** *could be heard quite far off.*

5 **macie et squalore confectus:** *in a wretched state of emaciation and filth.*
**promissa barba** and **horrenti capillo** are ablatives describing the old man (Ablatives of Description).

6 **cruribus:** *on his legs.*

8 **inhabitantibus:** present participle used with the force of a noun – *those who lived there.* This dative is to be taken with **noctes vigilabantur:** *sleepless nights were spent by the occupants* (literally *nights were spent on watch*).

10 **sequebatur** has two subjects: **morbus** and **mors.**

11 **oculis inerrabat:** *haunted them,* literally *wandered in front of their eyes.*

12 **causis:** Ablative of Comparison after **longior.**

13 **damnata solitudine:** *condemned to lie empty.* Supply **est** with **deserta, damnata** and **relicta.**
**illi monstro:** *to that ghost.* The noun **monstrum** was used in religious language for any evil omen.

14 **seu quis . . . vellet:** *to see whether anyone might want.*

15 **ignarus tanti mali:** *not knowing that it was under such a curse.*

# 65
# A Ghost Story

erat Athenis spatiosa et capax domus, sed infamis et pestilens. per silentium noctis sonus ferri et (si attenderes acrius) strepitus vinculorum longius primo, deinde e proximo reddebatur. mox apparebat idolon, senex

5 macie et squalore confectus, promissa barba, horrenti capillo. cruribus compedes, manibus catenas gerebat quatiebatque.

inde inhabitantibus tristes diraeque noctes per metum vigilabantur. vigiliam morbus et, crescente formidine,

10 mors sequebatur. nam interdiu quoque, quamquam abscesserat imago, memoria imaginis oculis inerrabat, longiorque causis timoris timor erat. deserta inde et damnata solitudine domus totaque illi monstro relicta.

proscribebatur tamen seu quis emere seu quis conducere

15 ignarus tanti mali vellet.

---

**spatiosus, -a, -um,** spacious
**capax, capacis,** roomy
**infamis, -is, -e,** with a bad reputation
**pestilens, -entis,** haunted
**sonus, -i** (*m*), sound, noise
**attendo** (3), to pay attention to
**idolon, -i** (*n*), ghost
**macies, -ei** (*f*), emaciation
**squalor, -oris** (*m*), filth
**promissus, -a, -um,** allowed to grow long, long
**barba, -ae** (*f*), beard
**horrens, -entis,** rough
**crus, cruris** (*n*), leg
**compes, -edis** (*f*), shackle

**catena, -ae** (*f*), chain
**quatio** (3), to shake
**dirus, -a, -um,** dreadful
**vigilo** (1), to keep watch, lie awake
**formido, -inis** (*f*), fear
**imago, -inis** (*f*), apparition, ghost
**desertus, -a, -um,** abandoned
**proscribo** (3), to advertise for sale
**seu ... seu ...,** whether ... or ...
**conduco** (3), to rent
**ignarus, -a, -um,** not knowing, unaware

16 **titulum:** *the notice* posted beside the house, advertising it.

17 **suspecta vilitas:** Supply **est.** Literally *the cheapness was suspected,* i.e. *he was suspicious of the low price.*

18 **immo tanto magis:** *in fact, all the more eagerly.*

20 **sterni:** *bedding to be spread.*

   **in prima parte:** This was in the part of the house nearer the front door. Contrast the living-quarters farther inside the house. (See **interiora** in line 22.)

21 **pugillares stilum lumen:** Pliny frequently lists items in this way without any connecting word.

   **suos:** *his attendants.*

22 **animum oculos manum:** another list with no connecting word.

23 **vacua mens:** *his idle mind,* i.e. *having nothing to occupy it.*

   **audita simulacra:** *the images of which he had heard.*

25 **initio:** Supply **erat.**

   **concuti:** *was rattled.* Here, and in the next few lines, a series of present infinitives (Historic Infinitives) is used to heighten the excitement of the passage. (Cf. **moveri, tollere, remittere, offirmare, praetendere, crebrescere, adventare, audiri.**) Translate them as past tense indicative verbs.

26 **non remittere stilum:** *he did not stop writing.*

27 **animum:** *concentration.*

   **auribus praetendere:** Supply **animum.** Literally *he stretched his mind in front of his ears (to screen off his ears).* Translate *he closed his ears.*

28 **ut in limine:** *as if in the doorway.*

29 **narratam sibi effigiem:** *the ghost which had been described to him.*

31 **stabat:** The subject is the ghost.

   **similis vocanti;** *similar to someone calling (beckoning).*

   **hic contra:** *he* (i.e. *Athenodorus) in response.*

32 **ut exspectaret:** an Indirect Command depending on **significat.**

venit Athenas philosophus Athenodorus. legit titulum
auditoque pretio, quia suspecta vilitas, percunctatus
omnia docetur; ac nihilo minus, immo tanto magis
conducit.

20 ubi coepit advesperascere, iubet sterni sibi in prima
domus parte, poscit pugillares stilum lumen. suos omnes
in interiora dimittit. ipse ad scribendum animum oculos
manum intendit ne vacua mens audita simulacra et inanes
sibi metus fingeret.

25 initio silentium noctis, dein concuti ferrum, vincula
moveri. ille non tollere oculos, non remittere stilum,
sed offirmare animum auribusque praetendere. tum
crebrescere fragor, adventare et iam ut in limine, iam ut
intra limen audiri. respicit, videt agnoscitque narratam
30 sibi effigiem.

stabat innuebatque digito similis vocanti. hic contra
ut paulum exspectaret manu significat, rursusque ceris et

<table>
<tr><td>

**philosophus, -i** (*m*),
  philosopher
**titulus, -i** (*m*), notice
**pretium -i** (*n*), price
**vilitas, -atis** (*f*), cheapness
**percunctor** (1), to make
  enquiries
**nihilo minus,** none the less
**immo,** in fact
**advesperascere,** to grow dark
**sterno** (3), to spread
**pugillares, -ium** (*m.pl*),
  writing-tablets
**stilus, -i** (*m*), pen
**lumen, -inis** (*n*), light, lamp
**interior, -oris,** inner
**intendo** (3), to turn to, apply
**vacuus, -a, -um,** empty, idle

</td><td>

**inanis, -is, -e,** empty,
  worthless
**fingo** (3), to form, imagine
**initio,** at first
**concutio** (3), to shake
**offirmo** (1), to strengthen
**praetendo** (3), to stretch in
  front
**crebresco** (3), to become
  frequent, increase
**advento** (1), to approach
**agnosco** (3), to recognise
**effigies, -ei** (*f*), likeness,
  image
**innuo** (3), to nod, give a sign
**contra,** on the other hand
**significo** (1), to make a sign
**cera, -ae** (*f*), wax (tablet)

</td></tr>
</table>

33 **illa:** *it,* i.e. the ghost.

**scribentis capiti catenis insonabat:** literally *sounded with its chains over the head of him writing.* Translate *rattled its chains over his head as he continued to write.*

34 **idem quod prius innuentem:** *making the same gesture as before.*

**innuentem** is the object of **respicit:** *looked back at the (ghost) gesturing.*

37 **desertus:** *left on his own.*

38 **signum** is used in apposition to **herbas ... concerpta:** *as a sign.* In other words, he marked the spot.

39 **monet ut iubeant:** *advised (them) to give orders.*

40 **inserta catenis et implicata:** literally *inserted in chains and wound round,* i.e. *all tangled up in chains.*

41 **quae corpus reliquerat:** *which the body had left,* **corpus** referring to the flesh and the organs which had decomposed.

**nuda et exesa:** This agrees with **quae,** referring to the bones. (Compare **collecta** in line 42.)

43 **manibus caruit:** *was free from the ghost.*

**rite conditis:** *which had been properly buried.* It was believed that the soul could not rest till it had been laid to rest with due rites.

stilo incumbit.  illa scribentis capiti catenis insonabat.
respicit rursus idem quod prius innuentem;  nec moratus
35 tollit lumen et sequitur.  ibat illa lento gradu, quasi gravis
vinculis.  postquam deflexit in aream domus, repente dil-
apsa deserit comitem.  desertus herbas et folia concerpta
signum loco ponit.

postero die adit magistratus, monet ut illum locum
40 effodi iubeant.  inveniuntur ossa inserta catenis et implicata, quae corpus aevo terraque putrefactum nuda et
exesa reliquerat vinculis.  collecta publice sepeliuntur.
domus postea rite conditis manibus caruit.

**incumbo** (3), to apply oneself
**insono** (1), to make a sound
  or noise
**lentus, -a, -um,** slow
**gradus, -us** (*m*), step
**deflecto** (3), to turn aside
**dilabor** (3), **dilapsus sum,** to
  glide away
**desero** (3), to desert
**comes, -itis** (*m*), companion
**folium, -i** (*n*), leaf
**concerptus, -a, -um,** picked
  up, gathered
**effodio** (3), to dig up
**os, ossis** (*n*), bone

**insertus, -a, -um,** inserted
**implicatus, -a, -um,** wound
  round
**aevum -i** (*n*), age, time
**putrefactus, -a, -um,** rotted
**exesus, -a, -um,** eaten away
**colligo** (3), to collect
**publice,** at public expense
**sepelio** (4), to bury
**rite,** properly, duly
**condo** (3), to found, lay
**manes, -ium** (*m.pl*), spirit of a
  dead person
**careo** (2) ( + *abl.*), to lack, be
  free (from)

1 **Hipponensis:** Hippo was a settlement on the north coast of Africa, not far from Carthage.

2 **in modum fluminis:** *like a river.*

3 **vice alterna:** *alternately.*

**prout aestus aut repressit aut impulit:** *according to the ebb or flow of the tide.* There is little or no tide in the Mediterranean, but the change in water level would be more noticeable at this point because of the narrowness of the channel.

5 **omnis hic aetas piscandi studio tenetur:** *in this area, people of all ages* (literally *of every age*) *are very keen on fishing* (literally *are held by an enthusiasm for fishing*).

6 **quos otium lususque sollicitat:** literally *whom leisure and play attract,* i.e. *who are attracted by sport and have time to pursue it.*

7 **gloria:** Supply **est.**      **altissime provehi:** *to swim really far out to sea.*

8 **qui longissime ut litus ita simul natantes reliquit:** *who has left farthest behind both the shore and his fellow-swimmers* (literally *those swimming along with him*). **ut … ita …** means literally *as … so …* and is used to link two words which fall into similar categories; hence the meaning *both … and …* or *not only … but also ….*

10 **audentior ceteris:** *more daring than the others.*

**in ulteriora:** *farther out (than the rest).*

11 **praecedere:** an Historic Infinitive, used to add excitement to the description. In this sentence, there are seven examples; they should all be translated as past tenses of the indicative. Note how Pliny reverts to the indicative for the last two verbs in the sentence (**flectit** and **reddit**) since these two actions were much more leisurely.

12 **subire:** not just *it went under,* but *it took him on its back.*

13 **trepidantem:** *the frightened boy.*

14 **in altum:** *into the open sea* (literally *the deep*).

**reddit:** Supply **eum.**

15 **concurrere:** again, Historic Infinitive. (Cf. **aspicere … narrare.**)

17 **narrare:** Part of the thrill of being an eye-witness is telling others about it.

18 **si quid est mari simile:** literally *if there is anything similar to the sea,* i.e. *anything at all resembling sea* – a complicated way of referring to the lagoon.

**inter hos ille:** **hos** refers to **pueri,** and **ille** is the boy who is the hero of the incident.

19 **sed cautius:** Supply a suitable verb in English.

**delphinus rursus:** Again, verbs have to be supplied in both parts of the sentence.

**ad tempus:** The dolphin obviously came at a set time.

20 **quasi invitet, revocet:** Supply **et** between the two verbs. Pliny frequently lists words without linking them in any way.

# 66

# The Boy and the Dolphin

est in Africa Hipponensis colonia mari proxima. adiacet navigabile stagnum. ex hoc in modum fluminis aestuarium emergit, quod vice alterna (prout aestus aut repressit aut impulit) nunc infertur mari, nunc redditur
5 stagno. omnis hic aetas piscandi, navigandi atque etiam natandi studio tenetur, maxime pueri quos otium lususque sollicitat. his gloria et virtus altissime provehi. victor ille qui longissime ut litus ita simul natantes reliquit.
10 hoc certamine puer quidam audentior ceteris in ulteriora tendebat. delphinus occurrit, et nunc praecedere puerum, nunc sequi, nunc circumire, postremo subire, deponere, iterum subire, trepidantemque perferre primum in altum, mox flectit ad litus redditque terrae aequalibus.
15 serpit per coloniam fama. concurrere omnes, ipsum puerum tamquam miraculum aspicere, interrogare, audire, narrare. postero die obsident litus, prospectant mare et si quid est mari simile. natant pueri, inter hos ille, sed cautius. delphinus rursus ad tempus, rursus ad
20 puerum. fugit ille cum ceteris. delphinus (quasi invitet,

**colonia, -ae** (*f*), colony, community, settlement
**adiaceo** (2), to lie near
**stagnum, -i** (*n*), pool, lagoon
**aestuarium, -i** (*n*), channel
**emergo** (3), to come forth, emerge
**piscor** (1), to fish
**sollicito** (1), to attract, appeal to
**provehor** (3), to go forward
**certamen, -inis** (*n*), contest, competition

**tendo** (3), to stretch, swim out
**delphinus, -i** (*m*), dolphin
**postremo,** at last, finally
**aequalis, -is, -e,** of the same age, companion
**serpo** (3), to creep, spread
**interrogo** (1), to ask questions
**prospecto** (1), to look out at
**caute,** cautiously
**invito** (1), to invite, summon

21 **varios orbes implicat expeditque:** literally *tied and untied different circles,* i.e. *performed various twists and turns.*

23 **hoc:** Supply **fecit.** The repetition of **hoc** links the three phrases.

**tertio:** Supply **die.** With **pluribus** supply **diebus.**

**homines innutritos mari:** *people bred to the sea,* i.e. the sea was part of their lives.

24 **timendi pudor:** **timendi** is a gerund depending on **pudor.**

25 **pertrectant praebentem:** Supply **se** with **praebentem.** Literally *they stroked (it) offering (itself) – it allowed itself to be stroked.*

27 **adnatat nanti:** *swam up to it while it was swimming.*

28 **agnosci se, amari (se):** two Accusative and Infinitives depending on **putat** – *he thought he was recognised (by the dolphin) and liked (by it).*

29 **huius ... illius ...** *of the one* (i.e. *the boy)... of the other (the dolphin).*

30 **nec non:** The double negative produces a very strong positive – *also* or *in addition.*

31 **una:** *along with it.*

32 **tantum:** *only.*

33 **patiebatur:** *allowed to be done to it.*

**alterum illum ducebat:** *it used to escort the other one.*

34 **ut puerum ceteri pueri:** Supply **ducebant, reducebant.**

35 **incredibile:** Supply **est.** On this depend the Accusative and Infinitives – **delphinum ... extrahi solitum (esse)** and **(delphinum) harenis siccatum ... in mare revolvi (solitum esse).**

**tam verum tamen quam priora:** *but just as true as the previous incidents.*

36 **gestatorem collusoremque:** *the carrier and playmate.* There is some exaggeration since only one boy was actually carried.

37 **extrahi solitum:** *got into the habit of dragging itself out of the water* (to bask in the sun). Pliny describes this as incredible, since the Romans believed that dolphins died the moment they left the water.

**harenis siccatum:** *becoming dry on the sands.*

**in mare revolvi (solitum esse):** *it used to roll back into the sea.*

39 **mora:** *extended stay.* **mora** is ablative case and goes closely with **quorum adventu.**

**modica res publica:** *the modest resources of the community.* When Roman officials visited a town, they expected to have all their expenses met by that community.

41 **secretum:** *its seclusion.*

**placuit:** *it was decided,* the usual word describing a resolution of a body such as a senate or town-council.

**interfici ad quod coibatur:** literally *that (the object) to which there was a gathering should be killed,* i.e. *that the creature which was the centre of attraction should be killed.*

revocet) exsilit, mergitur variosque orbes implicat
expeditque.

hoc altero die, hoc tertio, hoc pluribus, donec homines
innutritos mari subiret timendi pudor. accedunt et ad-
25  ludunt et appellant, tangunt etiam pertrectantque
praebentem. crescit audacia experimento. maxime
puer, qui primus expertus est, adnatat nanti, insilit tergo,
fertur referturque, agnosci se, amari putat, amat ipse.
neuter timet, neuter timetur. huius fiducia, mansuetudo
30  illius augetur. nec non alii pueri dextra laevaque simul
eunt hortantes monentesque. ibat una (id quoque
mirum) delphinus alius, tantum spectator et comes. nihil
enim simile aut fecit aut patiebatur; sed alterum illum
ducebat, reducebat ut puerum ceteri pueri.

35  incredibile, tam verum tamen quam priora, delphinum
gestatorem collusoremque puerorum in terram quoque
extrahi solitum harenisque siccatum, ubi incaluisset, in
mare revolvi. confluebant omnes ad spectaculum magistratus, quorum adventu et mora modica res publica novis
40  sumptibus atterebatur. postremo locus ipse quietem
suam secretumque perdebat. placuit occulte interfici ad
quod coibatur.

| | |
|---|---|
| **exsilio** (4), to jump out of | **laevus, -a, -um,** left |
| **mergor** (3), to dive | **mirus, -a, -um,** strange, |
| **orbis, -is** (*m*), circle | wonderful |
| **donec,** until | **tam .. quam ...,** as ... as ... |
| **pudor, -oris** (*m*), shame | **gestator, -oris** (*m*), carrier |
| **tango** (3), to touch | **collusor, -oris** (*m*), playmate |
| **audacia, -ae** (*f*), daring, | **sicco** (1), to dry |
| courage | **incalesco** (3), to grow |
| **experimentum, -i** (*n*), | warm |
| trial, experience | **confluo** (3), to flock |
| **insilio** (4), to leap on | **sumptus, -us** (*m*), expense |
| **neuter, -tra, -trum,** | **attero** (3), to wear |
| neither | away, exhaust |
| **fiducia, -ae** (*f*), confidence | **secretum, -i** (*n*), seclusion |
| **mansuetudo, -inis** (*f*), | **occulte,** secretly |
| gentleness, tameness | **coeo, -ire, -ii, -itum,** to |
| **augeo** (2), to increase | assemble, gather |

**Tacito suo s.:** The letter **s** stands for **salutem dat,** *sends greetings to.* P. Cornelius Tacitus wrote several books dealing with the history of Rome in the first century AD. Tacitus had written to his friend Pliny asking for details about how Pliny's uncle had died in the eruption of Vesuvius in AD 79.

1 **avunculi mei:** Pliny's uncle (Pliny the Elder) in his earlier years had served in the army and held administrative positions in several provinces of the empire. He showed a remarkable eagerness to acquire more and more knowledge, so much so that he spent almost every moment of his spare time reading; and even when he was eating or bathing, he used to have someone read to him. In his later life, he gathered all this information together into a kind of encyclopedia called the **Naturalis Historia.**

**quo verius possis: quo** (rather than **ut**) is used to introduce this Purpose clause because the clause contains a comparative adverb.

2 **morti eius:** This dative depends on **propositam esse** *(is in prospect).*

3 **si celebretur:** *if it were to be made famous.*

4 **beatos:** Supply **eos** and **esse** to complete the Accusative and Infinitive.

**quibus datum est:** literally *to whom it has been given,* i.e. *who have the ability to.*

5 **scribenda:** neuter plural of the gerundive – *things worth writing.* (Cf. **legenda.**)

6 **beatissimos quibus utrumque:** Pliny's style of writing can be very compressed at times. The thought contained in this phrase balances everything in the Latin from **beatos** to **legenda.** In its expanded form, it would read:

**(eos) beatissimos vero (esse puto) quibus (datum est) utrumque (facere).**

**horum in numero:** *among the latter.* The pronouns **hic** and **ille** are often used to signify *the latter* and *the former.*

7 **suis libris:** ablative case; translate *because of his own writings.*

**quo libentius:** *all the more willingly* (literally *by which the more willingly*).

8 **quod iniungis:** Supply **id,** the object of both **suscipio** and **deposco.**

# 67
# The Eruption of Vesuvius

## Part 1

### Death of an Uncle

C. Plinius Tacito suo s.

petis ut tibi avunculi mei exitum scribam quo verius
tradere posteris possis.  gratias ago, nam video morti
eius, si celebretur a te, immortalem gloriam esse
propositam.  equidem beatos puto, quibus deorum
5  munere datum est aut facere scribenda aut scribere legenda, beatissimos vero quibus utrumque.  horum in numero avunculus meus et suis libris et tuis erit.  quo libentius suscipio, deposco etiam quod iniungis.

| | |
|---|---|
| **avunculus, -i** (*m*), uncle | **propono** (3), to set before |
| **exitus, -us** (*m*), end, death | **equidem,** for my part |
| **scribo** (3), to write, | **beatus, -a, -um,** happy |
| describe | **munus, muneris** (*n*), gift |
| **posteri, -orum** (*m.pl*), | **suscipio** (3), to undertake |
| future generations | **deposco** (3), to ask, demand |
| **celebro** (1), to make famous | **iniungo** (3), to charge, impose |

Mt Vesuvius. (*Photo: The Photo Source*)

9 **erat:** The subject is *my uncle* (understood).

**Miseni:** Misenum was on a promontory at the north end of the Bay of Naples. It provided a harbour for a section of the Roman fleet. Pliny the Elder was the admiral in supreme command **(imperio)** and he was there in person **(praesens).**

10 **nonum Kal. Septembres:** The more common form would have been **ante diem nonum Kalendas Septembres** (shortened to **a.d.ix Kal.Sep.**), i.e. 24th August.

**hora fere septima:** The Romans divided the period between sunrise and sunset into twelve equal parts or hours. The length of each hour depended on the time of year, the summer hours being longer than those in winter. Since the sixth hour was at noon, the seventh hour in August would have been some time between 1 and 2 p.m.

11 **apparere nubem:** an Accusative and Infinitive depending on **indicat.**

**inusitata magnitudine:** an Ablative of Description giving more detail about the **nubes.**

12 **usus sole:** *he had been sunbathing.* Note how the English translation of **utor, uti, usus sum** changes to suit the context.

**frigida:** Supply **usus aqua:** i.e. *he had taken a cold bath.*

13 **poscit soleas:** It was customary to remove one's sandals before reclining at table.

14 **nubes** is the subject of **oriebatur** (in line 16).

**incertum:** Supply **erat.**

15 **intuentibus:** *to people watching.* (Cf. **adstantes,** *bystanders,* for the present participle used in Latin where English would more naturally use a noun.) From where he stood, Vesuvius was 29 kilometres away across the bay.

16 **cuius ... expresserit:** literally *whose likeness and shape no other tree than the pine would better represent.* The Italian pine has a flat top like an umbrella. A modern writer would undoubtedly have called it a "mushroom" effect.

The "mushroom cloud" effect of an atomic bomb explosion.
(*Photo: Popperfoto*)

erat Miseni classemque imperio praesens regebat.
10 nonum Kal. Septembres hora fere septima mater mea indicat ei apparere nubem inusitata et magnitudine et
specie. usus ille sole, mox frigida, gustaverat iacens
studebatque; poscit soleas, ascendit locum ex quo
maxime miraculum illud conspici poterat. nubes – in-
15 certum procul intuentibus ex quo monte (Vesuvium fuisse
postea cognitum est) – oriebatur, cuius similitudinem et
formam non alia magis arbor quam pinus expresserit.

**praesens, -entis,** present, in
person
**rego** (3), to rule, command
**indico** (1), to point out
**nubes, -is** (*f*), cloud
**inusitatus, -a, -um,** unusual
**species, -ei** (*f*), appearance
**gusto** (1), to eat, have a
light meal
**studeo** (2), to study

**solea, -ae** (*f*), sandal
**miraculum, -i** (*n*), wonder,
strange sight
**incertus, -a, -um,** uncertain
**intueor** (2), to look at
**similitudo, -inis** (*f*), likeness
**forma, -ae** (*f*), shape
**pinus, -i** (*f*), pine-tree
**exprimo** (3), **expressi,
expressum,** to express

Flat-topped pine trees on the Bay of Naples. (*Photo: Popperfoto*)

18 **longissimo velut trunco:** It was not actually a tree-trunk; hence the insertion of **velut** to indicate that it looked like that.

**elata in altum:** *carried high up into the sky.* **elata** agrees with **nubes** (understood).

19 **credo:** a parenthesis, *I suppose.* He is not really sure but is trying to give a rational explanation of what he saw.

**evecta, destituta** and **victa** all agree with **nubes** (understood).

20 **senescente eo** balances **recenti spiritu,** with **eo** referring to **spiritu,** *as the force of the blast weakened.*

21 **candida:** The adjectives **candida, sordida** and **maculosa** all describe **nubes.**

22 **prout:** *according as,* i.e. *depending on whether.*

23 **propius noscendum:** *requiring closer investigation.*

**ut eruditissimo viro:** Take this dative with **visum** – *it seemed to my uncle as being* (i.e. *since he was*) *a very learned man.*

24 **visum:** Supply **est** – *it* (i.e. *the phenomenon*) *seemed.* Take with **magnum (esse)** and **noscendum (esse).**

**liburnicam:** Supply **navem.** This was a light vessel designed for speed. Later (line 30), when he changed his plans, he used the much heavier warship (**quadriremis**). The Liburnian ship was named after the Liburnian pirates who used ships of this design.

**mihi facit copiam:** *he gave me the opportunity (of going).*

26 **quod scriberem dederat:** *he had given me what I was to write,* i.e. *some writing to do.*

**accipit:** The switch from past tenses to Historic Presents here and in lines 30–34 **(vertit, deducit, ascendit, properat, fugiunt, tenet)** adds vividness to the story.

27 **Rectinae Tasci:** Although **Rectinae** is genitive, English would say *from Rectina.* **Tasci** means *the wife of Tascius;* this was the normal way of referring to a married woman.

28 **subiacebat:** Supply **monti Vesuvio.**     **fuga:** Supply **erat.**

**ut ... eriperet:** Indirect Command depending on **orabat.**

29 **discrimini:** dative case, as is normal with a verb of *taking away (from).*

32 **amoenitas orae:** *this beautiful part of the coast.*

**laturus:** (future participle) *intending to bring.*

33 **rectum cursum recta gubernacula:** The two expressions, depicting the same idea, are used for dramatic effect.

34 **illius mali** refers to the *disaster.* Note how Latin does not need a word for "and" between **omnes motus** and **omnes figuras** (line 31.)

35 **dictaret enotaretque:** He always had near him a slave to whom he would dictate notes on anything interesting that he had seen or thought of.

nam longissimo velut trunco elata in altum quibusdam
ramis diffundebatur (credo quia recenti spiritu evecta),
20  dein senescente eo destituta aut etiam pondere suo victa in
latitudinem vanescebat, candida interdum, interdum sordida et maculosa prout terram cineremve sustulerat.

magnum propiusque noscendum ut eruditissimo viro
visum. iubet liburnicam aptari. mihi, si venire una vel-
25  lem, facit copiam. respondi studere me malle, et forte
ipse quod scriberem dederat. egrediebatur domo; accipit
codicillos Rectinae Tasci imminenti periculo exterritae
(nam villa eius subiacebat, nec ulla nisi navibus fuga). ut
se tanto discrimini eriperet orabat.

30  vertit ille consilium. deducit quadriremes, ascendit
ipse non Rectinae modo sed multis (erat enim frequens
amoenitas orae) laturus auxilium. properat illuc unde
alii fugiunt, rectumque cursum recta gubernacula in periculum tenet, adeo solutus metu ut omnes illius mali motus
35  omnes figuras dictaret enotaretque.

---

**velut,** as if, as though

**truncus, -i** (*m*), tree-trunk

**diffundo** (3), to spread out

**recens, -entis,** recent, fresh

**spiritus, -us** (*m*), blast (of air)

**eveho** (3), to carry out, raise
aloft

**dein,** then

**senesco** (3), to grow old, fail

**destitutus, -a, -um,** left
unsupported

**vanesco** (3), to vanish,
disperse

**candidus, -a, -um,** white

**interdum,** sometimes

**sordidus, -a, -um,** dirty

**maculosus, -a, -um,** spotted,
mottled

**cinis, -eris** (*m*), ash, cinders

**-ve,** or

**eruditus, -a, -um,** learned,
scholarly

**liburnica, -ae** (*f*), light vessel

**apto** (1), to get ready

**codicilli, -orum** (*m.pl*), note

**imminens, -entis,** imminent,
threatening

**subiaceo** (2), to lie under

**discrimen, -inis** (*n*), danger

**verto** (3), to turn, change

**deduco** (3), to launch

**quadriremis, -is** (*f*),
quadrireme

**frequens, -entis,** crowded,
well-populated

**amoenitas, -atis** (*f*), charm
(of scenery)

**propero** (1), to hasten

**rectus, -a, -um,** straight, direct

**gubernaculum -i** (*n*), rudder,
helm

**solutus, -a, -um,** free from

**motus, -us** (*m*), movement

**figura, -ae** (*f*), shape

**dicto** (1), to dictate

**enoto** (1), to take notes

37 **calidior et densior:** Supply **eo** with these words to balance **quo propius:** *the nearer . . . the hotter . . .*

**iam pumices:** Supply **incidebant.** (Cf. also **lapides.**)

38 **vadum:** Supply **fuit.** As the debris **(ruina)** came down from Vesuvius, it extended the shoreline **(litora),** thus making it shallow **(vadum)** and blocking **(obstantia)** the way ahead.

39 **an retro flecteret:** *whether to turn back.*

40 **ut ita faceret:** Indirect Command depending on **monenti,** which agrees with **gubernatori.** **ita,** of course, refers back to **an retro flecteret.**

41 **Pomponianum:** Pomponianus was a friend of Pliny the Elder and lived at Stabiae, which lay across the bay south of Vesuvius. We have to assume that Pliny had not abandoned Rectina but had either already rescued her or had sent one of the quadriremes to help her.

42 **erat:** The subject is Pomponianus.

**diremptus sinu medio:** *separated (from Pliny) by the bay which lay between them.* Normally, the adjective **medius** is translated *the middle of;* here, it means *intervening.* Pomponianus was at Stabiae, Pliny at Misenum.

44 **certus fugae:** The use of **certus** with the genitive (to denote *determined on* something) began with the poets and is imitated here by Pliny: *determined on flight* or *determined to flee.*

**quo secundissimo invectus:** *carried by the same wind blowing strongly behind him.* **quo** is a Linking Relative referring back to **ventus.** It was blowing across the bay from the north-west.

46 **trepidantem:** Supply **eum.** Note how the three verbs **complectitur, consolatur** and **hortatur** are used without any conjunction. (Cf. lines 33–35.)

**timorem eius sua securitate:** An excellent example showing the difference between **eius** (here referring to Pomponianus) and **sua** (referring to the subject of the clause, Pliny).

47 **deferri iubet:** *he ordered that he (Pliny) be taken.* Pliny is obviously trying to reassure Pomponianus by acting very calmly himself.

**lotus:** *after taking his bath.* Note that again there is no conjunction between **accubat** and **cenat.**

iam navibus cinis incidebat, quo propius accederent, calidior et densior. iam pumices etiam nigrique et ambusti et fracti igne lapides. iam vadum subitum ruinaque montis litora obstantia. cunctatus paulum an retro flecteret, mox gubernatori ut ita faceret monenti "fortes" inquit "fortuna iuvat. Pomponianum pete!"

Stabiis erat diremptus sinu medio. ibi quamquam nondum periculo appropinquante, sarcinas contulerat in naves, certus fugae si contrarius ventus resedisset. quo tunc avunculus meus secundissimo invectus, complectitur trepidantem consolatur hortatur; utque timorem eius sua securitate leniret, deferri in balneum iubet. lotus

**calidus, -a, -um,** hot
**pumex, -icis** (*m*), pumice-stone
**ambustus, -a, -um,** burnt
**obsto** (1), to block (the way)
**an,** whether
**retro,** back
**flecto** (3), to turn
**gubernator, -oris** (*m*), pilot, helmsman
**iuvo** (1), to help
**diremptus, -a, -um,** separated
**sinus, -us** (*m*), bay
**sarcina, -ae** (*f*), baggage

**contrarius, -a, -um,** opposing, contrary
**resido** (3), to sit, sink, abate
**invehor** (3), to sail in
**complector** (3), to embrace
**trepido** (1), to panic, be excited
**consolor** (1), to console
**securitas, -atis** (*f*), lack of concern
**lenio** (4), to soothe, calm
**lavo** (1), **lavi, lotum,** to wash

*Map 11* The neighbourhood of Mt Vesuvius

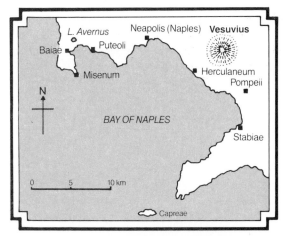

48 **quod aeque magnum:** *what is equally remarkable.*

50 **pluribus locis:** *in several places.* The omission of the preposition, a common practice in poetry, had also become common in prose by Pliny's time.

51 **quorum** refers back to **flammae** and **incendia.**

52 **excitabatur:** literally *was stirred up*, i.e. *was intensified.*

53 **dedit:** The subject is Pliny the Elder (the writer's uncle).

54 **meatus animae:** literally *the passage of his breath*, i.e. *his breathing*, which is possibly a polite way of referring to his snoring.

 **illi** is dative singular. Translate *in his case.*

56 **cinere mixtisque pumicibus:** *with a mixture of ash and pumice-stone.*

57 **si ... mora:** Supply **esset.**

58 **negaretur:** literally *would be denied*, i.e. it would be impossible to get out.

59 **seque:** Take **se** with **reddit** – *he restored himself* to them, i.e. *he joined* them.

60 **consultant:** Supply **utrum** *(whether)* after this word, introducing a double Indirect Question.

61 **subsistant:** *whether they should stay.* (Compare **vagentur.**)

64 **capitibus:** dative case, going with **imposita.**

 **linteis:** ablative case, going with **constringunt.**

65 **adversus incidentia:** *against falling debris.* (**incidentia** is neuter plural.)

 **iam dies alibi:** It was now 25th August and past what would normally have been dawn. The towns around Vesuvius **(illic),** however, were still in darkness. They had first noticed the eruption early in the afternoon of the previous day.

The people of Pompeii fleeing from the eruption. A scene from the film *The Last Days of Pompeii.* (*Photo: Ronald Grant*)

accubat cenat, aut hilaris aut (quod aeque magnum) similis hilari.

50 interim e Vesuvio monte pluribus locis latissimae flammae altaque incendia relucebant, quorum fulgor et claritas tenebris noctis excitabatur.

tum se quieti dedit et quievit verissimo quidem somno; nam meatus animae, qui illi propter amplitudinem cor-
55 poris gravior et sonantior erat, ab iis qui limini obversabantur audiebatur. sed area ita iam cinere mixtisque pumicibus oppleta surrexerat ut, si longior in cubiculo mora, exitus negaretur.

excitatus procedit, seque Pomponiano ceterisque qui
60 pervigilaverant reddit. in commune consultant intra tecta subsistant an in aperto vagentur. nam crebris vastisque tremoribus tecta nutabant et, quasi emota sedibus suis, nunc huc nunc illuc abire aut referri videbantur.

cervicalia capitibus imposita linteis constringunt; id
65 munimentum adversus incidentia fuit. iam dies alibi, illic

---

**accubo** (1), to recline at table

**hilaris, -is, -e,** cheerful

**aeque,** equally

**reluceo** (2), to blaze, shine out

**fulgor, -oris** (*m*), glare, flashes

**claritas, -atis** (*f*), brightness

**tenebrae, -arum** (*f.pl*), darkness

**meatus, -us** (*m*), passage

**amplitudo, -inis** (*f*), size, bulk

**sonans, -antis,** sonorous, loud

**obversor** (1) (+ *dat.*), to be near, hover about

**mixtus, -a, -um,** mixed

**oppletus, -a, -um,** completely filled

**pervigilo** (1), to spend the night awake

**in commune,** together, among themselves

**consulto** (1), to consult

**subsisto** (3), to stay, remain

**vastus, -a, -um,** huge, violent

**nuto** (1), to totter

**emotus, -a, -um,** moved

**sedes, -ium** (*f.pl*), foundations

**cervical, -alis** (*n*), pillow

**linteum, -i** (*n*), linen cloth, sail

**constringo** (3), to bind, tie

**munimentum, -i** (*n*), protection, defence

**incido** (3), to fall upon

**alibi,** elsewhere

66 **quam:** Linking Relative referring back to **nox.**

67 **placuit:** Supply **ei** – *he (Pliny) decided.*

68 **ecquid iam mare admitteret:** an Indirect Question depending on **adspicere:** *what (course of action), if any, the sea would now permit.* The next part of the sentence tells us how stormy it still was. The hot air rising from Vesuvius was replaced by cold air rushing in from the sea, which made it difficult for them to set sail from land.

69 **quod:** Linking Relative referring back to **mare.**

**vastum et adversum:** The waves were huge and there was a strong current running towards the shore.

72 **odor sulpuris** explains what the **flammarum praenuntius** is.

74 **ut ego colligo** is a parenthesis explaining that what follows is conjecture rather than established fact.

75 **spiritu obstructo** and **clauso stomacho** are both Ablative Absolutes, while **crassiore caligine** is ablative depending on **obstructo.** Note the use of the comparative to show that the smoke (smog, fumes) were *too thick* for him to breathe.

**illi:** Compare line 54.

**natura** is ablative: *by nature,* i.e. *naturally.*

76 **frequenter aestuans:** *frequently inflamed.* He probably suffered from asthma.

77 **redditus:** Supply **est.**

**is ab eo quem novissime viderat tertius:** Supply **erat dies** with **tertius** and **die** with **ab eo.** The Roman "inclusive" way of calculating (i.e. counting the first and last in a series) would make the "third day" 26th August. The eruption had started on 24th August; Pliny died on 25th August, but there had been no actual daylight **(dies)** for him to see on that day. The last day, therefore, which he had actually seen was the 24th.

78 **inventum:** Supply **est.**

**opertum:** This agrees with **corpus** (his lifeless corpse), whereas **ut fuerat indutus** *as he had been dressed* is masculine, thinking of him as he was when he was alive.

79 **quiescenti** *(someone sleeping)* and **defuncto** *(someone who had died).* Both of these datives are to be taken with **similior.** For this use of the participle compare **intuentibus** in line 15.

81 **nihil ad historiam:** *but this has nothing to do with the account you are writing.*

nox omnibus noctibus nigrior densiorque;  quam tamen faces multae variaque lumina solabantur.  placuit egredi in litus et ex proximo adspicere ecquid iam mare admitteret; quod adhuc vastum et adversum permanebat.  ibi
70  super abiectum linteum recubans semel atque iterum frigidam aquam poposcit hausitque.  deinde flammae flammarumque praenuntius odor sulpuris alios in fugam vertunt, excitant illum.  innitens servulis duobus adsurrexit et statim concidit, ut ego colligo, crassiore caligine
75  spiritu obstructo clausoque stomacho, qui illi natura invalidus et angustus et frequenter aestuans erat.

ubi dies redditus (is ab eo quem novissime viderat tertius), corpus inventum integrum inlaesum opertumque ut fuerat indutus.  habitus corporis quiescenti quam de-
80  functo similior.

interim Miseni ego et mater – sed nihil ad historiam, nec tu aliud quam de exitu eius scire voluisti.  finem ergo faciam.  vale!

**solor** (1), to comfort, relieve
**adspicio** (3), to observe
**permaneo** (2), to remain, persist
**recubo** (1), to recline
**semel atque iterum,** once or twice
**haurio** (4), to drain, drink
**praenuntius, -i** (*m*), forewarning, harbinger
**odor, -oris** (*m*), scent, smell
**sulpur, -uris** (*n*), sulphur
**innitor** (3) ( + *abl.*), to lean upon
**servulus, -i** (*m*), young slave
**adsurgo** (3), to rise up
**concido** (3), to fall
**colligo** (3), to gather
**crassus, -a, -um,** dense

**caligo, -inis** (*f*), mist, vapour, fumes
**obstructus, -a, -um,** blocked
**stomachus, -i** (*m*), windpipe
**frequenter,** frequently
**aestuans, -antis,** inflamed
**novissime,** last
**integer, -gra, -grum,** intact, unharmed, with no injuries
**inlaesus, -a, -um,** unharmed
**opertus, -a, -um,** covered
**habitus, -us** (*m*), appearance, condition
**defunctus, -a, -um,** dead
**historia, -ae** (*f*), story, account

2 **mox balineum, cena, somnus:** Although these are nominative, in English we would probably say *I took a bath, etc.*

4 **quia Campaniae solitus:** Supply **est.** Small tremors were common in the area, and there had been a very serious earthquake in AD 63.

**ut non moveri omnia sed verti crederentur:** *that everything seemed* (literally *was believed*) *not (only) to be shaken but turned upside down.*

6 **in vicem:** Translate *for my part.*

7 **si quiesceret** depends on **excitaturus** *intending to wake.*

**area:** This was not so much a courtyard as an open space between the house and the sea, only partially surrounded by the building.

8 **dividebat:** *separated.*

**dubito:** Supply **utrum** to introduce an Alternative Indirect Question.

**constantiam vocare:** *to call (what I did) courage.*

9 **agebam enim ...:** This parenthetical remark tells us that Pliny was born in either AD 61 or 62, making him 17 at the time of the eruption.

10 **Titi Livi:** The historian Livy wrote 142 books dealing with the history of Rome from its foundation in 753 BC to 9 BC. He had died in AD 17. (See also page 190.)

11 **excerpo:** *I copied extracts.* There was no law of copyright in Roman times. From one original manuscript by the author, other people would make copies for themselves. Educated Greek slaves were often used as copyists.

12 **ecce:** literally *behold.* Translate *suddenly along came.*

Two of the victims. During the excavation of the buried city, archaeologists found cavities left by the decayed bodies of people who had died. By carefully pouring plaster into these cavities the shapes and attitudes of the bodies were revealed. (*Photo: The Mansell Collection*)

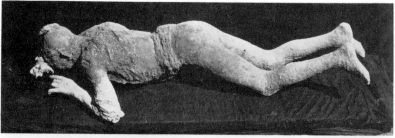

# 68

# The Eruption of Vesuvius

## Part 2

### Pliny's Own Experiences

*When Tacitus received Pliny's letter about his uncle's death, he wrote back asking him to describe his own experiences during the eruption.*

profecto avunculo, ipse reliquum tempus studiis impendi.
mox balineum, cena, somnus inquietus et brevis. praeces-
serat per multos dies tremor terrae minus formidulosus
quia Campaniae solitus.   illa vero nocte ita invaluit ut
5   non moveri omnia sed verti crederentur.
　　inrumpit cubiculum meum mater; surgebam in vicem,
si quiesceret, excitaturus. resedimus in area domus, quae
mare a tectis modico spatio dividebat.   dubito constantiam vocare an imprudentiam debeam (agebam enim
10   duodevicesimum annum).   posco librum Titi 'Livi et
quasi per otium lego atque etiam, ut coeperam, excerpo.
　　ecce amicus avunculi, qui nuper ad eum ex Hispania

**impendo** (3), to spend
**inquietus, -a, -um,**
　disturbed, restless
**praecedo** (3), to precede
**formidulosus, -a, -um,**
　terrifying
**invalesco** (3), to increase,
　grow strong
**inrumpo** (3), to burst in
**in vicem,** in turn
**quiesco** (3), to rest, sleep

**modicus, -a, -um,**
　moderate, slight
**constantia, -ae** (*f*),
　courage, resolution
**imprudentia, -ae** (*f*),
　imprudence, rashness
**duodevicesimus, -a. -um,**
　eighteenth
**otium, -i** (*n*), leisure
**excerpo** (3), to make
　extracts

*line*

14 **illius:** *her.*

**patientiam:** not so much *patience* as *forbearance* in allowing her son to loiter there. **patientia** is from the same root as the verb **pati,** *to allow.*

15 **nihilo segnius:** literally *by nothing more sluggishly.* Take with **intentus** and translate *concentrated no less earnestly.*

16 **hora diei prima:** Supply **erat.** See Chapter 67 line 10 for details of how the Roman day was divided into hours.

17 **dies:** *daylight.*

**circumiacentibus:** The present participle has the force of an adjective here. Translate *surrounding.*

18 **ruinae metus:** *risk from the falling masonry.*

19 **visum:** Supply **est nobis.** Translate *we decided.*

**egressi tecta:** *having passed beyond the buildings.*

20 **patimur:** *we experienced.*

21 **quamquam in planissimo campo:** *although (they were standing) on perfectly level ground.*

22 **ne ... quidem fulta:** *not even when wedged.*

24 **processerat litus:** *the shore-line had advanced* as the sea receded.

26 **ab altero latere:** *on the other side,* i.e. *inland.*

**ignei spiritus tortis vibratisque discursibus rupta:** *torn by twisted, zig-zag flashes* (literally *running about*) *of fiery vapour.*

Pompeii: the peristyle of the House of the Gilded Cupids. (*Photo: The Mansell Collection*)

venerat, ut me et matrem sedentes (me vero etiam legen-
tem) videt, illius patientiam, securitatem meam corripit.
15  nihilo segnius ego intentus in librum.

iam hora diei prima, et adhuc dubius et quasi languidus
dies.  iam quassatis circumiacentibus tectis, magnus et
certus ruinae metus.  tum demum excedere oppido
visum.  egressi tecta consistimus.  multa ibi miranda,
20  multas formidines patimur:  nam vehicula quae produci
iusseramus, quamquam in planissimo campo, in con-
trarias partes agebantur ac ne lapidibus quidem fulta in
eodem vestigio quiescebant.  praeterea mare in se resor-
beri et tremore terrae quasi repelli videbamus.  certe pro-
25  cesserat litus multaque animalia maris siccis harenis det-
inebat. ab altero latere nubes atra et horrenda, ignei spiritus tortis vibratisque discursibus rupta, in longas flammarum figuras dehiscebat.  fulguribus illae et similes et
maiores erant.
30  tum vero idem ille ex Hispania amicus acrius et instant-
ius "si frater" inquit "tuus, tuus avunculus vivit, vult esse

**securitas, -atis** (*f*),
  nonchalance, lack of
  concern
**corripio** (3), to rebuke,
  criticise
**segniter,** lazily, sluggishly
**dubius, -a, -um,** uncertain
**languidus, -a, -um,**
  weak, faint
**quasso** (1), to shake
  violently
**circumiaceo** (2), to lie
  around
**demum,** at last
**mirandus, -a, -um,**
  wonderful
**produco** (3), to bring
  forward
**campus, -i** (*m*), plain,
  ground

**fultus, -a, -um,** propped up
**resorbeo** (2), to suck back
**siccus, -a, -um,** dry
**harena, -ae** (*f*), sand
**detineo** (2), to hold back
**ater, atra, atrum,** dark, black
**horrendus, -a, -um,**
  terrifying, frightening
**igneus, -a, -um,** fiery
**tortus, -a, -um,** twisted
**vibratus, -a, -um,** quivering
**discursus, -us** (*m*),
  running to and fro
**ruptus, -a, -um,** broken
**dehisco** (3), to yawn,
  gape open
**fulgur, -uris** (*n*), lightning
**instanter,** urgently,
  earnestly

32 **superstites:** Supply **vos esse.**

34 **nos non commissuros (esse) ut:** *that we would not act in such a way that.*

**de salute illius incerti nostrae (saluti) consuleremus:** *we would look after our own safety while uncertain about his safety.*

35 **ultra:** Take with **moratus** – *any longer.*

36 **periculo aufertur:** *he hurried away from the danger.*

37 **descendere** and **operire** are Historic Infinitives. Translate as if they were indicatives.

38 **Miseni quod procurrit:** literally *what of Misenum runs forward (into the sea),* i.e. *the promontory of Misenum.* **Miseni** is Partitive Genitive.

40 **orare, hortari, iubere:** Historic Infinitives. (Cf. line 37.)

**quoquo modo fugerem:** an Indirect Command – *to flee by whatever means (I could).*

41 **posse iuvenem:** Supply **fugere.** This Accusative and Infinitive has no verb of speaking to introduce it, as is normal following on other indirect speech. Likewise, **se ... morituram (esse).**

**annis et corpore gravem:** She was apparently heavily built like her brother, Pliny the Elder.

43 **ego contra:** *I countered this by saying that.* Supply **esse** with **futurum.**

44 **addere gradum:** Supply **gradui** – literally *to add step to step,* i.e. *quicken her pace.*

47 **torrentis modo infusa terrae:** *spread over the earth like* (literally *in the manner of*) *a torrent.*

48 **in via strati:** literally *strewn on the road,* i.e. *knocked over on the road.* The participle **strati** agrees with the subject *we.*

50 **nox:** Supply **fuit.**

**non qualis inlunis:** *not like (a night) when there is no moon.*

51 **audires:** *you could hear.*

vos salvos. si periit, superstites voluit. proinde quid ces-
satis evadere?"

35    respondimus non commissuros nos ut de salute illius
incerti nostrae consuleremus. non moratus ultra proripit
se effusoque cursu periculo aufertur. nec multo post illa
nubes descendere in terras, operire maria. cinxerat
Capreas et absconderat, Miseni quod procurrit
abstulerat.

40    tum mater orare, hortari, iubere quoquo modo
fugerem: posse enim iuvenem, se et annis et corpore
gravem bene morituram, si mihi causa mortis non
fuisset. ego contra salvum me nisi una non futurum. dein
manum eius amplexus, addere gradum cogo. paret aegre
45    incusatque se quod me moretur.

iam cinis, adhuc tamen rarus. respicio. densa caligo
tergis imminebat, quae nos torrentis modo infusa terrae
sequebatur. "deflectamus," inquam "dum videmus, ne in
via strati comitantium turba in tenebris obteramur."

50    vix consederamus et nox, non qualis inlunis aut nubila,
sed qualis in locis clausis, lumine exstincto. audires ululatus feminarum, infantium quiritatus, clamores

| | |
|---|---|
| **salvus, -a, -um,** safe | **amplector** (3), to embrace |
| **superstes, -stitis,** surviving | **addo** (3), to add |
| **proinde,** accordingly, therefore | **incuso** (1), to accuse, |
| **quid?** why? | reproach |
| **cesso** (1), to hesitate | **rarus, -a, -um,** thinly scattered |
| **evado** (3), to go out, escape | **torrens, -entis** (*m*), torrent |
| **consulo** (3) (+ *dat.*), to consult, | **infusus, -a, -um,** spread over |
| consider | **stratus, -a, -um,** strewn |
| **ultra,** further | **comitantes, -ium** (*m.pl*), |
| **se proripere,** to rush out | companions |
| **effusus, -a, -um,** let | **turba, -ae** (*f*), crowd |
| loose, hurried | **obtero** (3), to crush |
| **operio** (4), to cover | **inlunis, -is, -e,** moonless |
| **cingo** (3), to surround | **nubilus, -a, -um,** cloudy |
| **Capreae, -arum** (*f.pl*), Capri | **exstinctus, -a, -um,** |
| **abscondo** (3), to hide | exstinguished |
| **procurro** (3), to run | **ululatus, -us** (*m*), howling |
| forward | **quiritatus, -us** (*m*), wailing |

(*Opposite*) Pompeii: a bar on the Via dell' Abbondanza. Note the graffiti on the
walls! (*Photo: The Mansell Collection*)

*line*

54 **noscitabant:** Since it was too dark to see them clearly, they had to recognise them by their voices.

**hi ... illi:** *some ... others.* With **suorum** supply **casum.**

55 **erant qui:** *there were some who.*

56 **tollere** is an Historic Infinitive.

**nusquam deos ullos:** Supply **esse.**

58 **nec defuerunt qui:** Compare line 55, *there was no lack of people who.*

60 **quod:** *which.* The antecedent is the whole clause **paulum reluxit.** It is also possible to translate *but this.*

61 **longius substitit:** *stayed quite a distance away* (literally *halted rather far off*).

62 **hunc** refers to the ash.

63 **operti:** Take with **essemus** – *we would have been covered over.*

67 **cum deficit:** *when there is an eclipse.*

**occursabant:** The subject is **omnia** in line 68.

68 **mutata:** Everything looked different because of the ruined buildings, and possibly because of some land movement caused by the earthquake.

70 **spe ac metu:** Take with both **suspensam** and **dubiam** – *(torn) between hope and fear.*

73 **expertis** and **exspectantibus:** *having experienced* and *still expecting.* Both participles agree with **nobis** and are to be taken with **quamquam.** English would probably translate them by clauses.

**abeundi consilium:** Supply **erat** and take with **nobis** (line 72) – literally *there was a plan to us of departing,* i.e. *had we any intention of leaving.*

A street with cobbles and stepping stones. The stepping stones were so placed that the wheels of carts could pass on either side of them. (*Photo: The Mansell Collection*)

virorum. alii parentes, alii liberos, alii coniuges vocibus
requirebant, vocibus noscitabant. hi suum casum, illi
55 suorum miserabantur. erant qui metu mortis mortem
precarentur. multi ad deos manus tollere, plures nusquam deos ullos aeternamque illam et novissimam noctem mundo interpretabantur. nec defuerunt qui fictis
mentitisque terroribus vera pericula augerent.

60 paulum reluxit, quod non dies nobis, sed adventantis
ignis indicium videbatur. et ignis quidem longius substitit, tenebrae rursus, cinis rursus multus et gravis. hunc
identidem adsurgentes excutiebamus. operti alioqui
atque etiam oblisi pondere essemus.

65 tandem illa caligo tenuata quasi in fumum nebulamve
discessit. mox dies verus. sol etiam effulsit, luridus
tamen, qualis esse, cum deficit, solet. occursabant trepi-
dantibus adhuc oculis mutata omnia altoque cinere tamquam nive obducta.

70 regressi Misenum suspensam dubiamque noctem spe
ac metu exegimus. metus praevalebat, nam tremor terrae
perseverabat. nobis tamen ne tunc quidem, quamquam
et expertis periculum et exspectantibus, abeundi consilium donec de avunculo nuntius.

---

**coniunx, -iugis** (*m/f*), husband,
  wife
**requiro** (3), to search for, ask
**noscito** (1), to recognise
**miseror** (1), to bewail, pity
**precor** (1), to pray
**nusquam,** nowhere
**novissimus, -a, -um,** last, final
**mundus, -i** (*m*), world, universe
**interpretor** (1), to interpret,
  believe
**fictus, -a, -um,** pretended,
  imagined
**mentitus, -a, -um,** feigned,
  false
**augeo** (2), to increase
**indicium, -i** (*n*), sign,
  indication

**excutio** (3), to shake off
**alioqui,** otherwise
**oblisus, -a, -um,** crushed
**tenuatus, -a, -um,** thinned out
**nebula, -ae** (*f*), mist
**effulgeo** (2), to shine forth
**luridus, -a, -um,** pale, sickly
  yellow
**occurso** (1) (+ *dat.*), to run
  up to, meet
**tamquam,** as if
**nix, nivis** (*f*), snow
**obductus, -a, -um,** covered
**exigo** (3), to spend
**praevaleo** (2), to prevail
**expertus, -a, -um,** having
  experienced

The Younger Pliny, like his uncle, was born at Comum (modern Como) in AD 61 or 62. In his teens he went to Rome to enter upon a public career which involved him first of all in the study of the law.

By his nineteenth year, he was already speaking in the law-courts, and from then onwards he progressed through the various public offices (quaestorship, praetorship, etc), which continued under the emperors to be the road to advancement, although the real power now resided not in them but in the hands of the emperor. Even when Pliny attained the consulship in AD 100, he held office for only the months of September and October. Indeed, hardly anyone was allowed more than four months' tenure as consul.

However, Pliny continued to be employed by the Emperor Trajan in increasingly responsible positions, and about AD 112 he was appointed governor of Bithynia. The following letter about the Christians is one of many he wrote from that province to the Emperor.

This most interesting imperial correspondence – we possess Trajan's replies as well as Pliny's letters to him – was published posthumously as the tenth book of Pliny's letters. Pliny himself seems to have died about AD 114, perhaps still on active service as a provincial governor.

1 **sollemne est mihi:** *It is my usual practice* (literally *it is usual for me*).

2 **cunctationem meam regere:** *guide my doubts,* i.e. *guide me when I am in doubt.* (Cf. **ignorantiam instruere.**)

3 **cognitionibus:** A **cognitio** was not so much a trial, which required a jury, but rather an inquiry where the presiding magistrate had the power to pass judgment, although he might take advice from a group of advisers.

4 **quid et quatenus:** Both these words go naturally with **puniri soleat:** *what is usually punished and how severe the punishment is.*

5 **nec mediocriter haesitavi:** The negative expression makes the statement a strong one – *I have had considerable doubts.* Pliny then states these in the form of three alternative questions:

    (a) **sitne ( = utrum sit) aliquod discrimen aetatum**
        **an quamlibet teneri nihil a robustioribus differant**
    (b) **(utrum) detur paenitentiae venia**
        **an ei, qui omnino Christianus fuit, desisse non prosit**
    (c) **(utrum) nomen ipsum, si flagitiis careat, (puniatur)**
        **an flagitia cohaerentia nomini puniantur.**

6 **discrimen aetatum:** Should more leniency be shown towards the young (**teneri**) or should no distinction be made (**nihil differant**)?

8 **ei desisse non prosit:** literally *it does not benefit him to have ceased (to be one),* i.e. does renouncing Christianity not save him from being convicted?

# 69
# Pliny and the Christians

C. Plinius Traiano Imperatori

sollemne est mihi, domine, omnia de quibus dubito ad
te referre.  quis enim potest melius vel cunctationem
meam regere vel ignorantiam instruere?  cognitionibus
de Christianis interfui numquam.  ideo nescio quid et
5    quatenus aut puniri soleat aut quaeri.  nec mediocriter
haesitavi sitne aliquod discrimen aetatum an quamlibet
teneri nihil a robustioribus differant, detur paenitentiae
venia an ei, qui omnino Christianus fuit, desisse non prosit, nomen ipsum, si flagitiis careat, an flagitia cohaerentia
10   nomini puniantur.

**sollemnis, -is, -e,** customary
**cunctatio, -onis** (*f*),
   hesitation
**instruo** (3), to instruct,
   inform
**intersum, -esse, -fui** ( + *dat.*),
   to take part in
**ideo,** therefore
**quatenus,** how far
**mediocriter,**
   moderately, in a
   small degree
**haesito** (1), to doubt,
   hesitate
**quamlibet,** however much

**tener, -a, -um,** tender,
   young
**robustus, -a, -um,**
   strong
**paenitentia, -ae** (*f*),
   repentance
**venia, -ae** (*f*), pardon
**prosum, prodesse,**
**profui** ( + *dat.*), to
benefit
**careo** (2) ( + *abl.*), to be
   free (from), not
   involved (in)
**cohaereo** (2), to stick
   together, associate with

---

9  **nomen ipsum, si flagitiis careat, (puniatur):** *is the mere name* (i.e. calling
oneself a Christian) *to be punished, if it is free from (involvement in)
disgraceful acts.* Besides being accused of atheism, because they did not
believe in the traditional Roman gods or in the deity of the emperor
himself, they were sometimes accused of incest and cannibalism. These
slanders may have been based on a misunderstanding of the
Communion Service in which the bread and wine are described as "the
body and blood of Christ."

11 **in iis:** *in the case of those.*

**deferebantur: deferre** was the technical term used when an individual brought an accusation against someone else to the governor.

12 **hunc modum:** *the following procedure.*

**an** is used in place of the more normal **num.**

13 **confitentes:** *if they confessed.* The participle is the direct object of **interrogavi.** (Cf. **perseverantes** in line 14.)

14 **duci:** i.e. to execution.

15 **qualecunque esset quod faterentur:** *whatever the nature of the crime to which they confessed.*

**pertinaciam, obstinationem, amentiae:** All three words illustrate Pliny's indignation that all his efforts to treat the Christians reasonably were rejected by them. Romans admired **constantia,** but only when it upheld the cults and creeds of the state. Firm adherence to beliefs which came into conflict with the state was not regarded as **constantia** but as **pertinacia,** a pejorative word.

17 **quia cives Romani erant:** Roman citizens had the right to be given a trial in Rome. (Cf. St Paul in Acts 25, 11–12.)

19 **mox ipso tractatu ... inciderunt:** *soon in the mere handling, as usually happens, the charge* (of being a Christian) *became more widespread and more cases came to light.* In other words, this became a common way for individuals to try to ruin their personal enemies.

**diffundente se crimine** is an Ablative Absolute: literally *the accusation spreading itself abroad.*

20 **sine auctore:** *anonymously.*

21 **qui negabant:** Supply **eos** as the antecedent, to be taken with **dimittendos esse putavi** (in line 25).

22 **praeeunte me:** Ablative Absolute meaning literally *me going ahead.* Translate *repeating (the prayer) after me.*

**deos appellarent:** *they called upon the gods,* i.e. the traditional gods of Rome.

23 **imagini tuae:** In the provinces, worship of the emperor was officially encouraged, although Trajan discouraged this cult in Rome itself. The cult was not compulsory, but the fact that they did not take part in it could be a useful piece of evidence against accused Christians.

24 **quorum nihil:** *none of which acts.*

26 **ab indice nominati:** *named by the informer,* i.e. in the anonymous booklet.

27 **fuisse:** Supply **se** to give an Accusative and Infinitive continuing the indirect speech.

28 **non nemo:** literally *not no one,* i.e. *some.*

31 **affirmabant hanc fuisse summam culpae quod:** *they claimed that the sum total of their guilt was that,* i.e. *all they had done was ...*

interim in iis, qui ad me tamquam Christiani deferebantur, hunc sum secutus modum. interrogavi ipsos an essent Christiani. confitentes iterum ac tertio interrogavi, supplicium minatus. perseverantes duci iussi. neque
15 enim dubitabam (qualecunque esset quod faterentur) pertinaciam certe et inflexibilem obstinationem debere puniri. fuerunt alii similis amentiae quos, quia cives Romani erant, adnotavi in urbem remittendos.

mox ipso tractatu, ut fieri solet, diffundente se crimine,
20 plures species inciderunt. propositus est libellus sine auctore multorum nomina continens. qui negabant esse Christianos aut fuisse, cum praeeunte me deos appellarent et imagini tuae ture ac vino supplicarent, praeterea maledicerent Christo (quorum nihil posse cogi dicuntur,
25 qui sunt re vera Christiani), dimittendos esse putavi.

alii, ab indice nominati, esse se Christianos dixerunt et mox negaverunt: fuisse quidem sed desisse, quidam ante triennium, quidam ante plures annos, non nemo etiam ante viginti. hi quoque omnes et imaginem tuam deor-
30 umque simulacra venerati sunt et Christo male dixerunt. affirmabant autem hanc fuisse summam vel culpae suae

**confiteor** (2), to confess
**supplicium, -i** (*n*),
    punishment.
**qualiscunque,** whatever
    kind of
**fateor** (2), to confess
**pertinacia, -ae** (*f*),
    persistence
**obstinatio, -onis** (*f*),
    obstinacy
**adnoto** (1), to note,
    comment upon
**tractatus, -us** (*m*),
    handling
**crimen, -inis** (*n*), charge,
    accusation
**incido** (3), to fall upon,
    come to light

**libellus, -i** (*m*), little
    book, pamphlet
**praeeo, -ire, -ii, -itum,**
    to go ahead
**tus, turis** (*n*),
    frankincense
**supplico** (1) ( + *dat.*), to
    pray (to)
**maledico** (3) ( + *dat.*), to
    curse
**index, -icis** (*m*),
    informer
**affirmo** (1), to affirm,
    claim
**summa, -ae** (*f*), chief
    point, whole of
**culpa, -ae** (*f*), blame,
    guilt

32 **stato die:** *on a fixed day,* i.e. the day which is now called Sunday.

**ante lucem:** The working day began at dawn and, for the Roman, one day was no different from any other day. The timing of the service therefore was particularly important for slaves who became Christians.

33 **carmen dicere secum in vicem:** *to sing a hymn with responses,* i.e. one group of singers sang one set of words and the other group sang other words in response (**in vicem**) – antiphonal singing.

34 **sacramento se obstringere:** *to bind themselves by an oath.* That is, no doubt, the meaning that Pliny took out of what he had been told, but for the Christians the phrase had much greater significance – the Sacrament of the Lord's Supper.

**in scelus aliquod:** *for some criminal purpose.*

35 **ne furta ... abnegarent:** Although Pliny was obviously unaware of it, these statements include references to the Ten Commandments.

36 **(ne) depositum appellati abnegarent:** *not to refuse (to return) a deposit when called upon (to do so).* Before the creation of banks, valuables were often deposited with friends for safe-keeping. It was not unknown for the friend to deny that this had ever taken place.

37 **morem sibi fuisse discedendi:** The Accusative and Infinitive continues their statement – *(They said that) it had been their custom to depart.* (Literally *There had been a custom to them of departing.*)

38 **rursus coeundi:** *to meet again* for the *agape* in the evening. The Greek word ἀγάπη meant *love feast.* It was a social meal designed to bind the Christians together as a community.

**promiscuum tamen et innoxium:** These words agree with **cibum** – *but (it was) ordinary and harmless food.* They are refuting the slanderous accusation of cannibalism. (See line 9.)

39 **quod ipsum facere desisse:** Supply **se** with **desisse** – continuing the indirect speech. **quod** is a linking relative.

40 **quo** refers to **edictum:** *in which.*

**hetaerias:** The emperors regarded all "clubs" or "secret societies" as politically dangerous. For example, when Pliny as governor asked the emperor's permission to form a guild of firemen to fight the fires that were common in Nicomedia, it was refused.

42 **quo magis necessarium credidi quaerere:** *I thought it all the more necessary to enquire.*

**quae ministrae dicebantur:** *called deaconesses.*

43 **et per tormenta:** *and (to do this) by torture.* Roman law required slaves to be tortured when giving evidence.

44 **superstitionem pravam, immodicam:** *a debased religious cult carried to excess.*

47 **periclitantium numerum:** *the number of people at risk.*

vel erroris, quod essent soliti stato die ante lucem convenire carmenque Christo quasi deo dicere secum in
vicem seque sacramento non in scelus aliquod ob-
35  stringere, sed ne furta, ne latrocinia, ne adulteria commit-
terent, ne fidem fallerent, ne depositum appellati
abnegarent: quibus peractis, morem sibi discedendi
fuisse rursusque coeundi ad capiendum cibum, promiscuum tamen et innoxium; quod ipsum facere desisse post
40  edictum meum, quo secundum mandata tua hetaerias
esse vetueram.

quo magis necessarium credidi ex duabus ancillis (quae
ministrae dicebantur) quid esset veri et per tormenta
quaerere. nihil aliud inveni quam superstitionem
45  pravam, immodicam. ideo dilata cognitione, ad consul-
endum te decucurri. visa est enim mihi res digna consul-
tatione, maxime propter periclitantium numerum. multi
enim omnis aetatis, omnis ordinis, utriusque sexus etiam

**carmen, -inis** (*n*), song,
hymn
**sacramentum, -i** (*n*),
oath
**obstringo** (3), to bind
**furtum, -i** (*n*), theft
**latrocinium, -i** (*n*),
robbery with violence
**fidem fallere,** to break
one's word
**abnego** (1), to refuse,
deny
**perago** (3), to
accomplish
**promiscuus, -a, -um,**
common, ordinary
**innoxius, -a, -um,**
harmless
**edictum, -i** (*n*), decree
**secundum** (+ *acc.*), in
accordance with

**mandatum, -i** (*n*), order
**ministra, -ae** (*f*),
serving woman,
deaconess
**superstitio, -onis** (*f*),
religious belief,
superstition
**pravus, -a, -um,**
depraved, warped
**immodicus, -a, -um,**
excessive
**dilatus, -a, -um,** having
been postponed
**dignus, -a, -um** (+ *abl.*),
worthy (of)
**consultatio, -onis** (*f*),
deliberation
**periclitor** (1), to run
risks
**sexus, -us** (*m*), sex

49 **neque civitates tantum:** *not only cities.*

51 **quae videtur sisti et corrigi posse:** *but it seems (to me) that it* (**quae**) *can be checked and cured.*

52 **satis constat:** *it is generally agreed.*

**templa coepisse celebrari:** *that the temples have begun to be filled (with worshippers).*

53 **sacra sollemnia repeti:** *sacred rites are being revived.*

54 **pastum venire victimarum:** This could have two meanings: (*a*) *food for the victims is being sold* (i.e. to fatten them up before sacrifice); or (*b*) *the flesh of victims is being sold* (i.e. after the sacrifice was over there was a good trade in selling off the meat, although Christians would not touch this). Either way, it would suggest that the old religion was picking up again. Note that **venire** is the infinitive of **veneo**, not of **venio.**

55 **quae turba:** *what a large number.*

56 **si sit locus:** *if there were an opportunity.*

vocantur in periculum, et vocabuntur.   neque civitates
50   tantum, sed vicos etiam atque agros superstitionis istius
contagio pervagata est;   quae videtur sisti et corrigi
posse.   certe satis constat prope iam desolata templa
coepisse celebrari, et sacra sollemnia diu intermissa repeti
pastumque venire victimarum, cuius adhuc rarissimus
55   emptor inveniebatur.   ex quo facile est opinari quae turba
hominum emendari possit, si sit paenitentiae locus.

**periculum, -i** (*n*), trial
**contagio, -onis** (*f*),
  infection, contact
**pervagor** (1), to wander,
  spread
**sisto** (3), to check, stop
**corrigo** (3), to correct,
  reform
**desolatus, -a, -um,**
  deserted
**sacra, -orum** (*n.pl*), rites
**intermitto** (3), to
  interrupt, discontinue

**repeto** (3), to seek
  again, revive
**pastus, -us** (*m*), food
**veneo, -ire, -ii,** to be up
  for sale
**victima, -ae** (*f*),
  victim
**emptor, -oris** (*m*), buyer
**opinor** (1), to suppose
**emendo** (1), to improve,
  reform

Trajan's reply was short and to the point:

"My dear Pliny, you have followed the right course in investigating
the cases of those who were denounced to you as Christians, for no
hard and fast rule can be laid down to deal with every case. The
Christians should not be hunted down, but they must be punished if
they are accused and found guilty; with this reservation, however,
that anyone who denies he is a Christian and proves by his actions
that he is not (i.e. by offering prayers to our gods) should be pardoned
because he has repented, no matter how seriously he was suspected in
the past. Anonymous pamphlets should carry no weight whatsoever,
whatever the charge, for that is a very bad precedent to set and is not
in keeping with the spirit of our age."

# 70
# Hannibal invades Italy

Livy's moving description of the death of Cicero comes from his history of Rome, AB URBE CONDITA *(From the Founding of the City)* which covers the period from 753 BC to 9 BC, i.e. from the foundation of Rome right up to Livy's own day.

Livy spent forty years of his life on the composition of this mammoth work, which ran into 142 books; but such is the uncertainty of survival of ancient manuscripts that we now possess only thirty-five books: I-X dealing with the years 753 BC to 293 BC, and Books XXI-XLV which cover the period 219 BC to 167 BC. Tantalising fragments of other books have survived, such as the description of Cicero's murder from Book CXX (see page 150), and every so often lost books of Livy come to light – the work unfortunately of some ambitious literary forger!

The Livy extracts which follow all come from Books XXI and XXII in which Livy tells how Rome was brought to the very brink of defeat by the great Carthaginian general, Hannibal.

*(Photo: The Mansell Collection)*

Carthage, on the North African coast, lies only 210 kilometres from Sicily, and it was over the control of Sicily that the First Punic War broke out between Rome and Carthage. (The word Punic comes from **Poeni,** a Latin word for the Carthaginians.)

Carthage had been founded at about the same date as Rome, but by the third century BC its position as a thriving seaport on the main east-west Mediterranean route had given it a population three times as great as that of Rome. It had a large land empire in North Africa, a foothold in Spain, at least four trading-posts in Sardinia and a secure base in Sicily: but in the bitter First Punic War, which dragged on from 264–241 BC, Carthage not only lost Sicily but suffered invasion of her own African territories.

In the Second Punic War, which began in 219 BC, the tables were turned. Italy was overrun and the very survival of Rome itself hung in the balance. Between the two wars Hamilcar (Hannibal's father) and Hasdrubal (his brother-in-law) had between them established a powerful empire in Spain. In 229 BC, however, Hamilcar was drowned and in 220 BC Hasdrubal was murdered by a slave; so at the age of twenty-five Hannibal found himself in sole command of the Carthaginian army in Spain, poised to advance on Italy.

His first act on taking command in Spain had been to besiege and capture Saguntum, a city which was under Rome's protection, thus in effect declaring war on Rome. After that he crossed first the Ebro and then the Pyrenees, before advancing through the territory of the Volcae as far as the Rhône. There he found Gallic forces drawn up on the opposite bank to bar his way.

*Map 12* The Mediterranean area

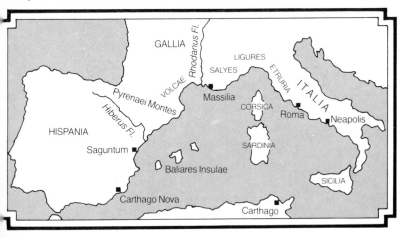

1 Publius Cornelius Scipio, one of the two consuls in 218 BC, had been given Spain as his **provincia** (i.e. his sphere of command).

4 **superasse = superavisse.**

5 **ceteris** refers to the other tribes through whose territory he passed before reaching the Volcae.

6 **gentis validae:** genitive case in apposition to **Volcarum.**

7 **colunt:** *they live.*

**autem:** *now,* used in the explanatory sense. Livy is fond of parentheses like this, giving background information which is not strictly necessary for the narrative.

8 **pro munimento:** *as a defence.*

**omnibus ferme suis:** *almost all their families and possessions.* Note the position of **ferme,** immediately after the word it qualifies.

9 **ulteriorem:** *farther,* looking at it from Hannibal's point of view.

12 **est:** Take with **coacta,** *was assembled.*

13 **novas alias:** Supply **lintres,** although it is clear from the rest of the sentence that they were "dug-outs" rather than boats.

**primum Galli inchoantes:** This is balanced by **deinde et ipsi milites.** The Gauls set the example and the Carthaginians imitated what they did; their efforts, however, were rough-and-ready.

16 **nihil:** direct object of **curantes.**

**innare aquae:** *to float on the water.* As usual, the compound verb governs the dative case.

## Hannibal reaches the Rhône

P. Cornelius, profectus ab urbe sexaginta longis navibus
praeter oram Etruriae Ligurumque et inde Salyum
montes, pervenit Massiliam et ad ostium Rhodani castra
locat, vixdum satis credens Hannibalem superasse
5 Pyrenaeos montes. Hannibal, ceteris metu aut pretio
pacatis, iam in Volcarum pervenerat agrum, gentis
validae. colunt autem circa utramque ripam Rhodani;
sed, ut flumen pro munimento haberent, omnibus ferme
suis trans Rhodanum traiectis, ulteriorem ripam amnis
10 armis obtinebant. ceteros accolas fluminis Hannibal
pellicit donis ad naves undique contrahendas
fabricandasque. itaque ingens coacta vis navium est
lintriumque; novasque alias primum Galli inchoantes
cavabant ex singulis arboribus, deinde et ipsi milites,
15 simul copia materiae simul facilitate operis inducti, alveos
informes (nihil dummodo innare aquae et capere onera
possent curantes) raptim faciebant.

| | |
|---|---|
| **sexaginta,** sixty | **accolae, -arum** (*m.pl*), |
| **navis longa,** warship | inhabitants, people |
| **praeter** (*+ acc.*), past, | living near |
| along | **pellicio** (3), to allure, |
| **Massilia, -ae** (*f*), | entice |
| Marseilles | **linter, -tris** (*f*), boat |
| **ostium, -i** (*n*), entrance, | **inchoo** (1), to begin, |
| river-mouth. | commence |
| **vixdum,** scarcely yet | **cavo** (1), to hollow out |
| **pretium, -i** (*n*), price, | **simul... simul...,** |
| bribe | both... and... |
| **validus, -a, -um,** strong | **facilitas, -atis** (*f*), ease, |
| **colo** (3), to dwell | easiness |
| **pro** (*+ abl.*), instead of, | **alveus, -i** (*m*), hollow, |
| as, for | small boat |
| **ferme,** almost | **informis, -is, -e,** |
| **traicio** (3), to put | shapeless, crude |
| across, take across | **inno** (1), to swim in, |
| **amnis, -is** (*m*), river | float on |
| **obtineo** (2), to hold, | **raptim,** hurriedly |
| keep possession of | |

*line*

18 **terrebant:** *what terrified them was . . .* The subject of this verb is **hostes.**

19 **ex adverso:** *opposite,* i.e. *facing them from the other side of the river.*

    **equites virique** are nominative in apposition to **hostes,** giving a more detailed description of the enemy – *cavalry and foot-soldiers.*

20 **quos:** a Linking Relative referring back to **hostes.** Hannibal is the subject of **averteret** and **iubet.**

21 **vigilia prima noctis:** The night (i.e. from sunset to sunrise) was divided into four equal watches. They set out, therefore, in the early evening.

22 **adverso flumine:** *upstream.*

24 **cum opus facto sit:** literally *when there was need of the deed,* i.e. *at the right moment.*

    **ad id dati duces:** *provided as guides for that purpose.*

25 **milia quinque et viginti ferme:** With **milia,** supply **passuum.** As in line 8, **ferme** comes immediately after the words it qualifies: "almost 25 miles."

26 **supra:** *higher up (the river).*

    **parvae insulae circumfusum:** literally *poured round a little island,* i.e. *where it flowed round a little island.* The participle **circumfusum,** which agrees with **amnem,** governs the dative case.

    **amnem ostendere:** Accusative and Infinitive depending on **edocent.** Translate **ostendere** as *offered.*

27 **ibi:** Livy does not waste any space describing the march northwards. He launches straight into what happened when they reached their destination.

    **caesa materia:** not an Ablative Absolute, as might appear at first sight. **caesa materia** and **rates fabricatae** are closely linked by **-que;** both are therefore nominative and we must supply **est** and **sunt** respectively with them. Livy is fond of this sort of omission.

28 **equi virique:** Compare line 19. Note that here he uses *horses* rather than *horsemen.*

    **traicerentur:** subjunctive, since this is a Purpose clause.

29 **mole:** *trouble, difficulty.* In its physical sense, **moles** describes any massive object, frequently one which creates an obstruction and which requires great effort to handle.

    **caetris superpositis incubantes:** *lying on their shields which had been laid on top* of the skin bags which acted as floats.

30 **tranavere = tranaverunt.**

    **alius = reliquus,** *the rest of,* as frequently in Livy.

## Native resistance circumvented

iamque omnibus satis comparatis ad traiciendum, terrebant ex adverso hostes omnem ripam equites virique
20 obtinentes. quos ut averteret, Hannonem Bomilcaris
filium vigilia prima noctis cum parte copiarum (maxime
Hispanis) adverso flumine ire iter unius diei iubet et,
quam occultissime traiecto amni, circumducere agmen ut,
cum opus facto sit, adoriatur ab tergo hostes. ad id dati
25 duces Galli edocent inde milia quinque et viginti ferme
supra parvae insulae circumfusum amnem transitum
ostendere. ibi raptim caesa materia ratesque fabricatae,
in quibus equi virique et alia onera traicerentur. Hispani
sine ulla mole, in utres vestimentis coniectis, ipsi caetris
30 superpositis incubantes flumen tranavere. et alius

**terreo** (2), to terrify
**ex adverso,** opposite
**averto** (3), to turn
  away, outflank
**adverso flumine,**
  upstream
**occulte,** secretly
**circumduco** (3), to lead
  around
**factum, -i** (*n*), deed
**ab tergo,** in the rear,
  from behind
**edoceo** (2), to inform,
  point out

**supra,** above
**circumfundo** (3), to
  pour round
**transitus, -us** (*m*),
  crossing, way across
**moles, -is** (*f*), mass,
  trouble, difficulty
**uter, utris** (*m*), bag
  made of animal hide
**caetra, -ae** (*f*), shield
**superpono** (3), to place
  above, lay on top
**incubo** (1), to lie on
**trano** (1), to swim
  across

*line*

31 **ratibus iunctis:** This does not mean that they tied several rafts together
to create a kind of bridge. It refers to the tying together of logs to form
rafts.

**traiectus** *(carried across)* and **fessus** *(tired out)* both agree with
**exercitus.**

32 **operis** refers to the task of preparing the camp and building the rafts.

35 **transisse** = **transiisse.** Supply **se.**

36 **paratas** agrees with both **lintres** and **naves; habebat** has two subjects –
**pedes** and **eques.**

37 **eques fere:** literally *the cavalry, generally speaking,* i.e. *most of the
cavalry.* The **lintres,** although suitable for the infantry, were too small
to carry horses. They obviously did not have enough **naves** since, as we
see later, some of the horses swam across.

The singular words **pedes** (foot-soldier) and **eques** (horseman) are often
used by Livy as collective nouns meaning *infantry* and *cavalry.*

38 **ad excipiendum adversi impetum fluminis:** *to break the force of the
current.* (**adversi fluminis** means literally *of the river flowing against them.*)

**parte superiore:** *at a point higher up (the river).*

39 **transmittens:** *crossing over.* This participle agrees with **agmen** which is
the subject of **praebebat** in line 40. There is no suggestion that the line
of boats was tied together to create a kind of breakwater. Simply by
crossing higher up they created calmer water for the smaller boats
which crossed lower down.

**infra** is an adverb: *lower down (the river).*

40 **equorum pars magna:** *many of the horses.* Although the subject **(pars)** is
singular, the verb **(trahebantur)** and the participle **(nantes)** are plural
because of the sense.

41 **instratos frenatosque:** *ready saddled and bridled,* agreeing with **quos.**

42 **ut extemplo usui essent:** *in order to be immediately of use,* i.e. the cavalry
could use them as soon as they landed.

44 **occursant:** *rushed down to meet them.* This verb is used to describe a
disorderly attack, each man operating on his own rather than in
formation as a disciplined army would fight.

**cantu:** *battle songs.*

46 **quamquam:** *despite the fact that.*     **ex adverso:** *in front of them*

**terrebat:** Supply **eos.**     **cum:** *accompanied by.*

48 **et qui … et qui …:** *both those who … and those who …* The first **qui**
refers to the sailors and soldiers who were actually struggling across the
river; the second refers to the soldiers who were still on the bank
waiting to start the crossing.

49 **traicientes suos:** *their comrades who were crossing.*

exercitus ratibus iunctis traiectus, castris prope flumen positis, nocturno itinere atque operis labore fessus, quiete unius diei reficitur.

postero die profecti, ex loco edito fumo significant
35   transisse et haud procul abesse.   quod ubi accepit Hannibal dat signum ad traiciendum.   iam paratas habebat pedes lintres, eques fere propter equos naves.   navium agmen ad excipiendum adversi impetum fluminis parte superiore transmittens tranquillitatem infra traicientibus
40   lintribus praebebat.   equorum pars magna nantes loris a puppibus trahebantur, praeter eos quos, instratos frenatosque ut extemplo egresso in ripam equiti usui essent, imposuerant in naves.

Galli occursant in ripa cum variis ululatibus cantuque,
45   quatientes scuta super capita vibrantesque dextris tela, quamquam ex adverso terrebat tanta vis navium cum ingenti sono fluminis et clamore vario nautarum militumque, et qui nitebantur perrumpere impetum fluminis et qui ex altera ripa traicientes suos hortabantur.   iam satis

fessus, -a, -um, tired out
reficio (3), to refresh,
   revive
editus, -a, -um, lofty,
   rising
pedes, peditis (m), foot-
   soldier, infantry
excipio (3), to receive,
   catch
transmitto (3), to cross
   over
tranquillitas, -atis (f),
   peace, quiet
infra, beneath, lower
   down
no (1), to swim

lorum, -i (n), thong,
   rein
puppis, -is (f), ship,
   stern
instratus, -a, -um,
   saddled
frenatus, -a, -um,
   bridled
extemplo, at once
cantus, -us (m), song,
   singing
quatio (3), to shake
vibro (1), to brandish
nauta, -ae (m), sailor
nitor (3), to strive

50 **paventes adverso tumultu:** *terrified (as they were) by the confusion in
front of them.* English idiom is quite different from the Latin idiom. In
Latin, **paventes** is the object of **adortus (est).** English needs to insert
*them* as the object.

**terribilior:** *(even) more terrifying.*

51 **et ipse aderat:** *Hanno himself arrived.* The force of the **et** is *as well as the
shouts* which had been previously heard.

52 **anceps terror:** literally *a two-headed terror,* i.e. the fact that they were
being attacked from two directions. The explanation of their two fears
is provided by the two Ablative Absolutes: **tanta vi evadente** and
**premente acie.**

**et e navibus ... et ab tergo ...:** Compare line 48 for **et ... et ...**

**tanta vi armorum:** literally *such a great force of arms,* i.e. *of armed men.*

54 **utroque vim facere:** *to offer resistance on both sides.*

**pellebantur:** Note the use of the imperfect tense – *(when) they were
being driven back.*

55 **qua patere visum maxime iter:** Take this clause with **perrumpunt** –
literally *where a way seemed to lie open most,* i.e. *wherever they could
most easily find a gap.*

56 **passim:** The position of this word is interesting. By placing it within the
phrase **in vicos suos** Livy has skilfully described not only their headlong
flight in all directions but also the scattered nature of their village
communities.

57 **per otium:** literally *at his leisure,* i.e. *without any opposition.* As in line
27, Livy wastes few words on what was probably the major part of the
operation. His matter-of-fact statement **(castra locat)** highlights even
more the frenzy and hurly-burly of the original crossing.

58 **tumultus:** The word is used contemptuously of a disorganised rather
than a concerted and planned attack.

59 **elephantorum traiciendorum consilia:** *suggestions for getting the
elephants across.* This has to be contrasted with **memoria actae rei,**
*recollections of what actually happened* or *accounts of what actually
happened.*

60 **quidam tradunt:** *some say.* The Accusative and Infinitive which depends
on this is **ferocissimum ex eis traxisse gregem,** *the fiercest elephant drew
the whole herd after it.* According to the ancient historian Polybius,
there were thirty-seven elephants.

62 **refugientem:** *as he retreated,* agreeing with **rectorem** (understood). The
driver deliberately provoked the elephant until it turned on him and
chased him into the water. The subject of **sequeretur** is *the elephant.*

63 **magis constat:** *the more generally held view (is that).*

64 **traiectos:** Supply **eos ... esse.**

66 **quam:** a Linking Relative, referring to **ratem.** It is the object of
**constraverunt** in line 69: *they covered it.*

**secunda aqua:** *downstream* or *by the current.*

50 paventes adverso tumultu terribilior ab tergo adortus
clamor, castris ab Hannone captis.  mox et ipse aderat
ancepsque terror circumstabat, et e navibus tanta vi
armorum in terram evadente et ab tergo improvisa premente acie.  Galli, postquam utroque vim facere conati pel-
55 lebantur, qua patere visum maxime iter perrumpunt
trepidique in vicos passim suos diffugiunt.  Hannibal,
ceteris copiis per otium traiectis, spernens iam Gallicos
tumultus, castra locat.

**Getting the elephants across**

elephantorum traiciendorum varia consilia fuisse
60 credo;  certe variat memoria actae rei.  quidam tradunt,
congregatis ad ripam elephantis, ferocissimum ex iis irri-
tatum ab rectore suo, cum refugientem in aquam sequeretur, traxisse gregem.  ceterum magis constat ratibus
traiectos.
65 ratem unam ducentos longam pedes quinquaginta
latam a terra in amnem porrexerunt; quam, ne secunda

**pavens, -entis,** terrified
**tumultus, -us** (*m*), din,
  confusion, uprising,
  attack
**anceps, ancipitis,** two-
  headed, double
**improvisus, -a, -um,**
  unforeseen, unex-
  pected
**acies, aciei** (*f*), line of
  battle
**utroque,** on both sides
**trepidus, -a, -um,**
  alarmed, panic-
  stricken
**passim,** in every
  direction

**diffugio** (3), to flee in
  different directions
**sperno** (3), to despise
**tradunt,** (they) say
**irritatus, -a, -um,**
  provoked
**rector, -oris** (*m*), driver,
  mahout
**refugio** (3), to flee back
**grex, gregis** (*m*), herd
**ceterum,** however, but
**ducenti, -ae, -a,** two
  hundred
**quinquaginta,** fifty
**porrigo** (3), to stretch
  out

67 **parte superiore ripae religatam:** literally *tied from a higher part of the bank*, i.e. *to a point higher upstream*. Note that the Latin idiom is *tied from* whereas English says *tied to*.

68 **pontis in modum:** *like a bridge*.

69 **velut per solum:** *as if over solid ground*.

72 The subject of the **ubi** clause is **sex elephanti**.

**per stabilem ratem:** This was the raft which was moored to the bank, whereas **minorem** refers to the raft which had been tied to the far end of the bigger raft.

74 **vinculis:** These were the ropes which tied the two rafts together.

75 **pertrahitur:** The subject is *the smaller raft*.

**primis:** Supply **elephantis**.

76 **repetiti:** literally *they were gone back for*, i.e. *the operation was repeated*.

77 **donec:** *as long as*.

**continenti velut ponte:** *on what seemed to be a continuous bridge*.

78 **soluta:** *separated*.

79 **in altum raperentur:** literally *they were being snatched into deep water*, i.e. *they were being towed swiftly into midstream*.

**urgentes inter se:** *pushing against each other*.

**extremis:** These were the elephants which were near the edge of the raft.

80 **edebant:** The subject is all the elephants on the raft.     **donec:** *until*.

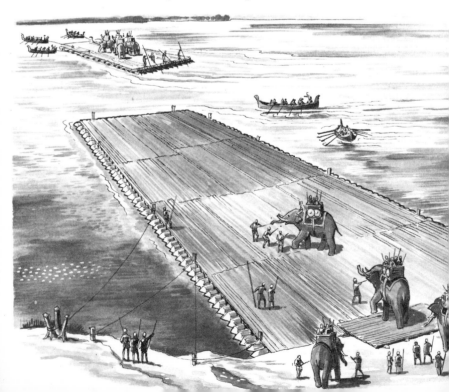

aqua deferretur, pluribus validis retinaculis parte superiore ripae religatam pontis in modum humo iniecta
constraverunt ut beluae audacter velut per solum
70 ingrederentur. altera ratis aeque lata, longa pedes centum, ad traiciendum flumen apta, huic copulata est. sex
tum elephanti ubi per stabilem ratem tamquam viam,
praegredientibus feminis, acti in minorem transgressi
sunt, extemplo resolutis vinculis, ab actuariis aliquot
75 navibus ad alteram ripam pertrahitur. ita, primis expos-
itis, alii deinde repetiti ac traiecti sunt.

nihil sane trepidabant donec continenti velut ponte
agerentur. primus erat pavor cum, soluta ab ceteris rate,
in altum raperentur. ibi urgentes inter se, cedentibus ex-
80 tremis ab aqua, trepidationis aliquantum edebant, donec

**retinaculum, -i** (*n*),
  cable
**religo** (1), to fasten
**humus, -i** (*f*), earth, soil
**inicio** (3), to throw
  upon
**consterno** (3), to strew,
  cover
**belua, -ae** (*f*), beast
**solum, -i** (*n*), ground
**ingredior** (3), to go on
**aptus, -a, -um,** suitable
**copulo** (1), to join
**stabilis, -is, -e,** steady
**tamquam,** as though
**praegredior** (3), to go in
  front

**femina, -ae** (*f*), woman,
  female
**resolvo** (3), to unfasten
**actuarius, -a, -um,** swift
**pertraho** (3), to drag
  over
**continens, -entis,**
  continuous
**pavor, -oris** (*m*), fear,
  panic
**cedo** (3), to withdraw,
  move back
**trepidatio, -onis** (*f*),
  fear, fright
**aliquantum,** (a) con-
  siderable (amount)
**edo** (3), to cause

81 **quietem circumspectantibus aquam fecisset:** literally *caused stillness among them looking at the water around them,* i.e. *fear itself caused them to stand still as they looked at the water round about them.*

82 **excidere = exciderunt.** (Cf. **evasere** in line 84.)

**etiam saevientes:** *still wildly uncontrolled.*

83 **quaerendis pedetentim vadis:** *by feeling for the shallow water foot by foot.* According to Polybius, they held their trunks out of the water, breathing through them like snorkels. Livy obviously did not know that elephants can, in fact, swim.

85 **ab Druentia:** The Druentia was a tributary of the Rhône.

**campestri:** *over flat country,* rather than *over plains.*

86 **cum bona pace Gallorum:** The phrase does not refer to a formal peace treaty. It suggests that the Gauls did not interfere with their progress rather than that they actually cooperated with them. (Cf. **pace tua,** *by your leave, if you don't object.*) Translate *unmolested by the Gauls.*

87 **fama prius praecepta res erat:** *what they encountered* (**res**) *had been anticipated by what they had heard* (**fama**) *previously.* The account which follows is obviously exaggerated if applied to the first sighting of the Alps. Livy, who had not inspected the area himself, combines impressions of various parts of the journey for dramatic effect.

88 **prope immixtae:** literally *almost mixed,* i.e. *blending.*

89 **tecta informia:** *crude huts.*

90 **torrida:** *shrivelled.* This adjective is normally associated with heat.

**animalia inanimaque:** *animate and inanimate.*

91 **visu quam dictu foediora:** *more dreadful to see than to speak about.*

92 **renovarunt = renovaverunt.** There are several subjects: **altitudo, nives, tecta, pecora iumentaque, homines, animalia inanimaque** and **cetera.**

quietem ipse timor circumspectantibus aquam fecisset. excidere etiam saevientes quidam in flumen: sed pondere ipso stabiles, deiectis rectoribus, quaerendis pedetentim vadis in terram evasere.

## Approaching the Alps

After crossing the Rhône, Hannibal did not take the easier route to Italy along the coast, presumably because he thought it would be easier for the Romans to oppose him. Instead, he went north from the mouth of the Rhône and entered Italy over the high passes of the Alps. It has not been possible to establish the exact route he followed since Livy does not give precise geographical details; but the general picture is clear, and we are given a vivid account of the difficulties Hannibal surmounted and the privations he and his army suffered.

85   Hannibal ab Druentia campestri maxime itinere ad Alpes cum bona pace incolentium ea loca Gallorum pervenit. tum, quamquam fama prius praecepta res erat, tamen ex propinquo visa montium altitudo nivesque caelo prope immixtae, tecta informia imposita rupibus, pecora iumen-
90   taque torrida frigore, homines intonsi et inculti, animalia inanimaque omnia rigentia gelu, cetera visu quam dictu foediora, terrorem renovarunt.

**circumspecto** (1), to
  look round
**excido** (3), to fall out of
**saevio** (4), to rage
**pedetentim,** step by
  step, gradually
**campester, -tris, -tre,** on
  level ground
**praecipio** (3), to
  anticipate
**rupes, -is** (*f*), rock, crag
**pecus, pecoris** (*n*),
  cattle, herd of cattle

**torridus, -a, -um,**
  parched, shrivelled
**intonsus, -a, -um,**
  shaggy, unshaven
**incultus, -a, -um,**
  unkempt
**inanimus, -a, -um,**
  inanimate
**rigens, -entis,** stiff
**gelu, -us** (*n*), frost, cold
**foedus, -a, -um,**
  horrible, horrid
**renovo** (1), to renew

93 **perventum:** Supply **est.** For this use of the impersonal passive see page 98.

    **ad frequentem alium populum:** literally *to another district crowded with inhabitants,* i.e. *to another district (which was) densely populated.* The adjective **frequens** is qualified by the phrase **ut inter montanos** *for a mountain region.*

94 **suis artibus:** *by his own methods.* The subject of **est circumventus** is, of course, Hannibal, whom the Romans regarded as very treacherous.

96 **memorantes:** *stating.* On this depends the Accusative and Infinitive **(se) malle.**    **doctos** agrees with **se** (understood).

98 **facturos:** Supply **se ... esse,** another Accusative and Infinitive depending on **memorantes.**

99 **ad fidem promissorum:** *as a guarantee of their promises.*

    **obsides:** Generals who were occupying a country took hostages as a guarantee that the people would not attempt any treachery. In more recent times, the word "hostage" has acquired a new meaning – someone held by, say, terrorists to blackmail others into meeting their demands.

100 **acciperet:** The indirect speech continues with a command *(they asked him) to accept.*

101 **nec temere credendum nec aspernandum:** Supply **esse** with each of these impersonal passives to form two Accusative and Infinitive clauses depending on **ratus** – literally *that it should neither be believed ...,* i.e. *that he should neither believe ....*

102 **ne fierent:** *in case they became.*

103 **commeatu** is ablative depending on **usus.**

104 **nequaquam ... agmine: nequaquam** should be taken closely with both **ut inter pacatos** and **composito agmine** – *with his army drawn up in no way (as it would be drawn up) had he been among a peaceful people.* In other words, he did not trust them and was ready for attacks at any time. Translate *with a marching formation very different from what it would have been if he had been among friendly peoples.*

105 **primum agmen:** *the front of the column.*

106 **post cum robore peditum:** *behind with the main body of the infantry.* Normally, the infantry would have been at the head of the column and the baggage would have been at the rear. On this occasion, Hannibal reversed the order by sending the cavalry and the baggage on in front.

108 **in angustiorem viam:** *into a narrower pass.*

109 **petunt:** *attacked.* The object is *the Carthaginians* (understood). Note how the omission of linking words (e.g. **et, -que, atque, ac**) between the pairs of words **(a fronte ab tergo; comminus eminus; petunt, devolvunt)** creates an impression of speed of action.

perventum inde ad frequentem cultoribus alium, ut
inter montanos, populum. ibi non bello aperto sed suis
95 artibus, fraude et insidiis, est prope circumventus.
principes castellorum ad Poenum veniunt memorantes
alienis malis doctos amicitiam malle quam vim experiri
Poenorum: itaque obedienter imperata facturos; com-
meatum itinerisque duces et ad fidem promissorum ob-
100 sides acciperet.

Hannibal nec temere credendum nec aspernandum
ratus ne repudiati aperte hostes fierent, benigne cum re-
spondisset, obsidibus acceptis et commeatu (quem in
viam ipsi detulerant) usus, nequaquam ut inter pacatos
105 composito agmine duces eorum sequitur. primum
agmen elephanti et equites erant. ipse post cum robore
peditum circumspectans omnia sollicitusque incedebat.

ubi in angustiorem viam ventum est, undique ex insidiis
barbari, a fronte ab tergo coorti, comminus eminus pet-
110 unt, saxa ingentia in agmen devolvunt. maxima ab tergo

**cultor, -oris** (*m*),
  inhabitant
**montani, -orum** (*m.pl*),
  mountain dwellers
**fraus, fraudis** (*f*), trick,
  treachery
**insidiae, -arum** (*f.pl*),
  ambush
**circumvenio** (4), to trap,
  catch out
**Poenus, -i** (*m*), Carthaginian
**memoro** (1), to declare
**alienus, -a, -um,** of
  another, of others
**imperatum, -i** (*n*), order
**commeatus, -us** (*m*),
  supplies, provisions
**promissum, -i** (*n*), promise
**temere,** unthinkingly
**aspernor** (1), to reject,
  spurn

**repudio** (1), to reject,
  refuse
**aperte,** openly
**benigne,** kindly, in a
  friendly way
**nequaquam,** by no
  means, in no way
**pacatus, -a, -um,**
  pacified
**robur, roboris** (*n*),
  strength
**sollicitus, -a, -um,**
  anxious
**incedo** (3), to march,
  advance
**coorior** (4), to rise
**comminus,** at close
  quarters
**eminus,** from a distance
**saxum, -i** (*n*), rock
**devolvo** (3), to roll
  down

113 **agmen:** This refers to the rest of the column, i.e. the infantry. The cavalry and the elephants had already entered the pass. In line 114, however, **agmine** refers to the whole column.

**per obliqua:** *at an angle (to the column),* i.e. *on the flanks.*

114 **viam insedere:** *(they) took control of the road,* by cutting the column in two. **(insedere = insederunt.)**

115 **nox una Hannibali acta est:** *one night was spent by Hannibal,* i.e. *Hannibal spent one night.* This use of the dative **(Hannibali)** with the perfect passive is similar to its use with gerundives.

117 **segnius intercursantibus barbaris:** literally *the natives running between (the front and the rear of the column) more lazily,* i.e. *since the natives were less determined in their attacks.*

118 **iunctae:** Supply **sunt.** Similarly, supply **est** with **superatus** in line 119.

**haud sine clade:** *not without loss.* The double negative produces a very strong positive, i.e. he suffered considerable losses.

119 **superatus:** literally *was overcome,* i.e. they won their way through the pass.

120 **nono die:** i.e. eight days from the time they started climbing into the Alps.

**iugum:** literally *the ridge,* i.e. *the top of the pass* or *the highest point in their ascent.*

121 **stativa:** Supply **castra.** In other words, they built a proper camp instead of the makeshift arrangements they had had to make for sleeping during the ascent.

**habita:** Supply **sunt.**      Supply **est** with **data** in line 22.

122 **in rupibus:** *among the rocks.* These were not the animals which had fallen over precipices, but those which had stumbled on the rough ground and had been left behind.

124 **pervenere = pervenerunt.**

**fessis taedio terrorem adiecit:** literally *added fear to them being weary with the weariness.* **fessis** refers to the Carthaginian soldiers. Translate *caused fear among the soldiers who were already weighed down by the depressing effect....*

125 **per omnia nive oppleta;** *over ground which was completely covered with snow.*

**cum** *(since)* governs two verbs: **incederet** and **emineret.**

127 **praegressus signa:** *having gone ahead of the standards,* i.e. right out in front of the column.

129 **prospectus:** This is a nice dramatic touch but, in fact, it is impossible to see the plains of Northern Italy from any of the Alpine passes. Compare the use of **ostentat** in line 130, although in this case he possibly could have persuaded them to believe that they were looking down on Italy.

vis hominum urgebat. tunc ad extremum periculi ac
prope perniciem ventum est; nam, dum cunctatur Hannibal demittere agmen in angustias, occursantes per obliqua montani, interrupto medio agmine, viam insedere,
115  noxque una Hannibali sine equitibus atque impedimentis
acta est.

postero die, iam segnius intercursantibus barbaris,
iunctae copiae saltusque haud sine clade, maiore tamen
iumentorum quam hominum pernicie, superatus.

120  nono die in iugum Alpium perventum est. biduum in
iugo stativa habita, fessisque labore ac pugnando quies
data militibus. iumentaque aliquot, quae prolapsa in
rupibus erant, sequendo vestigia agminis in castra
pervenere. fessis taedio tot malorum nivis etiam casus
125  ingentem terrorem adiecit. per omnia nive oppleta cum,
signis prima luce motis, segniter agmen incederet pigrit-
iaque et desperatio in omnium vultu emineret, praegressus signa Hannibal in promuntorio quodam, unde longe ac
late prospectus erat, consistere iussis militibus Italiam

---

**urgeo** (2), to press
**pernicies, -ei** (*f*),
    destruction, disaster
**angustiae, -arum** (*f.pl*),
    narrows, pass, defile
**obliquus, -a, -um,**
    slanting
**interrumpo** (3), to break
    through
**insideo** (2), to beset,
    occupy
**segniter,** lazily
**intercurso** (1), to run
    between
**saltus, -us** (*m*), pass
**clades, -is** (*f*), disaster
**biduum, -i** (*n*), (a period
    of) two days
**stativus, -a, -um,**
    standing

**prolabor** (3), to fall
    down
**taedium, -i** (*n*),
    weariness
**casus, -us** (*m*), fall
**adicio** (3), to add
**oppletus, -a, -um,**
    covered, filled
**signa movere,** to begin
    marching
**pigritia, -ae** (*f*),
    weariness, lethargy
**desperatio, -onis** (*f*),
    despair
**emineo** (2), to stand
    out, be obvious
**promuntorium, -i** (*n*),
    peak, height
**prospectus, -us** (*m*),
    view

131 **eos transcendere:** Accusative and Infinitive depending on a verb which has to be supplied. The colon which follows **campos** indicates that indirect speech is to follow (lines 131–134) with the introductory verb of speaking understood from **ostentat.**

132 **plana, proclivia:** Besides their literal meaning these words also indicate *plain-sailing and easy.*

    **fore** is future infinitive of **esse.**

133 **summum** is used adverbially: *at most.*

134 **habituros:** Supply **eos** and **esse.**

138 **titubassent = titubavissent.**

    **haerere affixi vestigio suo:** literally *to stick fixed to their track,* i.e. *to keep their footing.*

140 **succiderent:** There are two subjects – **iumenta** and **homines,** and the phrase **alii super alios** *(on top of each other)* applies to both.

    **hoc maxime modo:** *very much in this manner.*

141 **a Carthagine Nova:** It was from this Spanish city that Hannibal had launched the attack on Saguntum.

    **Alpibus superatis:** Compare line 119 for this use of **superare.**

*Map 13* Hannibal's route from the Alps to Lake Trasimene

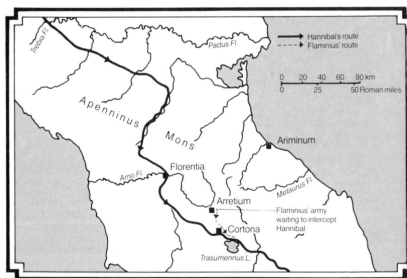

130     ostentat subiectosque Alpinis montibus Circumpadanos
      campos: moenia eos tum transcendere non Italiae modo
      sed etiam urbis Romanae; cetera plana, proclivia fore;
      uno aut summum altero proelio arcem et caput Italiae in
      manu ac potestate habituros.
135     procedere inde agmen coepit. ceterum iter multo,
      quam in ascensu fuerat, difficilius fuit. omnis enim ferme
      via praeceps, angusta, lubrica erat ut neque sustinere se a
      lapsu possent nec, qui paulum titubassent, haerere affixi
      vestigio suo, aliique super alios et iumenta et homines
140     succiderent. hoc maxime modo in Italiam perventum est,
      quinto mense a Carthagine Nova, Alpibus quinto decimo
      die superatis.

**ostento** (1), to point
  out, show
**subicio** (3), to place
  beneath (below)
**Circumpadanus, -a, -um,**
  of the Po valley
**transcendo** (3), to cross
  over
**proclivis, -is, -e,** steep,
  sloping down
**arx, arcis** (*f*), citadel
**caput, capitis** (*n*),
  capital
**ascensus, -us** (*m*), ascent

**praeceps, -itis,**
  precipitous
**lubricus, -a, -um,**
  slippery
**lapsus, -us** (*m*), fall
**titubo** (1), to stumble,
  stagger
**affixus, -a, -um,**
  fastened, fixed
**succido** (3), to fall
**mensis, -is** (*m*), month
**quintus decimus,**
  fifteenth

### The Battle of Lake Trasimene

When Hannibal reached northern Italy, he defeated the Romans in
two battles, at the River Ticinus and at the River Trebia, both in 218
BC. By this time, winter was upon him. It was the following spring
(217 BC) before he continued his advance south. The consul Flaminius tried to intercept him at Arretium, south of Florence, but Hannibal eluded him by taking a different route. Flaminius pursued him
southwards and caught up with him at Lake Trasimene. Here, Hannibal lured Flaminius into an ambush and inflicted a crushing defeat
on the Roman army.

143 **nata:** literally *born*, i.e. *naturally suited* or *ideal*.

**maxime subit:** literally *comes most under*, i.e. *comes very close to*.

**montes Cortonenses:** *the mountains near (the town of) Cortona*.

145 **velut spatio relicto:** *as if a space had been left*.

**ad id ipsum:** *for that very purpose*, i.e. to make the road.

146 **deinde:** *after that*, i.e. as you travel along the road. (Cf. **inde** in this line.)

147 **ibi:** at the end of the plain where the hills begin.

**locat:** The subject is Hannibal.

**ubi ipse consideret:** a Purpose clause – *where he himself planned to encamp*.

**modo:** *only*. The Africans and Spaniards were the strongest part of his army.

148 **Baliares:** *the Balearic slingers*. The Balearic Islands include the modern Majorca and Minorca.

150 **tumulis apte tegentibus:** literally *small hills suitably hiding (them)*. Translate *where the hills gave them convenient cover*.

**ut clausa omnia essent:** *so that everything might be blocked*, i.e. there would be no escape routes at all.

151 **intrassent = intravissent.**

154 **vixdum satis certa luce:** literally *when the light was scarcely certain enough(to see things clearly)*, i.e. *when it was not quite daylight*.

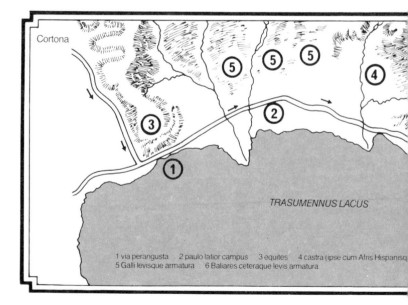

iam pervenerant ad loca nata insidiis, ubi maxime montes
Cortonenses Trasumennus subit.  via tantum interest
145  perangusta, velut ad id ipsum de industria relicto spatio;
deinde paulo latior patescit campus; inde colles insurgunt.
ibi castra in aperto locat, ubi ipse cum Afris modo
Hispanisque consideret.  Baliares ceteramque levem
armaturam post montes circumducit.  equites ad ipsas
150  fauces saltus, tumulis apte tegentibus, locat ut, ubi
intrassent Romani, obiecto equitatu clausa omnia lacu ac
montibus essent.

Flaminius cum pridie solis occasu ad lacum perven-
isset, inexplorato postero die, vixdum satis certa luce,

**tantum,** only
**interesse,** to be
  between, lie between
**perangustus, -a, -um,**
  very narrow
**de industria,** deliberately
**patesco** (3), to be open
**insurgo** (3), to rise up
**consido** (3), to sit down,
  settle

**fauces, -ium** (*f.pl*),
  mouth, entrance
**apte,** suitably
**obicio** (3), to throw in
  the way of
**solis occasus, -us** (*m*),
  sunset
**inexplorato,** without
  reconnaissance

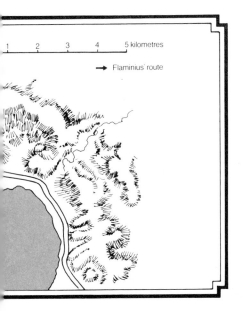

1  2  3  4  5 kilometres

→ Flaminius' route

*Map 14* The Battle of
Lake Trasimene

155 **angustiis superatis:** Compare lines 119 and 142 for this use of **superare.**

156 **pandi** is present infinitive passive.

    **id tantum hostium:** *only that part of the enemy.*

    **ex adverso** refers to the infantry encamped with Hannibal in the open plain ahead of them; **ab tergo** refers to the cavalry which would block the entrance to the pass as soon as they had gone through; **super caput** refers to the light-armed troops who were hiding in the hills above the plain.

157 **deceptae:** Supply **sunt** – *went unnoticed.*

158 **Poenus:** *the Carthaginian,* i.e. Hannibal.

    **clausum** agrees with **hostem** in the next line: *hemmed in.*

159 **suis copiis:** *by his own troops.*

160 **qui,** a Linking Relative referring back to **omnibus,** is subject of **decucurrerunt.**

    **qua cuique proximum fuit:** literally *where it was shortest for each man,* i.e. *each by the shortest route.*

161 **eo magis... quod:** *all the more... because.*

162 **res:** *the attack.*    **campo:** *on the plain.*

164 **ipsa inter se satis conspecta (sunt):** *were fairly clearly* **(satis)** *seen by one another.*

165 **pariter:** *in good formation.* When taken with **eo magis,** the phrase means *for that reason* **(eo)** *in better formation.*

    **Romanus:** either *the Roman (general),* i.e. Flaminius (corresponding to **Poenus** in line 158) or possibly *the Romans* generally.

    **prius... quam:** This word is regularly split in this way. Although **prius** appears in the previous clause, take it closely with **quam** when translating. (Compare **ante... quam** in line 167.)

    **priusquam satis cerneret:** *before they could see clearly* **(satis).**

167 **pugnari coeptum est:** a double use of the impersonal passive. Literally it means *it was begun to be fought,* i.e. *the fighting began.*

    **antequam** governs both **instrueretur** and **possent; possent** has two subjects – **arma** and **gladii.**

170 **satis:** Take with **impavidus.**

    **ut in re trepida:** *considering the alarming situation.* For this "limiting" use of **ut** compare line 104.

171 **ut** used with indicative here means *as.*

173 The colon again indicates that indirect speech is to follow, with no introductory word of speaking. (Cf. line 131.)

174 **deum = deorum.**

175 **viam fieri:** Flaminius is speaking in general terms, not about the particular situation in which they found themselves.

    **quo minus... eo minus...:** *the less... the less...*

176 **ferme:** *generally speaking.*

155 angustiis superatis, postquam in patentiorem campum
pandi agmen coepit, id tantum hostium quod ex adverso
erat conspexit. ab tergo ac super caput deceptae insidiae.
Poenus ubi (id quod petierat) clausum lacu ac montibus
et circumfusum suis copiis habuit hostem, signum omni-
160 bus dat simul invadendi. qui ubi, qua cuique proximum
fuit, decucurrerunt, eo magis Romanis subita atque improvisa res fuit quod orta ex lacu nebula campo quam
montibus densior sederat; agminaque hostium ex pluribus collibus ipsa inter se satis conspecta eoque magis
165 pariter decucurrerant. Romanus clamore prius undique
orto quam satis cerneret, se circumventum esse sensit; et
ante in frontem lateraque pugnari coeptum est quam satis
instrueretur acies aut expediri arma stringique gladii
possent.
170 consul, perculsis omnibus, ipse satis ut in re trepida
impavidus, turbatos ordines instruit, ut tempus locusque
patitur; et, quacunque adire audirique potest, adhortatur
ac stare ac pugnare iubet: nec enim inde votis aut im-
ploratione deum, sed vi ac virtute evadendum esse; per
175 medias acies ferro viam fieri, et quo timoris minus sit, eo
minus ferme periculi esse.
ceterum prae strepitu ac tumultu nec consilium nec im-

**patens, -entis,** open
**pando** (3), to open,
   spread out
**decipio** (3), to deceive
**qua,** where
**eo magis,** all the more
**inter se,** one another
**priusquam,** before
**cerno** (3), to perceive
**antequam,** before
**aciem instruere,** to draw
   up a line of battle
**expedio** (4), to make ready
**gladium stringere,** to
   draw a sword

**percello** (3), to terrify
**impavidus, -a, -um,**
   unafraid, calm
**turbo** (1), to throw into
   confusion
**quacunque,** wherever
**adhortor** (1), to
   encourage
**votum, -i** (*n*), vow,
   prayer
**imploratio, -onis** (*f*),
   prayer, appeal for help
**ferrum, -i** (*n*), sword
**prae** ( + *abl.*), because of
**consilium, -i** (*n*), advice

178 **tantum aberat ut noscerent ut . . .:** *so far were they from recognising . . . that . . .*

179 **vix competeret animus:** literally *the mind was scarcely capable,* i.e. *they scarcely had the presence of mind.*

181 **iis:** *by their armour.*

182 **ad** governs **gemitus, ictus** and **clamores.**

183 **ictus corporum aut armorum:** *blows landing on bodies or armour.*

184 **strepentium paventiumque:** literally *of men shouting out or being afraid.* An abstract noun is often the neatest way of translating this use of the present participle: *of triumph and fear.*

   **circumferebant ora oculosque:** literally *they kept turning round their faces and eyes,* i.e. *they kept turning and looking (towards).*

186 **capti:** Supply **sunt**—*had been tried.*

188 **claudebat** is also governed by **ubi.** Note the change of tense from perfect to imperfect. This verb has three subjects **(montes ac lacus, acies)** but is singular, agreeing with the nearest. Translate *were hemming (them) in.*

   **apparuit** is also governed by **ubi.** The tense changes back to perfect to indicate the sudden realisation.

   **nullam** agrees with **spem.**

189 **tum:** *it was then that.* After the three **ubi** clauses which describe the difficulties facing the soldiers, Livy uses **tum** to emphasise this important stage in the battle when individual soldiers realised they would have to take their own decisions.

190 **factus:** Supply **est.**

   **exorta:** Take with **est.**

192 **qui** is the subject of **prostravit, avertit, invexit** and **proruit.** The clauses indicate the usual effects of an earthquake – collapsed buildings, changed geographical features, tidal waves and landslides.

197 **eum et . . . et:** Despite its position outside **et . . . et . . .,** **eum** is the object of only **sequebantur.** The construction changes at the second **et** and **ipse** becomes the subject.

198 **robora virorum:** *the flower of his troops* or *the best of his soldiers.*

199 **premi ac laborare suos:** *that his men were being hard pressed and were struggling.*

200 **insignem** (agreeing with **eum** understood) is object of both **petebant** and **tuebantur,** as can be seen from its position outside **et . . . et . . .** (Contrast lines 197–8.)

perium accipi poterat; tantumque aberat ut sua signa atque ordines et locum noscerent ut vix ad arma capienda

180 aptandaque pugnae competeret animus, opprimerenturque quidam onerati magis iis quam tecti. et erat in tanta caligine maior usus aurium quam oculorum. ad gemitus vulneratorum ictusque corporum aut armorum et mixtos strepentium paventiumque clamores circumferebant ora

185 oculosque.

deinde, ubi in omnes partes nequiquam impetus capti et ab lateribus montes ac lacus, a fronte et ab tergo hostium acies claudebat, apparuitque nullam nisi in dextera ferroque salutis spem esse, tum sibi quisque dux adhortator-

190 que factus ad rem gerendam, et nova de integro exorta pugna est. tantusque fuit ardor animorum, adeo intentus pugnae animus, ut eum motum terrae, qui multarum urbium Italiae magnas partes prostravit avertitque cursu rapidos amnes, mare fluminibus invexit, montes lapsu in-

195 genti proruit, nemo pugnantium senserit.

tres ferme horas pugnatum est et ubique atrociter. circa consulem tamen acrior infestiorque pugna est. eum et robora virorum sequebantur et ipse, quacunque in parte premi ac laborare senserat suos, impigre ferebat opem,

200 insignemque armis et hostes summa vi petebant et

| | |
|---|---|
| **nosco** (3), to get to know | **rem gerere,** to carry on |
| **apto** (1), to fit on | the fight |
| **competo** (3), to be capable | **de integro,** anew, afresh |
| **oneratus, -a, -um,** weighed | **exorior** (4), to rise up, begin |
| down, burdened | **ardor, -oris** (*m*), eagerness |
| **caligo, -inis** (*f*), mist | **prosterno** (3), to |
| **usus, -us** (*m*), use | overthrow, lay low |
| **auris, -is** (*f*), ear | **rapidus, -a, -um,** swift |
| **gemitus, -us** (*m*), groan | **inveho** (3), to carry in (into) |
| **ictus, -us** (*m*), blow | **proruo** (3), to cast down |
| **strepo** (3), to shout | **atrociter,** fiercely |
| triumphantly | **infestus, -a, -um,** hostile |
| **nequiquam,** in vain | **impigre,** energetically |
| **ab lateribus,** on the flanks | **opem** (*acc.*), help |
| **dextera, -ae** (*f*), right hand | **insignis, -is, -e,** conspicuous, |
| **adhortator, -oris** (*m*), | easily recognised |
| encourager | |

201 **cives:** *the Romans,* contrasted with **hostes.**

**Ducario** is dative, agreeing with **ei** (understood). Ducarius saw a chance to avenge the defeat inflicted on his people (the Insubrian Gauls) by Flaminius in 223 BC, seven years before this, after they had settled near Milan.

203 **legiones nostras:** *our troops.* Livy uses a term which should, strictly speaking, be applied only to the Roman army.

**cecidit:** The fact that the verb has an object shows that it is the perfect of **caedere,** *to kill, cut down* and not of **cadere,** *to fall.*

204 **hanc victimam:** literally *this victim.* Translate *this man as a sacrificial victim.* It was customary in ancient times to offer up a sacrifice to appease the souls of the dead.

205 **peremptorum foede:** In the campaign against the Insubrians, Flaminius had faced certain defeat. He was given a free retreat on condition that he withdrew from their territory. He did, but returned later with more troops and won the victory mentioned by Ducarius.

208 **infesto venienti obviam:** literally *in the way of (him) coming hostile,* i.e. *in the way of his hostile charge.* **venienti** agrees with **Ducario** (understood).

210 **magnae partis fuga:** literally *the flight of a great part,* i.e. *the flight of very many.*

211 **per omnia:** Supply **loca.**

212 **super alium alii:** *on top of one another.*

216 **fuere quos:** *there were some whom.* **fuere** = **fuerunt.**

217 **quae:** Linking Relative referring back to **fuga.**

218 **deficientibus animis:** *as their spirits failed.*

221 **sex milia:** These contrast with those who took flight. (See line 210 – **magnae partis.**)

223 **evasere** = **evaserunt.** (Compare **ostendere** in line 228.)

225 **quae fortuna pugnae esset:** Indirect Question depending on **nec scire nec perspicere.** Translate **fortuna** here as *outcome.*

---

**tueor** (2), to protect
**en!** look! see!
**popularis, -is** (*m*), fellow-countryman
**depopulor** (1), to ravage, devastate
**manes, -ium** (*m.pl*), spirits of the dead
**peremptus, -a, -um,** killed, slain

**foede,** shamefully, treacherously
**subdo** (3), to plunge into
**calcar, -is** (*n*), spur
**obtrunco** (1), to kill
**armiger, -eri** (*m*), armour-bearer
**obviam** ( + *dat.*), in the way (of)
**lancea, -ae** (*f*), lance, spear
**transfigo** (3), to pierce through

tuebantur cives, donec Insuber eques (Ducario nomen
erat) facie quoque noscitans consulem "en!" inquit "hic
est" popularibus suis "qui legiones nostras cecidit
agrosque et urbem est depopulatus.  iam ego hanc vict-
205 imam manibus peremptorum foede civium dabo." sub-
ditisque calcaribus equo, per confertissimam hostium tur-
bam impetum facit obtruncatoque prius armigero qui se
infesto venienti obviam obiecerat, consulem lancea
transfixit.

210      magnae partis fuga inde primum coepit.  et iam nec
lacus nec montes pavori obstabant.  per omnia arta
praeruptaque velut caeci evadunt, armaque et viri super
alium alii praecipitantur.   pars magna, ubi locus fugae
deest, per prima vada paludis in aquam progressi, quoad
215 capitibus humerisve exstare possunt, sese immergunt.
fuere quos inconsultus pavor nando etiam capessere
fugam impulerit; quae ubi immensa ac sine spe erat, aut
deficientibus animis hauriebantur gurgitibus aut nequiquam fessi vada retro aegerrime repetebant;  atque ibi ab
220 ingressis aquam hostium equitibus passim trucidabantur.

      sex milia ferme primi agminis, per adversos hostes
eruptione impigre facta, ignari omnium quae post se agerentur, ex saltu evasere et, cum in tumulo quodam constit-
issent, clamorem modo ac sonum armorum audientes,
225 quae fortuna pugnae esset neque scire nec perspicere prae

**obsto** (1) ( + *dat.*), to
   oppose, stand in the
   way (of)
**artus, -a, -um,** narrow
**praeruptus, -a, -um,** steep
**caecus, -a, -um,** blind
**praecipito** (1), to hurl
   headlong
**vadum, -i** (*n*), shallow
**palus, -udis,** (*f*), marsh
**quoad,** as long as
**humerus, -i** (*m*), shoulder
**exsto** (1), to stand out

**immergo** (3), to plunge into
**inconsultus, -a, -um,**
   unthinking, rash
**fugam capessere,** to
   take to flight
**immensus, -a, -um,** endless
**haurio** (4), to swallow up
**gurges, -itis** (*m*), deep water
**aegre,** with difficulty
**primum agmen,** the
   vanguard
**eruptio, -onis** (*f*), sortie
**sonus, -i** (*m*), sound

226 **inclinata re:** *when the battle had been lost.*

228 **stratam:** This is the perfect participle passive of **sternere.** The word contains two ideas: *scattered* and *slaughtered.* Taken along with **foede** it suggests *hideous carnage.*

229 **ne:** *fearing that.*

**in conspectos procul:** *against (them) seen from afar.* This refers to the 6000 Romans.

230 **eques:** singular for plural – *cavalry.* (Cf. line 37.)

**quam citatissimo poterant agmine:** *with all possible speed.* Like Caesar, Livy chooses to insert **poterant.** (Compare Chapter 56, line 68.)

233 **Maharbale:** Maharbal was one of Hannibal's senior officers. He had pursued the retreating Romans during the night.

234 **passurum:** Supply **se ... esse** – an Accusative and Infinitive depending on **fidem dante.**

**quae fides:** *this promise.*

235 **Punica religione:** *with typical Carthaginian scrupulousness.* Livy is writing from a biased Roman point of view. The Romans traditionally regarded the Carthaginians as a very treacherous nation. Hannibal claimed that Maharbal had no authority to make the promise and so it was not binding on Hannibal.

236 **omnes:** In fact, this happened only to the Roman captives. In the hope of winning the support of the Italians during his march on Rome, Hannibal released the Italian troops who had been in the Roman army he had defeated.

237 **nobilis:** *famous.*

**inter paucas memorata:** literally *remembered among few,* i.e. *one of the most memorable.*

243 **ad:** *at.*

244 **populi:** Take with **concursus.**

245 **quae ... quaeve ...:** These two Indirect Questions depend on **percunctantur.**

246 **obvios:** *those they met.*

247 **versa:** *turned.*

**magistratus:** accusative plural.

caligine poterant. inclinata denique re, cum incalescente sole dispulsa nebula aperuisset diem, tum liquida iam luce montes campique perditas res stratamque ostendere foede Romanam aciem. itaque ne in conspectos procul
230 immitteretur eques, sublatis raptim signis, quam citatissimo poterant agmine, sese abripuerunt.

postero die, cum super cetera extrema fames etiam instaret, fidem dante Maharbale, si arma tradidissent, abire cum singulis vestimentis passurum, sese dediderunt. quae
235 Punica religione servata fides ab Hannibale est, atque in vincula omnes coniecti.

haec est nobilis ad Trasumennum pugna atque inter paucas memorata populi Romani clades. quindecim milia Romanorum in acie caesa; decem milia sparsa fuga
240 per omnem Etruriam diversis itineribus urbem petiere; duo milia quingenti hostium in acie, multi postea ex vulneribus periere.

Romae ad primum nuntium cladis eius cum ingenti terrore ac tumultu concursus in forum populi est factus.
245 matronae vagae per vias, quae repens clades adlata quaeve fortuna exercitus esset, obvios percunctantur. et cum turba in comitium et curiam versa magistratus vocaret, tandem haud multo ante solis occasum M. Pomponius praetor "pugna" inquit "magna victi sumus."

| | |
|---|---|
| **inclino** (1), to lean, incline | **memoro** (1), to record |
| **incalesco** (3), to grow hot | **clades, -is** (*f*), |
| **dispello** (3), to disperse |   disaster, defeat |
| **liquidus, -a, -um,** clear | **sparsus, -a, -um,** scattered |
| **perdo** (3), to destroy | **diversus, -a, -um,** |
| **foede,** foully, horribly |   different, various |
| **immitto** (3), to send in | **quingenti, -ae, -a,** 500 |
| **fames, -is** (*f*), hunger | **matrona, -ae** (*f*), |
| **insto** (1), to press on |   married woman |
| **fidem dare,** to promise, | **vagus, -a, -um,** wandering |
|   give one's word | **repens, -entis,** sudden |
| **singuli, -ae, -a,** one each | **adferre,** to bring |
| **patior** (3), to allow | **percunctor** (1), to ask |

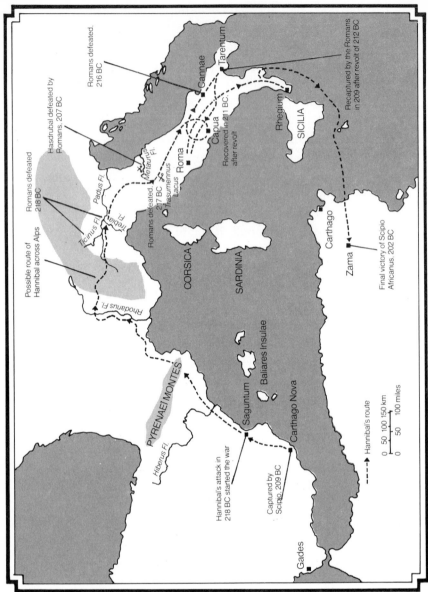

*Map 15* Hannibal's route during the Second Punic War, 218–202 BC

Romans defeated. 216 BC

Hasdrubal defeated by Romans. 207 BC

Romans defeated 218 BC

Possible route of Hannibal across Alps

Recaptured by the Romans in 209 after revolt of 212 BC

Cannae

Tarentum

Rhegium

SICILIA

Capua

Recovered in 211 BC after revolt

Roma

Romans defeated. 217 BC

*Metarus Fl.*

*Trasumennus Lacus*

*Padus Fl.*

*Trebia Fl.*

*Ticinus Fl.*

*Rhodanus Fl.*

CORSICA

SARDINIA

Carthago

Zama

Final victory of Scipio Africanus. 202 BC

PYRENAEI MONTES

Saguntum

Baliares Insulae

Carthago Nova

*Hiberus Fl.*

Hannibal's attack in 218 BC started the war

Captured by Scipio. 209 BC

Gades

Hannibal's route

0   50  100 150 km

0      50      100 miles

220

## The rest of the war

To deal with the extreme crisis after the disaster at Trasimene, the Romans appointed a dictator, Quintus Fabius Maximus, to take sole command of the army. His tactics were to avoid fighting pitched battles with Hannibal in the hope that this would gradually wear him down, while Rome rebuilt its forces. These tactics proved very successful and earned Fabius the **cognomen** Cunctator. However, by 216 BC, some of the Romans were becoming impatient at the thought that no attempt was being made to drive the aggressor out of Italy. When Fabius' term of office expired, he was replaced by two consuls, and one of these committed the Roman army to battle at Cannae in Apulia. Despite its superior numbers, the Roman army was out-manoeuvred and virtually wiped out.

Hannibal chose not to attack the city of Rome, assuming that Rome's allies would desert her. Fortunately for Rome, however, the majority of her allies remained loyal and, in the years following Cannae, Rome was able to rebuild her forces while employing Fabian tactics once more. Hannibal was now losing the initiative.

Another important factor was the war in Spain. Even while Hannibal was invading Italy, the Romans had maintained an army in Spain to pin down the forces of Hannibal's brother, Hasdrubal, so that the latter was unable to send reinforcements to Italy. By 208 BC it was clear that Hannibal needed support, and so Hasdrubal moved his army into Italy to join his brother. He was intercepted by the consuls at the River Metaurus in northern Italy in 207 BC. His army was defeated and he was killed. Hannibal was now very much on his own since the government at Carthage was unable to send him reinforcements.

While still containing the efforts of Hannibal in Italy, the Romans went on the offensive in Spain. Publius Cornelius Scipio (son of the Scipio mentioned in line 1 of this chapter) first drove the Carthaginians out of Spain and then invaded Africa. By 203 BC, the Carthaginians were under so much pressure that they withdrew Hannibal from Italy, much against his will, to defend Carthage. In 202 BC, however, he was defeated by Scipio at Zama, near Carthage, and this brought the Second Punic War to an end. In honour of his victory, Scipio was given the title Africanus.

**unus homo nobis cunctando restituit rem**
Lines written by the poet Ennius to praise Q. Fabius Maximus Cunctator.

# Medieval Latin

Most of the Latin we read is Classical Latin, by definition Latin written between roughly 100 BC and AD 150, the period which produced Rome's greatest writers—Cicero, Livy and Tacitus among the prose writers, and Virgil, Horace, Ovid and Juvenal among the poets. The Latin of this period has come to be called "Classical" because it was thought to have set a standard of excellence and correctness.

Latin written between roughly AD 200 and AD 500 is known as Late Latin. In this period, the gradual break-up of the Roman Empire and a decline in literacy following the barbarian invasions produced a language in which noun and verb groups and sentence constructions were beginning to fall into confusion. In fact, the various Latin-based languages which we call the Romance languages (e.g. Italian, Spanish and French) were just beginning to emerge as the Empire's central control weakened; and this process was speeded up as spoken Latin, called Vulgar or Popular Latin, began to influence writers more and more. Existing alongside the literary language, this simpler, racier, less formal tongue can be glimpsed in the plays of Plautus, in Cicero's letters and even in the graffiti which survive on the walls of buildings in Pompeii.

Throughout the Dark Ages, this transformation of Latin into the Romance languages went on almost unnoticed because most speakers of these fledgling languages were illiterate; but at the same time the Church continued its own development of the written language in the Latin Bible and in Christian literature generally.

The result of all these influences operating side by side is to be seen in Medieval Latin. Some writers oscillate uncertainly between Classical and non-Classical words and constructions. Others, who were better educated, aim at an almost Ciceronian elegance. Others again express themselves in a language which can scarcely be described as Latin at all.

The following examples illustrate some of the features of the changing language, the examples being taken from Chapters 71 and 72.

*1 Changes in spelling*

**ae** becomes **e**, e.g.  **haec → hec**
                           **praecepit → precepit**
                           **saepius → sepius**

**t** becomes **c**, e.g.   **militia → milicia**
                           **negotium → negocium**
                           **pulsatio → pulsacio**

**h** becomes **ch**, e.g.  **mihi → michi**

Doubling of consonants, e.g.  **oculus → occulus**
                                   **intolerabilis → intollerabilis**

One consonant for two, e.g.  **reddita → redita**
                                 **afferre → affere**

*2 Sentence construction*

Compare Chapter 71, line 11, where Classical Latin is used:

    **illum numquam antea se vidisse dicebat.**
    *He said he had never seen him before.*

with Chapter 71, line 1, where a **quod** clause is used instead of the Classical Accusative and Infinitive:

    **dictum mihi fuit quod quidam Hispanus perrexit Meccam.**
    *It was said to me that a Spaniard went to Mecca.*

*3 Meaning of Words and Forms*

(*a*)  Present participle: **audiens** = *while hearing* (Classical Latin)
                                       = *having heard* (Medieval)

    e.g. **quod audiens increpavit eum.**
    *Having heard this he rebuked him.*

(*b*)  Gerund: **laudando** = *by praising* (Classical)
                        = *while praising* (Medieval)

  Compare modern Italian *crescendo, (while) getting louder.*

(*c*)  Subjunctive use is unpredictable.

    e.g. **dum ibidem exspectat, venit quidam** (Classical)
    **dum ibidem exspectasset, venit quidam** (Medieval)

    *While he was waiting in the same place, someone came along.*

These notes illustrate only the processes that affected the language. Other points will be explained in the notes which accompany the passages.

1 **dictum mihi fuit:** literally *it was told to me*, i.e. *I was told*.

  **quod:** *that*. In Medieval Latin, a clause introduced by **quod** is often used where a Classical Latin writer would have used an Accusative and Infinitive. (Cf. line 3.)

  **Meccam:** Mecca, the birthplace of Mohammed, was a place of pilgrimage for Moslems.

2 **dum iret:** literally *while he was going*, i.e. *on his way*.

  **deserta:** Supply **loca.**

4 **dimitteret:** *he would deposit*.

  **voluisset:** *he was willing*.

7 **probitate fidelitatis:** In English we would probably say *honesty and trustworthiness*.

  **de suo: suum** is used here as a neuter noun. Translate *from his fortune*.

8 **talenta:** A talent was a very valuable coin. It is impossible to give an exact equivalent value, but the total he deposited would have amounted to over a million pounds at present day values.

10 **quod = id quod.**

13 **tractasset = tractavisset.**

  **eum** refers to the man who had deposited the money.

15 **nihil hoc esse:** *that there was nothing in this story*.

16 **qui:** *the man who*.

  **unaquaque die:** *every single day*.

19 **quod:** Linking Relative – object of **audiens.**

  **deceptor:** Nouns ending in **-tor** *(the person who . . .)* are often derived from the supine of a verb, in this case **deceptum,** supine of **decipere,** *to deceive*.

  **ne tale quid diceret:** *not to say anything like this*.

21 **poenas subiret:** literally *he would undergo punishment*, i.e. *he would be punished*.

---

**pergo** (3), to proceed
**dimitto** (3), to entrust, deposit
**noto** (1), to note
**probitas, -atis** (*f*), honesty, integrity
**committo** (3), to entrust
**talentum,** -i (*n*), a talent

**nequitia, -ae** (*f*), wickedness, villainy
**probus, -a, -um,** good, honest
**tracto** (1), to treat
**refero, referre,** to relate, report
**vicinus, -i** (*m*), neighbour
**perdo** (3), to lose

# 71
# The Deceiver Deceived

This story was written by Petrus Adolphus, a Christianised Jew who was godson of the King of Aragon. He lived in the twelfth century AD. He gathered together some Arab fables which had a moral in them, containing the kind of advice which a good father might give to his son. Some of these stories were used in later literature such as the Decameron of Boccaccio.

dictum mihi fuit quod quidam Hispanus perrexit Meccam et, dum iret, venit in Aegyptum. qui deserta terrae intrare volens et transire, cogitavit quod pecuniam suam in Aegypto dimitteret. et antequam dimittere voluisset, in-
5   terrogavit si aliquis homo fidelis esset in illa regione, cui posset pecuniam suam dimittere. tunc ostenderunt ei hominem antiquum notatum probitate fidelitatis, cui de suo mille talenta commisit. deinde perrexit.
      factoque itinere, ad illum rediit cui pecuniam commisit,
10  et quod commiserat ab eo quaesivit. at ille, plenus nequitia, illum numquam antea se vidisse dicebat. ille vero sic deceptus perrexit ad probos homines regionis illius, et quomodo tractasset eum homo ille cui pecuniam commiserat eis retulit. vicini vero illius de eo talia audientes
15  credere noluerunt, sed nihil hoc esse dixerunt.
      qui vero pecuniam perdiderat unaquaque die ad domum illius, qui iniuste retinebat pecuniam, ibat; blandisque precibus eum deprecabatur ut pecuniam redderet. quod deceptor audiens increpavit eum, dicens ne
20  tale quid de eo amplius diceret nec ad eum veniret; quod si amplius faceret, poenas ex merito subiret.

**blandus, -a, -um,** flattering, charming
**preces, -um** (*f.pl*), entreaties, pleas
**deprecor** (1), to beg, plead with, entreat
**increpo** (1), to rebuke
**ex merito,** deservedly

23 **eremitalibus pannis:** *in the clothes of a hermit (recluse)*.

24 **haec:** *she*

25 **laudando:** In Classical Latin, we would find the present participle rather than the gerund.

29 **at:** In Medieval Latin, **at** frequently means *and*, rather than the contrasting idea of *but* or *however*.

30 **inquit:** In Medieval Latin, **inquit** is frequently found outside the direct speech.

31 **qua** = **quae.**

33 **de terra tua:** *from your country*.

35 **decepti:** genitive singular of **deceptus**, *the deceived man*.
   **exterius:** *on the outside*.

37 **emere:** Take with **praecepit.**

40 **qui ... deferant:** a Purpose clause – *to take*.

43 **quam cito primus venerit** *as soon as the first man comes*.

44 **veni et tu: et** means *too*.

45 **in Domino:** *in the name of the Lord*.
   **redita fuerit** = **reddetur.**

47 **quae:** *she*. (Cf. **haec** in line 24.)
   **quod praedixerat:** This relative clause precedes its antecedent **iter.**

---

**mina, -ae** (*f*), threat
**obvio** (1), to meet
**vetula, -ae** (*f*), old woman
**pannus, -i** (*m*), garment
**fragilis, -is, -e,** frail
**artus, -us** (*m*), limb
**sustento** (1), to support
**laedo** (3), to hurt
**levo** (1), to pick up
**extraneus, -i** (*m*), foreigner
**pietas, -atis** (*f*), pity
**angiportus, -us** (*m*), lane, side-street

**ordinate,** in order, from beginning to end
**inde,** then
**factum, -i** (*n*), deed
**fidem habere** ( + *dat*.), to trust
**praecipio** (3) ( + *dat*.), to instruc
**cophinus, -i** (*m*), box
**pretiosus, -a, -um,** precious
**depictus, -a, -um,** decorated
**deargentatus, -a, -um,** silver-plated
**ligo** (1), to bind, fasten
**sera, -ae** (*f*), lock

auditis minis illius qui eum deceperat, tristis coepit abire, et in redeundo obviavit cuidam vetulae eremit-alibus pannis indutae.  haec autem baculo fragiles artus
25 sustentabat et per viam, laudando Deum, lapides ne transeuntium pedes laederentur levabat.  quae videns hominem flentem, cognovit eum esse extraneum.  com-mota pietate, in angiportum vocavit, et quid ei accidisset interrogavit.  at ille ordinate narravit.
30 femina vero, auditis illius verbis, inquit: "amice, si vera sunt qua retulisti, feram inde tibi auxilium."

et ille "quomodo potes hoc facere, ancilla Dei?"

at illa inquit "adduc mihi hominem de terra tua, cuius factis et dictis fidem habere possis."  at ille adduxit.  de-
35 inde decepti socio praecepit decem cophinos exterius pret-iosis depictos coloribus atque ferro deargentato ligatos cum bonis seris emere, et ad domum sui hospitis affere, lapidibusque comminutis implere.  at ipse ita egit.

mulier vero, ut vidit omnia quae praeceperat esse
40 parata, ait "nunc decem homines perquire qui, euntes ad domum illius qui deceperat te, mecum et cum socio tuo deferant scrinios, unus post alium, venientes ordine longo.  et quam cito primus venerit ad domum hominis qui te decepit et requiescet ibi, veni et tu et roga pro
45 pecunia tua, et ego promitto tibi in Domino quod redita tibi pecunia fuerit."  et ipse, sicut iusserat vetula, fecit.

quae, non oblita incepti operis, quod praedixerat iter incepit, et venit cum socio decepti ad domum deceptoris, et inquit "quidam homo de Hispania hospitatus est
50 mecum et vult Meccam adire;  quaeritque a me fidelem

---

**hospes, -itis** (*m*), friend
**comminuo** (3), to crush, crumble
**perquiro** (3), to look for
**scrinius, -i** (*m*), box
**ordo, -inis** (*m*), line
**requiesco** (3), to rest

**obliviscor** (3), **oblitus sum** (*+ gen.*), to forget
**incipio** (3), to begin
**praedico** (3), to mention earlier
**hospitor** (1), to stay as a guest

*line*

51 **cui tradat:** a Purpose clause – *to whom he may hand over.*

52 **servandam** agrees with **pecuniam** in line 51: translate *to keep.*

53 **mei causa:** *for me.*   **custodias:** Supply **eam.**

55 **commendatorem:** Compare line 19 for **-tor** ending (**commendare** means *to entrust*).

56 **adesse** = **esse.**

57 **aliis a longe apparentibus:** *the others appearing in the distance.*

61 **cui:** *whose.*

62 **alius:** *the other man.*

64 **contra eum:** *to meet him.* (Cf. line 70.)
   **dicendo:** Compare line 25.

66 **inveni:** Supply **te.**

68 **laetus effectus:** *made happy.*

74 **quod acceperat:** This clause is the object of **servavit.**

75 **eorum quae:** *of those things which.*
   **adhuc exspectabat:** *he kept on waiting.*

76 **bono ingenio:** *because of the good thinking,* i.e. the ingenious plan.

virum, cui tradat pecuniam suam, quae est in decem scriniis, servandam donec revertatur. precor itaque ut mei causa in aede tua custodias et, quia audivi et scio te bonum et fidelem esse hominem, nolo aliquem alium
55 praeter te solum huius pecuniae commendatorem adesse." et dum loqueretur, venit primus deferens scrinium, aliis a longe apparentibus.

interim deceptus, praeceptorum vetulae non oblitus, post primum scrinium, sicut ei praeceptum fuerat, venit.
60 ille vero qui pecuniam celaverat, plenus nequitiae et malae artis, ut vidit hominem venientem cui pecuniam celaverat, timens ne, si pecuniam suam requireret, alius qui pecuniam suam adducebat sibi non committeret, statim contra eum ita dicendo perrexit: "o amice, ubi tu tam diu
65 fuisti? et ubi moratus es? veni et accipe pecuniam tuam fidei meae iam diu commendatam, quoniam inveni et amodo taedet me custodire."

at ille laetus effectus recepit pecuniam gratias agens. vetula autem, ut vidit hominem pecuniam suam habere,
70 surrexit et inquit "ibimus ego et socius meus contra scrinios nostros, et festinare praecipiemus. tu vero ex-specta donec redeamus, et bene serva quod iam adduximus."

ille autem laetus animo quod acceperat servavit, adven-
75 tumque eorum quae restabant adhuc exspectabat. et ita bono ingenio vetulae reddita fuit viro summa pecuniae.

| | |
|---|---|
| **donec,** until | **moror** (1), to loiter, |
| **revertor** (3), to return | delay |
| **precor** (1), to beg, ask | **fides, -ei** (*f*), good faith, |
| **aedes, -is** (*f*), house | trust |
| **praecepta, -orum** (*n.pl*), | **amodo,** henceforth, any |
| instructions | longer |
| **ars, artis** (*f*), cunning | **resto** (1), to remain |
| **requiro** (3), to ask back | **summa, -ae** (*f*), sum, |
| | total |

The following story comes from a collection of moralising tales known as the **Gesta Romanorum**. These are not, as the title might suggest, stories about Romans. In fact, it is possible that many of them are oriental in origin, brought back from the East by Crusaders. No one knows who the original authors were, but one theory is that a monk (round about the 13th century) gathered them together for use in preaching. Later writers, including Chaucer and Shakespeare, found them a useful source of material for their own works.

*line*

4 **sim** is used instead of **sum.**

  **hiis** = **his.**

6 **karissimi** = **carissimi.**

10 **equitasset** = **equitavisset.**

  **in tantum quod:** *so much so that.*

11 **mori** is used instead of the future infinitive.

13 **remaneatis:** The present subjunctive is used to express a command.

17 **tamdiu ... quousque:** literally *so long ... until when.* Translate *until.*

22 **sicut persona imperatoris:** literally *as the person of the Emperor,* i.e. *as the person who was their Emperor.*

  **nullam suspicionem habebant nisi quod:** *they had no doubts about.*

26 **hec** = **haec.**

  **vestes nec equum:** Supply **nec** before **vestes.**

29 **ad se reversus:** literally *coming back to himself,* i.e. *recovering his composure.*

30 **unus:** not the number *one,* but simply *a.*

---

**semel,** once
**stratus, -us** (*m*), bed
**elevo** (1), to lift up
**cor, cordis** (*n*), heart
**ultra,** beyond
**venor** (1), to hunt
**adimpleo** (2), to fulfil
**calor, -oris** (*m*), heat
**balneor** (1), to bathe
**quousque,** until

**dextrarius, -i** (*m*), war-horse
**calcar, -aris** (*n*), spur
**ibidem,** in the same place
**gestus, -us** (*m*), bearing, movement
**ammiror** (1), to be amazed
**contristo** (1), to sadden
**ministro** (1), to serve, treat
**miles, -itis** (*m*), court-official, courtier

# 72

# A Bitter Lesson for the Emperor

Iovinianus imperator regnavit potens valde. qui cum semel in stratu suo iacuisset, elevatum est cor eius ultra quam credi potest, et dicebat in corde suo: "estne alter Deus quam sim ego?" hiis cogitatis dormivit.

5   mane vero surrexit, vocavit milites suos ac ceteros et ait: "karissimi, bonum est cibum sumere, quia hodie ad venandum volo pergere."

illi vero parati erant eius voluntatem adimplere. cibo sumpto, ad venandum perrexerunt. dum vero imperator
10  equitasset, calor intollerabilis arripuit eum, in tantum quod videbatur sibi mori, nisi in aqua frigida posset balneari. respexit, a longe vidit aquam latam. dixit militibus suis: "hic remaneatis quousque ad vos veniam!"

15  percussit dextrarium cum calcaribus et ad aquam festinanter equitavit. de equo descendit. omnia vestimenta deposuit, aquam intravit et tamdiu ibidem remansit, quousque totaliter refrigeratus fuisset.

dum vero ibidem exspectasset, venit quidam ei per
20  omnia similis in vultu, in gestu, et induit se vestimentis suis, dextrarium eius ascendit et ad milites equitavit. ab omnibus sicut persona imperatoris est receptus, quia nullam suspicionem de eo habebant, nisi quod dominus eorum esset, quia in omnibus ei similis erat. ludebant;
25  finito ludo, ad palacium cum militibus equitabat.

post hec Iovinianus de aqua exivit, vestes nec equum invenit. ammirabatur. contristatus est valde, quia nudus erat et neminem vidit. cogitabat intra se: "quid faciam ego? miserabiliter sum ministratus." tandem ad
30  se reversus dicebat: "hic prope manet unus miles, quem ad

*line*

36 **quesivit** = **quaesivit.** (Cf. **hec** in line 26.)

    **qualis:** *who.*

39 **vadas:** present subjunctive used to express a command. (Cf. line 13.)

40 **michi** = **mihi.**

45 **in mensa sedet:** *sits at table* or *is seated at his meal.*

46 **denunciabo** = **denuntiabo.**

48 **precepit** = **praecepit,** *he gave instructions.* (Cf. lines 26 and 36.)

---

**milicia, -ae** (*f*), a
    position at court
**taliter,** in such a way
**confundo** (3), to
    distress, embarrass
**castrum, -i** (*n*), castle
**vado** (3), to go

**a casu,** accidentally
**mentior** (4), to tell a lie
**ribaldus, -a, -um,** obscene
**parum,** a little
**noticiam habere,** to
    recognise
**peroptime,** very easily

miliciam promovi.  pergam ad eum et vestimenta habebo
et equum, et sic ad palacium meum ascendam et videbo
quomodo et per quem taliter sim confusus."

    Iovinianus totaliter nudus solus ad castrum militis
35  perrexit.  ad ianuam pulsavit.  ianitor causam pul-
sacionis quesivit.  at ille: "ianuam aperi et vide qualis
sim ego!"

    ille ianuam aperuit et, cum vidisset eum, ait:  "quis es
tu?" et ille: "ego sum Iovinianus imperator.  vadas ad
40  dominum tuum et dic ei ut michi vestes mittat, quia a casu
vestes et equum perdidi."

    qui ait:  "mentiris, pessime ribalde!  parum ante te
dominus meus imperator Iovinianus ad palacium suum
cum militibus equitavit, et dominus meus secum equitavit
45  et rediit et iam in mensa sedet.  sed quia imperatorem te
nominas, domino meo denunciabo."

    ianitor intravit et domino suo verba eius annunciavit.
ille hec audiens precepit ut introduceretur.  et sic factum
est.  miles cum eum vidisset, in nullo noticiam eius
50  habebat.  sed imperator eum peroptime cognovit.  ait ei
miles:  "dic michi, quis es tu, et quod est tibi nomen?" at
ille:  "imperator sum et Iovinianus dicor et te ad miliciam
promovi tali die et tali tempore."

    at ille:  "o ribalde pessime, qua audacia audes te ipsum

58 **rybalde:** The writer's spelling is inconsistent.

60 **presumpcionem = praesumptionem:** *presumption, audacity.*

64 **quid hoc esse potest quod:** *how can it be that.*

65 **cum hoc:** literally *with this,* i.e. *in addition to this.*

66 **dux consiliarius meus:** *one of the dukes who advise me.*

73 **fac negocium meum:** *plead my case.*

81 **presumit:** Compare line 60.

82 **hostium = ostium.** (See line 71.)

89 **apropriasti = appropriavisti,** *you have claimed.*

---

**associo** (1), to join (to)
**impune,** unpunished, without punishment
**egregie,** excellently, thoroughly
**flagello** (1), to whip
**amare,** bitterly
**necessitas, -atis** (*f*), need
**ostium, -i** (*n*), door
**quare?** why?

**ideo,** for that reason
**succurro** (3) (+ *dat.*), to help
**introitus, -us** (*m*), entry
**cito,** quickly
**ducatus, -us** (*m*), dukedom
**insanio** (4), to be crazy
**versus** (+ *acc.*), towards
**gradus, -us** (*m*), rank

55 imperatorem nominare? iam dominus meus, imperator
Iovinianus, ante te ad palacium cum militibus equitavit,
et ego per viam eram ei associatus et sum reversus. o
rybalde pessime! verum est quod tali die et hora factus
sum miles per dominum meum imperatorem. quia ad
60 tantam presumpcionem devenisti ut te ipsum imperatorem nominares, impune non transibis." et statim fecit
eum egregie verberari et postea expelli.

ille vero sic flagellatus et expulsus flevit amare et ait: "o
deus meus, quid hoc esse potest quod miles, quem ad
65 miliciam promovi, noticiam mei non habet et cum hoc me
graviter verberavit? hic prope est quidam dux consiliarius meus. ad eum pergam et necessitatem meam ei
ostendam. per quem potero indui et ad palacium meum
pergere."

70 cum vero ad ianuam ducis venisset, pulsabat. ianitor,
audiens pulsacionem, ostium aperuit et, cum hominem
nudum vidisset, ammirabatur et ait: "quis es tu et quare
sic totaliter nudus advenisti?" at ille: "rogo te, fac
negocium meum cum duce! ego sum imperator et a casu
75 vestimenta et equum perdidi et ideo ad eum veni ut michi
in hac necessitate succurrat."

ianitor cum verba eius audisset, ammirabatur, intravit
et domino suo annunciavit quod quidam homo nudus in
porta esset, qui diceret se imperatorem esse et introitum
80 peteret. ait dux: "cito eum introduc ut videamus quis sit
qui presumit se imperatorem nominare!" ianitor vero
hostium aperuit ac introduxit. imperator noticiam ducis
peroptime habebat, sed ille eius noticiam in nullo.

ait ei dux: "quis es tu?" et ille: "ego sum imperator
85 et te ad honores et ad ducatum promovi et consiliarium
meum inter alios constitui." ait dux: "insanis, miser!
parum ante te perrexi cum domino meo imperatore versus
palacium et reversus sum. et quia talem gradum tibi
apropriasti, impune non transibis."

90 fecit eum incarcerari et per aliquos dies pane et aqua

92 **verberare = verberari.**

96 **abieccio = abiectio,** *an object of scorn.*

98 **mei de curia:** literally *my people from the court,* i.e. *my courtiers.*

101 **apperuit = aperuit.**

103 **numquid non nostis me?:** *Do you not recognise me?* There is no exact equivalent for **numquid** in English; like **-ne,** it merely indicates a question. **nostis** is a shortened form of **novistis.** It will be noted that this is plural even though he is speaking to only one person. Medieval Latin has frequently "errors" like that.

104 **portas:** *you wear.*

106 **in signum huius:** *as a sign of this* (i.e. that he is the emperor).
   **dei amore:** *for the love of god.*

109 **dic ei quod:** *tell her that* ... In Medieval Latin, a **quod** clause frequently replaces an Accusative and Infinitive. In this case, however, the author changes the construction in mid-sentence and continues with an Indirect Command clause **(ut ...).**

110 **que = quae.**

112 **quia sis:** *that you are.* In Medieval Latin a clause introduced by **quia** (compare **quod** in line 109) may replace an Accusative and Infinitive.

117 **flexis genibus:** literally *on bending knees,* i.e. *kneeling.*

118 **non modicum:** *not a little,* i.e. *greatly.*

120 **sepius = saepius.**

125 **ante:** *previously.*

127 **impeditus quod eum non lesit:** *it was prevented from harming him.*

---

**carcer, -eris** (*m*), prison
**effusio, -onis** (*f*), a pouring out
**suspirium, -i** (*n*), a sigh
**opprobrium, -i** (*n*), (an object of) disgrace
**plebs, plebis** (*f*), the common people
**saltem,** at least

**imperatrix, -icis** (*f*), empress
**aula, -ae** (*f*), palace
**verumtamen,** however
**intimo** (1), to inform
**diligo** (3), **dilexi, dilectum,** to love
**guttur, -uris** (*n*), throat
**laedo** (3), to harm
**item,** also

sustentari.  deinde de carcere eum extraxit et usque ad effusionem sanguinis egregie verberare eum fecit et ab eius terra eum deiecit.

ille sic deiectus ultra quam credi potest, gemitus et sus-
95 piria emittebat et ait intra se:  "heu michi!  quid faciam? confusus sum.  sum enim opprobrium hominum et abiec-cio plebis.  melius est michi ad palacium meum pergere, et mei de curia noticiam mei habebunt.  si non illi, saltem domina uxor mea noticiam mei habebit per certa signa."
100     solus ad palacium totaliter nudus accessit, ad ianuam pulsavit.  audita pulsacione, ianitor ianuam apperuit. quem cum vidisset, ait: "dic michi, quis es tu?"  et ille: "numquid non nostis me?"  qui ait: "in nullo."  at ille: "de hoc ammiror, quia portas meas vestes."  qui ait:
105 "mentiris, quia vestes domini mei imperatoris porto."  et ille: "ego sum ille.  in signum huius rogo te dei amore ut ad imperatricem pergas et ei de adventu meo dicas, ut michi celeriter vestes mittat, quia aulam intrare volo.  si vero dictis tuis non credat, dic ei quod per ista signa et
110 ista, que nemo novit nisi nos duo, ut tibi per omnia credat!"

ait ianitor:  "non dubito quia sis insanus, quia iam dominus meus in mensa sedet et imperatrix iuxta eum. verumtamen, quia dicis te imperatorem esse, imperatrici
115 intimabo et certus sum quia graviter propter hoc punieris."

ianitor ad imperatricem perrexit, flexis genibus omnia ei retulit.  illa non modicum contristata ad dominum suum conversa, iuxta quem sedebat, ait:  "o domine mi,
120 audite mirabilia!  signa privata inter nos sepius acta quidam rybaldus per ianitorem michi recitat et dicit se imperatorem esse et dominum meum."

ipse cum hoc audisset, precepit ianitori ut eum intro-duceret in conspectum omnium.  qui cum introductus
125 fuisset totaliter nudus, canis quidam, qui ante eum mul-tum dilexit, ad guttur saltavit ut eum occideret, sed per homines impeditus quod eum non lesit.  item quendam

129 **imperator:** From this point on, it is sometimes not clear whether this word refers to the real emperor or the impostor. Here, it refers to the impostor and **isti** *(to him)* in line 131 refers to the real emperor.

133 **istius imperii:** *of this empire.*

138 **questio** = **quaestio:** *a question.*

139 **quod scimus:** *as far as we know.*

142 **ut de tali presumpcione se non intromittant:** *so that they do not allow themselves to get involved in such arrogant behaviour.*

152 **tam ausus fuisti:** *you have been so daring.*

153 **do pro iudicio ut:** *I give it as my judgment that,* i.e. *the sentence I impose is that.*

154 **ammodo:** *henceforth.*

156 **ita tamen quod:** *in such a way, however, that.*

159 **pereat dies:** literally *may the day perish,* i.e. *curse the day.*

160 **uxor mea nec filii:** In Classical Latin, there would be a **nec** in front of **uxor.**

163 **ipse:** an emphatic *he.*

---

**falco, -onis** (*m*), falcon
**pertica, -ae** (*f*), pole
**ligatura, -ae** (*f*), cord, rope
**volo** (1), to fly
**sive ... sive ...,** whether ... or ...
**iuramentum, -i** (*n*), oath
**nequam,** worthless, good for nothing

**proles, -is** (*f*), offspring, child
**perpetro** (1), to bring about, accomplish
**satelles, -itis** (*m*), attendant
**heremita, -ae** (*m*), hermit

falconem habebat in pertica, qui cum eum videret, liga-
turam fregit et extra aulam volavit.  ait imperator omni-
130 bus in aula, sedentibus in mensa sive stantibus: "karissimi," ait "audite mea verba que isti dicam!  dic michi,
karissime, quis es tu et ob quam causam huc venisti?"

at ille: "domine, imperator sum istius imperii et
dominus istius loci.  et ideo huc veni ad loquendum cum
135 imperatrice."  ait imperator omnibus circumstantibus:
"dicite michi per iuramentum quod fecistis, quis nostrum
est imperator et dominus?"  at illi: "o domine, ista est
questio mirabilis.  per iuramentum quod fecimus, numquam illum nequam vidimus, quod scimus.  sed tu es
140 dominus noster et imperator quem a iuventute
habuimus.  et ideo rogamus ut puniatur, ut omnes
exemplum capiant, ut de tali presumpcione se non
intromittant."

imperator ille conversus ad imperatricem et ait: "dic,
145 domina, michi per fidem qua teneris, nosti tu istum
hominem qui dicit se imperatorem et dominum tuum
esse?"  at illa:  "o bone domine, cur talia a me queris?
nonne plus quam XXX annis in societate tua steti et pro-
lem per te habui?  sed unum est quod miror, quomodo
150 rybaldus ille pervenit ad nostra secreta inter nos
perpetrata."

imperator ille dixit ei:  "quia tam ausus fuisti quod te
imperatorem nominasti, do pro iudicio ut ad caudas equi
hodie sis tractus.  et si ammodo talia audes affirmare,
155 turpissima morte te condempnabo!"  vocavit satellites,
precepit eis ut eum ad caudam equi traherent, ita tamen
quod non occideretur.  et sic factum est.

post hec vero ultra quam credi potest dolebat et quasi
desperatus de se ipso ait intra se: "pereat dies in qua
160 natus sum! a me amici mei recesserunt. uxor mea nec filii
noverunt me." dum hec dixisset, cogitabat: "hic prope
manet heremita, confessor meus.  vadam ad eum; forte
ipse noticiam mei habebit, quia sepius confessionem
meam audivit." perrexit ad heremitam et ad fenestram

239

*line*

165  **celle sue** = **cellae suae.**

172  **pre** = **prae,** *on account of.*

  **barbe** = **barbae.**

173  **celum** = **caelum.**

174  **heu ego!** an interesting variation for **heu michi!**

179  **clausa:** Supply **fenestra,** an Ablative Absolute meaning *with the window shut.*

  **audias:** present subjunctive used to express a command. Note that **audi** was used in line 178.

184  **Benedictus Altissimus:** Supply **sit** – *Blessed be the Lord Almighty.*

190  **habetis:** again, the plural for the singular. (Cf. line 103 and **vos** in line 192.)

191  **eciam** = **etiam:** *yes.*

200  **exi foras:** *go outside.*

---

**cella, -ae** (*f*), chamber, hut

**maledictus, -a, -um,** accursed

**dyabolus, -i** (*m*), the devil

**caelum, -i** (*n*), heaven

**recordor** (1), to remember

**crux, crucis** (*f*), cross

**finio** (4), to finish

**praecipue,** especially

**erigo** (3), to erect, set up

**honorifice,** with respect

**camera, -ae** (*f*), hall, chamber

**intime,** carefully

**assimilor** (1), to be like

**penitus,** completely

**foras,** outside

165 celle sue pulsavit. at ille: "quis est qui ibi pulsat?" qui
dixit: "ego sum Iovinianus imperator. aperi michi fenestram ut loquar tecum!"

ille vero cum vocem eius audisset, aperuit fenestram et,
cum eum vidisset, statim cum impetu fenestram clausit et
170 ait: "discede a me, maledicte! tu non es imperator, sed
dyabolus in specie hominis." ille hec audiens ad terram
pre dolore cecidit, crines capitis traxit et barbe, et lamen-
taciones usque ad celum dedit et dixit: "heu michi! quid
faciam? heu ego!" hoc dicto recordatus est quomodo
175 una nocte in stratu suo elevatum est cor eius et dixit:
"estne alter deus quam ego?"

pulsavit iterum ad fenestram heremite et dixit: "amore
illius qui pependit in cruce, audi confessionem meam!
saltem, si nolis fenestram aperire, clausa audias tamen
180 quousque finiero!" tunc de tota vita sua est confessus, et
precipue quomodo se contra Deum erexisset dicens quod
non crederet alium deum esse quam se ipsum.

facta confessione et absolucione, heremita fenestram
aperuit et statim noticiam eius habebat et ait: "Benedictus
185 Altissimus! iam noticiam tui habeo. paucas vestes hic
habeo. cito indue te et ad palacium tuum perge! ut
spero, omnes noticiam tui habebunt." imperator induit
se et ad palacium perrexit. ad ianuam pulsavit. ianitor
hostium apperuit et eum satis honorifice salutavit.

190 at ille: "numquid noticiam mei habetis?" qui ait:
"eciam, domine, peroptime. sed moror quod tota die hic
steti nec vidi vos exire." ille vero aulam intravit, et ecce
omnes capita inclinabant. sed alius imperator erat cum
domina in camera. quidam autem miles de camera exivit
195 et eum intime respexit, in cameram rediit et ait: "domine
mi, est quidam homo in aula cui omnes honorem faciunt,
qui tantum assimilatur vobis in omnibus, quod quis vestrum sit imperator penitus ignoramus."

imperator hec audiens ait imperatrici: "karissima
200 domina, exi foras et michi dic si noticiam eius habeas, et
michi renuncia!" illa vero foras exivit et, cum eum vidis-

241

*line*

203 **in periculo anime mee:** literally *in danger of my life,* i.e. *at risk to my life.*

205 **ex quo:** *since.*

    **discuciam = discutiam:** literally *I shall shake out,* i.e. *I shall reveal.*

211 **in celis:** Cf. line 173.

215 **unde:** *after which.*

217 **custos anime sue:** literally *the guardian of his soul,* i.e. *his conscience.*

219 **penitencia = paenitentia:** *penitence,* i.e. *penance,* the suffering he had to undergo to achieve repentance.

223 **occulis = oculis.**

224 **gracias = gratias:** *thanks.*

set, ammirabatur. statim cameram intravit et ait: "o domine, in periculo anime mee vobis unum dico, quod quis vestrum sit dominus meus penitus ignoro." at ille:
205 "ex quo sic est, foris pergam et veritatem discuciam."

cum aulam intrasset, eum per manum accepit et iuxta eum stare fecit et vocavit omnes nobiles in aula tunc existentes cum imperatrice et ait: "per iuramentum quod fecistis, dicite quis nostrum est imperator." imperatrix
210 primo respondit: "domine, michi incumbit primo respondere. testis est michi Deus in celis, quis vestrum sit dominus meus penitus ignoro!" et sic omnes dixerunt.

tunc ait ille qui de camera exivit: "audite me! iste homo est imperator vester et dominus; nam aliquo tem-
215 pore se contra Deum erexit, unde omnis noticia hominum ab eo recessit, quousque satisfaccionem Deo fecit. ego vero sum angelus eius, custos anime sue, qui imperium suum custodivi quamdiu penitenciam sustinuit. iam penitencia est completa et pro delictis suis satisfecit quia,
220 ut vidistis, illum ad caudas equi trahi feci." hiis dictis ait: "ammodo sitis ei obedientes! ad Deum vos recommendo."

statim ab occulis eorum disparuit. imperator vero gracias Deo reddidit et post hec omni tempore vite sue in
225 bona pace vixit et spiritum Deo tradidit.

---

**foris,** outside
**veritas, -atis** (*f*), truth
**existo** (3), to be
**michi incumbit,** it is
  incumbent upon me,
  it is my duty
**angelus, -i** (*m*),
  messenger, angel

**anima, -ae** (*f*), soul
**quamdiu,** as long as
**sustineo** (2), to bear,
  undergo, endure
**delictum, -i** (*n*), crime,
  offence
**satisfacio** (3), to make
  amends
**spiritus, -us** (*m*), soul

*line*

1 **vir beatus:** *the saint.*

2 **necesse habuit:** *he found it necessary.*

   **ad cuius ripam:** Take as one phrase.

3 **misellum homunculum:** Both of these words are diminutives (= **miserum hominem**). They are used here to express pity for the plight of the "poor fellow." (Cf. **contuli** in line 29, and **navicula** in line 31.)

4 **ut ferebant:** *as (they) said* or *according to what (they) said*

5 **quaedam** agrees with **bestia.**

   **paulo ante nantem:** Take with **quem.**

7 **sero licet:** *although too late.*

8 **praeripuere** = **praeripuerunt.**

# 73
# The Loch Ness Monster

The following extract is taken from Adamnan's Life of St Columba who in the 6th century AD brought Christianity across from Ireland to the west of Scotland and founded a monastery on the island of Iona where he died in AD 597. Adamnan lived in the 7th century AD.

cum vir beatus in Pictorum provincia per aliquot mora-
retur dies, necesse habuit fluvium transire Nesam.  ad
cuius cum accessisset ripam, alios ex accolis aspicit misellum humantes homunculum.  quem, ut ipsi sepultores
5  ferebant, quaedam paulo ante nantem aquatilis praeri-
piens bestia morsu momordit saevissimo.  cuius miserum
cadaver, sero licet, quidam in alno subvenientes porrectis
praeripuere uncinis.
    vir e contra beatus haec audiens praecipit ut aliquis ex
10  comitibus enatans caupulum, in altera stantem ripa, ad se
navigando reducat.  quo sancti audito viri praecepto,
Lugneus Mocumin nihil moratus obsecundans, depositis
excepta vestimentis tunica, immittit se in aquas.

**aliquot,** several
**fluvius, -i** (*m*), river
**accola, -ae** (*m*), one
    who lives near by,
    native
**aspicio** (3), to behold, see
**humo** (1), to bury
**no** (1), to swim
**aquatilis, -is, -e,** living
    in water
**praeripio** (3), to snatch
    and carry off
**morsus, -us** (*m*), bite

**mordeo** (2), to bite
**alnus, -i** (*m*), little boat
**subvenio** (4), to come to
    help
**uncinus, -i** (*m*), a hook
**e contra,** however
**enato** (1), to swim out
**caupulus, -i** (*m*), a small
    boat
**sanctus, -a, -um,** holy
**praeceptum, -i** (*n*),
    order
**obsecundo** (1), to obey

14 **non tam satiata quam in praedam accensa:** literally *not so much satiated as roused to plunder*, i.e. *with its appetite not so much satisfied as whetted for (another) kill.*

16 **turbatam supra aquam:** *that the water above had been disturbed.*

17 **in medio alveo:** The noun **alveus** is used for anything "hollow." Here it is used to describe the hollow channel of the river. Translate *in midstream.*

18 **cucurrit:** Although **currere** normally means *to run*, it can be used of an swift movement.

19 **omnibus qui inerant:** *all who were present.*

   **tam barbaris quam etiam fratribus:** *natives as well as members of his brotherhood.* The word "friars" is derived from **fratres.** Translate *natives and brothers alike.*

21 **salutare** is an adjective agreeing with **signum.** The basic idea of **salutari** is *bringing safety* **(salus).** Translate *the saving sign (of the cross).*

23 **noles:** future tense used as a command. (Cf. the Ten Commandments.)

   **tangas:** present subjunctive used to express a command.

24 **citius:** *quickly.*

   **revertere = reverteris,** *you will turn back.*

25 **ac si:** *as if.*

26 **velociori recursu:** *with a swifter retreat,* i.e. than its attack had been. Translate *more swiftly.*

27 **eo usque appropinquavit:** *approached so close.*

28 **inter:** preposition governing both **hominem** and **bestiam.**

32 **glorificaverunt Deum in beato viro:** *glorified God (as revealed) in the blessed man.*

33 **et:** *even.*

sed belua, quae prius non tam satiata quam in praedam
15 accensa in profundo fluminis latitabat, sentiens eo nante
turbatam supra aquam, subito emergens, natatilis ad
hominem in medio natantem alveo, cum ingenti fremitu,
aperto cucurrit ore.

vir tum beatus videns, omnibus qui inerant tam bar-
20 baris quam etiam fratribus nimio terrore perculsis, cum
salutare sancta elevata manu in vacuo aere crucis pinx-
isset signum, invocato Dei nomine, feroci imperavit
bestiae dicens: "noles ultra progredi, nec hominem tangas, retro citius revertere!"

25 tum vero bestia, hac Sancti audita voce, retrorsum, ac si
funibus retraheretur, velociori recursu fugit tremefacta.
quae prius Lugneo nanti eo usque appropinquavit ut
hominem inter et bestiam non amplius esset quam unius
contuli longitudo.

30 fratres tum, recessisse videntes bestiam Lugneumque
commilitonem ad eos intactum et incolumem in navicula
reversum, cum ingenti admiratione glorificaverunt Deum
in beato viro. sed et gentiles barbari, qui ad praesens
inerant, eiusdem miraculi magnitudine (quod et ipsi
35 viderant) compulsi Deum magnificaverunt Christian-
orum.

**profundum, -i** *(n)*, the
depths
**latito** (1), to lie in
hiding, lurk
**turbo** (1), to disturb
**natatilis, -is, -e,**
swimming
**fremitus, -us** *(m)*, a
roar(ing)
**nimius, -a, -um,**
excessive, very great
**percello** (3), to strike
(with consternation)
**elevo** (1), to raise
**aer, aeris** *(m)*, the air
**crux, crucis** *(f)*, cross

**pingo** (3), to draw
**ultra,** beyond, farther
**retro,** back
**retrorsum,** backwards
**funis, -is** *(m)*, rope
**tremefacio** (3), to terrify
**contulus, -i** *(m)*, a (little)
pole
**longitudo, -inis** *(f)*,
length
**commilito, -onis** *(m)*,
comrade
**navicula, -ae** *(f)*, small
boat
**gentilis, -is, -e,** heathen
**ad praesens,** at the time

# The Vulgate

Christianity became the official religion of the Roman Empire as the result of the decree issued in AD 325 by the Emperor Constantine after his conversion to Christianity. For roughly two centuries before then, however, that religion had been spreading throughout the Empire.

The Old Testament was originally written in Hebrew, the New Testament in Greek. The Old Testament had already been translated into Greek, and Greek became the main language of the early Church. Later on, Latin translations of both Testaments were produced from the Greek versions.

These Old Latin versions were unsatisfactory in several respects, however, and in AD 382 Pope Damasus commissioned St Jerome, the leading biblical scholar of the day, to produce a new Latin version of the entire Scriptures, which would be used universally within the Church. For this reason, it was called the **Editio Vulgata.** (The Latin verb **vulgare** means "to make public" and is from the same root as **vulgus**.) St Jerome went to Bethlehem to learn Hebrew so that he could make his translation of the Old Testament direct from the original language.

St Jerome's translation of the Scriptures, which was known as the Vulgate, became the official text of the Western Church but, since manuscripts had to be copied by hand, many mistakes were made over the centuries, and these errors were multiplied as more and more copies were made from faulty originals. Later scholars made various individual attempts at correcting these mistakes, but they did not have the original text available since it had been lost. Many more different versions were therefore produced and those also suffered from faulty copying by scribes and from further suggested amendments by other scholars, so that by the 16th century there were very many different versions of St Jerome's text. Even today, there are in existence more than 8000 Vulgate MSS.

In the latter half of the 16th century, therefore, Pope Clement VIII ordered a revision of the Vulgate which was published in AD 1593 and remained as the authorised text of the Roman Catholic Church until the vernacular was introduced after the Vatican II Council in 1963.

"The road from Jerusalem to Jericho" (Luke chapter 10, verse 30).
*(Photo: The Torrance Collection, University Library, Dundee)*

3 **in lege:** This refers to the religious laws by which the Jews governed their lives.

5 **diliges:** The future tense is used with the force of a command. (Cf. Chap. 73, line 23.)

7 **proximum** here means *neighbour*.

12 **in Hiericho:** *to Jericho*. Neither **Hiericho** nor **Hierusalem** declines.

16 **Levita:** Levites were priests in the Jewish church, but less important in rank than the **sacerdos** mentioned in the previous paragraph.

18 **Samaritanus:** The religion of the people of Samaria was slightly different from Judaism. The Samaritans tended to be despised by the orthodox Jews.

21 **iumentum:** In such a rugged country, where there were few roads, the handiest form of transport was on the back of an animal such as a mule. Most people walked.

**stabulum:** Although this gives us our word "stable", it is used of any place where one could stop. It is derived from **stare**.

22 **altera die:** *on the next day*. **alter** is frequently used in the sense *second*.
**denarios:** This was one of the more valuable coins in currency then.

---

**lex, legis** (*f*), law
**peritus, -a, -um**
 (*+ gen.*), skilled (in)
**possideo** (2), to possess
**lego** (3), to read
**diligo** (3), to love
**cor, cordis** (*n*), heart
**anima, -ae** (*f*), soul
**mens, mentis** (*f*), mind
**proximus, -a, -um,**
 nearest
**suscipio** (3), to take up,
 answer
**plaga, -ae** (*f*), blow
**sacerdos, -otis** (*m*),
 priest

**secus** ( *+ acc.*), beside
**misericordia, -ae** (*f*),
 pity
**alligo** (1), to bind
**oleum, -i** (*n*), oil
**iumentum, -i** (*n*), beast
 of burden, mule
**stabulum, -i** (*n*), inn
**profero,** to bring out
**denarius, -i** (*m*), silver
 coin
**supererogo** (1), to spend
 in addition
**vado** (3), to go

# 74

# Two Extracts from The Vulgate

## (a) The Good Samaritan

et ecce quidam legis peritus surrexit temptans illum et dicens: "magister, quid faciendo vitam aeternam possidebo?" at ille ei dixit: "in lege quid scriptum est? quomodo legis?"

5    ille respondens dixit: "diliges Dominum tuum ex toto corde tuo et ex tota anima tua et ex omnibus viribus tuis et ex omni mente tua; et proximum tuum sicut te ipsum."

dixitque illi: "recte respondisti. hoc fac et vives!" ille autem, volens iustificare se ipsum, dixit: "et quis est meus 10 proximus?"

suscipiens autem Iesus dixit: "homo quidam descendebat ab Hierusalem in Hiericho, et incidit in latrones qui etiam despoliaverunt eum et, plagis impositis, abierunt semivivo relicto.

15    "accidit autem ut sacerdos quidam descenderet eadem via et, viso illo, praeteriit. similiter et Levita, cum esset secus locum et videret eum, pertransiit.

"Samaritanus autem quidam iter faciens venit secus eum et videns eum misericordia motus est. et appropin-
20 quans alligavit vulnera eius, infundens oleum et vinum. et imponens eum in iumentum suum duxit in stabulum et curam eius egit. et altera die protulit duos denarios et dedit stabulario et ait: 'curam illius habe! et quodcunque supererogaveris, ego, cum rediero, reddam tibi'.

25    "quis horum trium videtur tibi proximus fuisse illi qui incidit in latrones?"

at ille dixit: "qui fecit misericordiam in illum." et ait illi Iesus: "vade et tu fac similiter!"

Luke, Chapter 10, verses 25–37

### (b) St Peter Denies his Master

comprehendentes autem eum duxerunt ad domum
principis sacerdotum.  Petrus vero sequebatur a longe.
accenso autem igni in medio atrio, et circumsedentibus
illis, erat Petrus in medio eorum.

5   quem cum vidisset ancilla quaedam sedentem ad lumen
et eum fuisset intuita, dixit: "et hic cum illo erat."  at ille
negavit eum, dicens: "mulier, non novi illum."
  et post pusillum alius videns eum dixit: "et tu de illis
es."  Petrus vero ait: "o homo, non sum."

10   et intervallo facto quasi horae unius, alius quidam af-
firmabat, dicens: "vere et hic cum illo erat, nam et
Galilaeus est."  et ait Petrus: "homo, nescio quid dicis."
  et continuo, adhuc illo loquente, cantavit gallus. et conversus Dominus respexit Petrum.  et recordatus est

15   Petrus verbi Domini, sicut dixit: "priusquam gallus can-
tet, ter me negabis."  et egressus foras Petrus flevit amare.

Luke Chapter 22, verses 54–62

**comprehendo** (3), to
  seize
**accendo** (3), to light
**lumen, -inis** (*n*), light,
  fire
**intueor** (2), to look at
**novi, novisse,** to know
**post pusillum,** soon
  after

**continuo,** immediately
**gallus, -i** (*m*), cock
**recordor** (1) ( + *gen.*),
  to recall, remember
**ter,** three times
**foras,** outside
**fleo** (2), to weep
**amare,** bitterly

---

1 **eum** refers to Jesus.

**principis sacerdotum:** literally *of the chief of the priests,* i.e. *of the high
priest.*

3 **igni** is ablative case.

6 **fuisset intuita = esset intuita.**

# Vocabulary

N.B. Where only the Present Indicative Active and the Group number of verbs have been given, you will find that the endings of the present infinitive, the perfect indicative active and the supine (where they exist) follow the set patterns for Principal Parts: *Group 1:* **-o, -are, -avi, -atum**
*Group 2:* **-eo, -ere, -ui, -itum**
*Group 4:* **-io, -ire, -ivi, -itum**

## A

**a, ab** (+ *abl.*), by, from, away from
  **a fronte,** at the front, in front
  **a lateribus,** on the flanks
  **a tergo,** in the rear, from behind
**abditus, -a, -um,** hidden
**abeo, -ire, -ii, -itum,** to go away, leave
**abicio** (3), **-ieci, -iectum,** to throw, throw away
**ablatum,** *see* **aufero**
**abnego** (1), to refuse, deny
**abripio** (3), **-ripui, -reptum,** to carry off
  **se abripere,** to rush off
**abscedo** (3), **-cessi, -cessum,** to depart, go away
**abscondo** (3), **-condi, -conditum,** to hide, conceal
**abstuli,** *see* **aufero**
**absum, abesse, afui,** to be away, be distant from
**abutor** (3), **-usus sum** (+ *abl.*), to abuse, take advantage of, exhaust
**ac,** and
**accedo** (3), **-cessi, -cessum,** to approach, come up to
  **accedit,** it is added
**accidit** (3), **accidit,** to happen
**accipio** (3), **-cepi, -ceptum,** to receive, take, get, suffer, sustain
**accola, -ae** (*m*), inhabitant, one who lives near
**accommodo** (1), to fit
**accubo** (1), **-cubui, -cubitum,** to sit, recline at table
**accurro** (3), **-curri, -cursum,** to run towards, run up to
**accusator, -oris** (*m*), accuser
**accuso** (1), to accuse
**acer, acris, acre,** fierce, spirited
**acies, aciei** (*f*), line of battle, battle
  **aciem instruere,** to draw up a line of battle
**acriter,** fiercely
**actuarius, -a, -um,** swift
**actum,** *see* **ago**
**ad** (+ *acc.*), to, at, near, towards, for, with a view to
**addo** (3), **-didi, -ditum,** to add

**adduco** (3), **-duxi, -ductum,** to lead on, bring
**adeo,** to such a degree, so much, so
**adeo, -ire, -ii, -itum,** to go to, approach
**adfero,** *see* **affero**
**adhaereo** (2), **-haesi, -haesum,** to stick to
**adhortator, -oris** (*m*), encourager
**adhortor** (1), **-atus sum,** to encourage
**adhuc,** still, as yet
**adiaceo** (2), **-iacui,** to lie near
**adicio** (3), **-ieci, -iectum,** to add
**adigo** (3), **-egi, -actum,** to hurl
**adimo** (3), **-emi, -emptum** (+ *dat.*), to take away (from)
**adipiscor** (3), **adeptus sum,** to obtain
**aditus, -us** (*m*), approach, landing-place
**adiutor, -oris** (*m*), helper
**adiuvo** (1), **-iuvi, -iutum,** to help
**administro** (1), to carry out, perform
**admirationi esse** (+ *dat.*), to be a cause of wonder/amazement (to)
**admitto** (3), **-misi, -missum,** to commit
**admodum,** about, very, exceedingly
**adnato** (1), to swim towards
**adnoto** (1), to note, comment upon
**adorior** (4), **adortus sum,** to attack
**adscisco** (3), **-scivi, -scitum,** to attach
**adspicio** (3), **-spexi, -spectum,** to look at, observe
**adstantes, -ium** (*m.pl*), bystanders
**adsum, adesse, adfui,** to be here, be present, be near, attend
**adsurgo** (3), **-surrexi, -surrectum,** to rise up
**adulescens, -entis** (*m*), young man
**adulterium, -i** (*n*), adultery
**adultus, -a, -um,** grown up, mature
**advenio** (4), **-veni, -ventum,** to reach, arrive, come to
**advento** (1), to approach
**adventus, -us** (*m*), arrival
**adversus** (+ *acc.*), against
**adversus, -a, -um,** facing, opposite, from the front
  **ex adverso,** opposite
  **adverso colle,** uphill
  **adverso flumine,** upstream
**advesperascit** (3), **-avit,** to grow dark

**advoco** (1), to call to, summon
**advolo** (1), to fly to, swoop down on
**aedificium, -i** (*n*), building
**aedifico** (1), to build
**aedilis, -is** (*m*), aedile
**aeger, aegra, aegrum**, sick, ill
**aegre**, with difficulty
**aequalis, -is, -e**, of the same age
   **aequales, -ium** (*m.pl*), companions
**aeque**, equally
**aes, aeris** (*n*), bronze
**aestas, -atis** (*f*), summer
**aestuans, -antis**, inflamed
**aestuarium, -i** (*n*), creek, channel, estuary
**aestus, -us** (*m*), tide
**aetas, -atis** (*f*), age
**aeternus, -a, -um**, everlasting
**aevum, -i** (*n*), age, time
**affero, -ferre, attuli, allatum**, to bring
**afficio** (3), **-feci, -fectum**, to affect, treat,
   fill, influence
   **affectus, -a, -um**, weak, weakened
**affirmo** (1), to affirm, claim, declare
**affixus, -a, -um**, fastened, fixed
**ager, agri** (*m*), field, district, territory
**agger, -eris** (*m*), rampart
**agmen, -inis** (*n*), line of march, (army)
   column
   **novissimum agmen**, rear, rearguard
   **primum agmen**, vanguard
   **quam citatissimo agmine**, with the
   greatest possible speed
**agnosco** (3), **-novi, -nitum**, to recognise
**ago** (3), **egi, actum**, to do, carry, drive,
   spend (time), discuss
   **quid agis?** What are you up to?
**agrestis, -is, -e**, wild, rustic
**ait, aiunt**, (he, she) says, said; they say,
   said
**ala, -ae** (*f*), wing
**alacritas, -atis** (*f*), keenness
**albus, -a, -um**, white
**alibi**, elsewhere
**alienus, -a, -um**, of another, of others
**alioqui**, otherwise
**aliquando**, at some time or other, at long
   last
**aliquanto post**, sometime later
**aliquantum**, considerable
**aliquis, -quis, -quid**, someone, something
**aliquo**, somewhere, to some place or other
**aliquot**, several
**alius, alia, aliud**, other, another, different
   **alii ... alii ...**, some ... others ...
**allatum**, *see* **affero**
**alligo** (1), to tie to, bind to
**Alpinus, -a, -um**, Alpine
**alter, -era, -erum**, the one, the other, the
   second

**alter ... alter ...**, the one ... the other
**altitudo, -inis** (*f*), height, depth
**altum, -i** (*n*), deep water, the deep
**altus, -a, -um**, high, deep
**alveus, -i** (*m*), small (hollowed-out) boat
**ambo, ambae, ambo**, both
**ambulo** (1), to walk
**ambustus, -a, -um**, burnt, scorched
**amentia, -ae** (*f*), madness
**amentum, -i** (*n*), thong
**amicitia, -ae** (*f*), friendship
**amicus, -i** (*m*), friend
**amitto** (3), **-misi, -missum**, to lose
**amnis, -is** (*m*), river
**amo** (l), to love, like
**amoenitas, -atis** (*f*), beauty, charm (of
   scenery)
**amphitheatrum, -i** (*n*), amphitheatre
**amplector** (3), **amplexus sum**, to embrace
**amplitudo, -inis** (*f*), size, stoutness, bulk
**amplius**, more, more (than)
**amputo** (1), to cut off
**an**, whether, if
**anceps, ancipitis**, two-headed, double
**ancora, -ae** (*f*), anchor
**angustiae, -arum** (*f.pl*), narrows,
   (mountain) pass, defile
**angustus, -a, -um**, narrow
**anima, -ae** (*f*), breath, soul
**animadverto** (3), **-verti, -versum**, to notice
**animal, -alis** (*n*), animal
**animus, -i** (*m*), mind, attitude, spirit, will,
   desire, temper
   **in animo habere**, to intend
**annus, -i** (*m*), year
**ante** ( + *acc.*), before, in front of
**antea**, before, previously, formerly
**antequam**, before
**antiquus, -a, -um**, ancient, very old
**aperte**, openly
**apertus, -a, -um**, open, exposed
**appareo** (2), to appear, be obvious
**apparo** (1), to prepare
**appello** (1), to call, name
**appropinquo** (1) ( + *dat.*), to approach,
   draw near (to)
**apte**, suitably
**apto** (1), to fit on, get ready
**aptus, -a, -um**, suitable
**apud** ( + *acc.*), among, at the house of, at,
   on, with
**aqua, -ae** (*f*), water
**aquila, -ae** (*f*), eagle, standard
**aquilifer, -i** (*m*), standard-bearer
**ara, -ae** (*f*), altar
**arator, -oris** (*m*), farmer
**arbiter, -tri** (*m*), umpire, judge
**arbitror** (1), **-atus sum**, to think, consider
**arbor, -oris** (*f*), tree

**arceo** (2), **arcui,** to keep away, exclude
**arcesso** (3), **-ivi, -itum,** to send for, summon
**ardor, -oris** (*m*), eagerness
**area, -ae** (*f*), courtyard
**argentum, -i** (*n*), silver
**aridus, -a, -um,** dry
**arma, -orum** (*n.pl*), arms, weapons
**armatura, -ae** (*f*), armour, equipment
**armatus, -a, -um,** armed
**armiger, -eri** (*m*), armour-bearer
**armo** (1), to arm
**arripio** (3), **-ripui, -reptum,** to snatch, seize
**ars, artis** (*f*), art, cunning, trick
**artificium, -i** (*n*), workmanship
**artus, -a, -um,** narrow
**arx, arcis** (*f*), citadel, fortress
**ascendo** (3), **-scendi, -scensum,** to climb, get up
**ascensus, -us** (*m*), ascent
**aspectus, -us** (*m*), sight, appearance
**asper, -era, -erum,** rough, desperate
**aspernor** (1), **-atus sum,** to reject, spurn
**asporto** (1), to carry off
**assido** (3), **-sedi,** to sit down beside
**astra, -orum** (*n.pl*), stars
**astutia, -ae** (*f*), cleverness, shrewdness
**astutus, -a, -um,** clever, cunning
**at,** but
**ater, atra, atrum,** black, dark
**Athenae, -arum** (*f.pl*), Athens
**atque,** and
**atqui,** and yet, however
**atrocitas, -atis** (*f*), brutality
**atrociter,** fiercely
**attendo** (3), **-tendi, -tentum,** to pay attention to, listen to
**attero** (3), **-trivi, -tritum,** to wear away, exhaust
**attexo** (3), **-texui, -textum,** to weave on, add by weaving
**attingo** (3), **-tigi, -tactum,** to touch, border on, reach
**attuli,** *see* **affero**
**auctor, -oris** (*m*), instigator, author
**auctoritas. -atis** (*f*), influence
**audacia, -ae** (*f*), daring, courage
**audacter,** boldly
**audax, -acis,** bold
**audens, -entis,** bold, daring
**audeo** (2), **ausus sum,** to dare
**audio** (4), to hear, listen, listen to
**aufero, -ferre, abstuli, ablatum,** to take away
**augeo** (2), **auxi, auctum,** to increase
**auris, -is** (*f*), ear
**aurum, -i** (*n*), gold
**aut,** or
  **aut ... aut ...,** either ... or ...

**autem,** however, but, now, moreover, on the other hand
**auxilia, -orum** (*n.pl*), reinforcements
**auxilium, -i** (*n*), help, assistance
  **auxilio esse** ( + *dat.*), to be of assistance (to), help
**avarus, -a, -um,** greedy
**averto** (3), **-verti, -versum,** to turn away, outflank
**avunculus, -i** (*m*), uncle

**B**

**balneum, -i** (*n*), bath
**balteus, -i** (*m*), belt
**barba, -ae** (*f*), beard
**barbarus, -a, -um,** savage, uncivilised
**barbarus, -i** (*m*), barbarian
  **barbari, -orum** (*m.pl*), the natives
**beatus, -a, -um,** happy
**bello** (1), to make war, go to war
**bellum, -i** (*n*), war
  **bellum gerere,** to wage war
**belua, -ae** (*f*), beast
**bene,** well
**beneficium, -i** (*n*), act of kindness, favour
**benigne,** kindly.
**bestia, -ae** (*f*), beast
**bibo** (3), **bibi,** to drink
**biduum, -i** (*n*), (period of) two days
**biennium, -i** (*n*), (period of) two years
**bona, -orum** (*n.pl*), property, possessions
**boni, -orum** (*m.pl*), the good (citizens), patriots
**bonus, -a, -um,** good
  **bono esse** ( + *dat.*), to be of advantage (to), benefit
**bracae, -arum** (*f.pl*), leather trousers
**brevis, -is, -e,** short
**brevitas, -atis** (*f*), shortness
**breviter,** briefly
**Britanni, -orum** (*m.pl*), Britons
**Britannia, -ae** (*f*), Britain
**bulla, -ae** (*f*), lucky charm, locket

**C**

**cadaver, -eris** (*n*), corpse, body
**cado** (3), **cecidi, casum,** to fall
**caecus, -a, -um,** blind
**caedes, -is** (*f*), slaughter, murder, death
**caedo** (3), **cecidi, caesum,** to kill, cut down, slash at, beat
**caelum, -i** (*n*), heaven, sky
**caementum, -i** (*n*), cement, mortar
**caespes, -pitis** (*m*), turf, sod of grass
**caetra, -ae** (*f*), shield
**calcar, -aris** (*n*), spur
**calceus, -i** (*m*), shoe

**calidus, -a, -um,** hot
**caligae, -arum** (*f.pl*), boots
**caligo, -inis** (*f*), mist, vapour, fumes
**calo, -onis** (*m*), camp-follower
**calor, -oris** (*m*), heat
**campester, -tris, -tre,** on level ground
**campus, -i** (*m*), plain, ground
**candidus, -a, -um,** white
**canto** (1), to sing
**cantus, -us** (*m*), song, singing
**capax, -acis,** roomy
**capesso** (3), **-ivi, -itum,** to seize, snatch at
**capilli, -orum** (*m.pl*), hair
**capio** (3), **cepi, captum,** to take, capture, seize
   **consilium capere,** to form (adopt) a plan
**Capreae, -arum** (*f.pl*), Capri
**captivus, -i** (*m*), prisoner
**caput, -itis** (*n*), head, capital
   **capitis condemnare,** to condemn to death
**careo** (2) ( + *abl*.), to lack, be free (from)
**carmen, -inis** (*n*), song, hymn
**carrus, -i** (*m*), (baggage) cart, wagon
**carus, -a, -um,** dear, precious, esteemed
**casa, -ae** (*f*), hut
**castellum, -i** (*n*), castle, fortress, fort
**castigo** (1), to rebuke, reprimand
**castra, -orum** (*n.pl*), camp
   **castra ponere,** to pitch camp
**casu,** by chance
**casus, -us** (*m*), fall
**catena, -ae** (*f*), chain
**cauda, -ae** (*f*), tail
**causa, -ae** (*f*), cause, reason
   **causa indicta,** without a trial
**causa** ( + *gen*.), for the sake of
**caute,** cautiously
**caveo** (2), **cavi, cautum,** to take care, beware of
**cavo** (1), to hollow out
**cecidi,** *see* **cado** and **caedo**
**cedo** (3), **cessi, cessum,** to yield, give way, withdraw, move back
**celebro** (1), to make famous, praise
**celeritas, -atis** (*f*), speed
**celeriter,** quickly
**cena, -ae** (*f*), dinner
**centum,** hundred
**centuria, -ae** (*f*), century, company of 100 soldiers (See p. 39.)
**centurio, -onis** (*m*), centurion
**cepi,** *see* **capio**
**cera, -ae** (*f*), wax, wax-tablet
**cerno** (3), **crevi, cretum,** to perceive
**certamen, -inis** (*n*), contest, competition
**certe,** at least, certainly, surely
**certus, -a, -um,** certain, definite

**certiorem facere,** to inform
**cervical, -alis** (*n*), pillow
**cessi,** *see* **cedo**
**cesso** (1), to stop, give over, hesitate
**ceteri, -ae, -a,** the rest, the others
**ceterum,** but, however
**Christus, -i** (*m*), Christ
**cibus, -i** (*m*), food
**cingo** (3), **cinxi, cinctum,** to surround
**cinis, cineris** (*m*), ash, cinders
**circa** ( + *acc*.), around
**circiter,** about
**circuitus, -us** (*m*), a way round, circuit, circumference
**circum** ( + *acc*.), round, around
**circumcido** (3), **-cidi, -cisum,** to cut (all) round
**circumduco** (3), **-duxi, -ductum,** to lead around
**circumeo, -ire, -ii, -itum,** to go round, surround
**circumfero, -ferre, -tuli, -latum,** to carry round
**circumfundo** (3), **-fudi, -fusum,** to pour round, surround
**circumiaceo** (2), **-iacui,** to lie around
**circumlatum,** *see* **circumfero**
**Circumpadanus, -a, -um,** of the Po valley
**circumsisto** (3), **-steti,** to surround
**circumspecto** (1), to look round
**circumsto** (1), **-steti,** to stand round, surround
**circumtuli,** *see* **circumfero**
**circumvenio** (4), **-veni, -ventum,** to surround, catch, trap
**cito,** quickly
**civis, -is** (*m*), citizen
**civitas, -atis** (*f*), state, city, people, citizens
**clades, -is** (*f*), defeat, disaster
**clam,** secretly, without being seen
**clamo** (1), to shout, cry, call
**clamor, -oris** (*m*), shout, shouting, noise
**claritas, -atis** (*f*), brightness
**clarus, -a, -um,** clear, famous, distinguished
**classis, -is** (*f*), fleet
**claudo** (3), **clausi, clausum,** to shut, shut in, close, block, enclose
**clava, -ae** (*f*), club, cudgel
**clavis, -is** (*f*), key
**clementer,** quietly, gently
**coacervo** (1), to pile up
**coactum,** *see* **cogo**
**codicilli, -orum** (*m.pl*), note(s)
**coegi,** *see* **cogo**
**coemo** (3), **-emi, -emptum,** to buy up, purchase
**coepi, -isse,** I began

**coeo, -ire, -ii, -itum,** to assemble, gather

**coetus, -us** (*m*), assembly, meeting

**cogito** (1), to think, ponder over

**cognitio, -onis** (*f*), inquiry

**cognosco** (3), **-novi, -nitum,** to learn, to find out, recall to mind

**cogo** (3), **coegi, coactum,** to force, compel, collect, assemble

**cohaereo** (2), **-haesi, -haesum,** to stick together, associate with

**cohors, -ortis** (*f*), cohort
**cohors praetoria,** the governor's staff

**cohortatio, -onis** (*f*), encouragement

**cohortor** (1), **-atus sum,** to exhort, encourage

**coicio** (3), **-ieci, -iectum,** to throw

**collatum,** *see* **confero**

**colligo** (3), **-legi, -lectum,** to collect, gather

**collis, -is** (*m*), hill, cliff

**colloco** (1), to station, place, arrange, deploy

**colloquor** (3), **-locutus sum,** to converse with, talk

**collusor, -oris** (*m*), playmate

**colo** (3), **colui, cultum,** to dwell, inhabit

**colonia, -ae** (*f*), colony, community, settlement, township

**color, -oris** (*m*), colour

**comburo** (3), **-bussi, -bustum,** to burn completely

**comes, -itis** (*m*), companion, comrade

**comitantes, -ium** (*m.pl*), companions, comrades

**comitatus, -us** (*m*), retinue

**comitium, -i** (*n*), (place of) assembly
**comitia, -orum** (*n.pl*), elections

**commeatus, -us** (*m*), supplies, provisions

**commemoro** (1), to mention, relate

**comminus,** at close quarters

**committo** (3), **-misi, -missum,** to entrust
**proelium committere,** to join battle

**commoror** (1), **-atus sum,** to delay

**commotus, -a, -um,** upset, excited, moved

**commoveo** (2), **-movi, -motum,** to move

**communio** (4), to fortify

**communis, -is, -e,** common
**in commune,** together, among themselves

**commutatio, -onis** (*f*), change

**comparo** (1), to get ready, obtain, acquire

**compello** (3), **-puli, -pulsum,** to drive

**comperio** (4), **-peri, -pertum,** to find out, ascertain

**compes, -edis** (*f*), shackle

**competo** (3), **-ivi, -itum,** to be capable

**complector** (3), **-plexus sum,** to embrace

**compleo** (2), **-evi, -etum,** to fill, complete

**complures, -es, -a,** several

**comporto** (1), to collect, gather together

**comprehendo** (3), **-endi, -ensum,** to seize, arrest

**comprimo** (3), **-pressi, -pressum,** to check, choke, suppress

**compuli,** *see* **compello**

**conatus, -us** (*m*), attempt

**concedo** (3), **-cessi, -cessum,** to yield, withdraw, concede, grant permission

**concerpo** (3), **-cerpsi, -cerptum,** to pick up, gather

**concido** (3), **-cidi,** to fall, collapse

**concito** (1), to rouse, stir up, cause

**conclamo** (1), to shout

**concurro** (3), **-curri, -cursum,** to run together, rush up

**concursus, -us** (*m*), rushing together, rallying

**concutio** (3), **-cussi, -cussum,** to shake

**condemno** (1), to condemn
**capitis condemnare,** to condemn to death

**condicio, -onis** (*f*), condition, term(s)

**condo** (3), **-didi, -ditum,** to found, bury, lay (a ghost)

**conduco** (3), **-duxi, -ductum,** to hire, rent

**confectus, -a, -um,** worn out, exhausted

**confero, -ferre, -tuli, collatum,** to confer, bestow

**confertus, -a, -um,** closely packed, crowded, thick

**confestim,** quickly, immediately

**conficio** (3), **-feci, -fectum,** to finish, exhaust completely

**confido** (3), **-fisus sum** ( + *dat*.), to trust, be confident

**confirmo** (1), to establish, confirm, pledge

**confiteor** (2), **-fessus sum,** to confess

**confluo** (3), **-fluxi,** to flock together

**confusus, -a, -um,** bewildered, disordered

**congredior** (3), **-gressus sum,** to meet, come together

**congregor** (1), **-atus sum,** to assemble

**conicio** (3), **-ieci, -iectum,** to hurl, throw, guess

**coniungo** (3), **-iunxi, -iunctum,** to join (together)

**coniunx, -iugis** (*m/f*), husband/wife, spouse

**coniuratio, -onis** (*f*), conspiracy

**conor** (1), **-atus sum,** to try

**conscendo** (3), **-scendi, -scensum,** to board, go on board

**conscribo** (3), **-scripsi, -scriptum,** to enrol, conscript, recruit

**consecro** (1), to dedicate

**consensio, -onis** (*f*), agreement, unanimity

**consensus, -us** (*m*), agreement

**consido** (3), **-sedi, -sessum,** to sit down

**consilium, -i** (*n*), plan, advice, resourcefulness
  **consilium capere,** to form (adopt) a plan
**consisto** (3), **-stiti,** to stand, halt, take up a position
**consolor** (1), **-atus sum,** to console
**conspectus, -us** (*m*), sight
**conspicio** (3), **-spexi, -spectum,** to catch sight of
**conspicor** (1), **-atus sum,** to notice
**constantia, -ae** (*f*), courage, resolution, determination
**constat,** it is agreed
  **satis constat,** it is generally agreed
**consterno** (3), **-stravi, -stratum,** to strew, cover
**constituo** (3), **-ui, -utum,** to decide, fix, draw up, anchor
**constringo** (3), **-strinxi, -strictum,** to bind, tie
**consuesco** (3), **-suevi, -suetum,** to grow (become) accustomed
**consuetudo, -inis** (*f*), custom, experience
**consul, -is** (*m*), consul
**consularis, -is, -e,** of consular rank
**consulatus, -us** (*m*), consulship
**consulo** (3), **-sului, -sultum** (+ *acc.*), to consult, consider; (+ *dat.*) to look after, consult the interests of
**consultatio, -onis** (*f*), deliberation, consideration
**consulto** (1), to consult
**consultum (senatus),** a decree (of the senate)
**consumo** (3), **-sumpsi, -sumptum,** to spend, use up, consume, destroy
**consurgo** (3), **-surrexi, -surrectum,** to get up, rise
**contabulo** (1), to cover with boards
**contactum,** *see* **contingo**
**contagio, -onis** (*f*), infection, contact
**contendo** (3), **-tendi, -tentum,** to strive, hasten, fight
**contestor** (1), **-atus sum,** to call to witness
**continens, -entis,** continuous
**continenter,** continually
**contineo** (2), **-tinui, -tentum,** to confine, hold
**contingo** (3), **-tigi, -tactum,** to touch
**continuo,** immediately, forthwith
**contio, -onis** (*f*), meeting, assembly
**contra,** on the other hand
**contra** (+ *acc.*), opposite, against
**contraho** (3), **-traxi, -tractum,** to gather into one place, muster
**contrarius, -a, -um,** opposite, contrary
**convenio** (4), **-veni, -ventum,** to meet, assemble, gather, be acceptable, be agreed upon

**conventus, -us** (*m*), gathering, assembly, meeting, court of justice
**converto** (3), **-verti, -versum,** to turn
**convertor** (3), **-versus sum,** to turn (*intransitive*)
**convinco** (3), **-vici, -victum,** to prove
**convoco** (1), to call together, invite
**cooperio** (4), **-operui, -opertum,** to cover over
**coopertus, -a, -um,** covered
**coorior** (4), **coortus sum,** to arise, rise, break out
**copia, -ae** (*f*), supply, quantity, opportunity
  **copiae, -arum** (*f.pl*), forces
**copulo** (1), to join
**cornu, -us** (*n*), horn, wing (of an army)
**corona, -ae** (*f*), crown, garland
**corpus, -oris** (*n*), body
**corrigo** (3), **-rexi, -rectum,** to correct, reform
**corripio** (3), **-ripui, -reptum,** to chide, reprove, criticise, rebuke
**cotidianus, -a, -um,** daily
**cotidie,** daily, every day
**crassus, -a, -um,** dense
**cratis, -is** (*f*), hurdle, wicker-work
**creber, crebra, crebrum,** frequent
**crebresco** (3), **crebrui,** to grow frequent, increase
**credo** (3), **credidi, creditum** (+ *dat.*), to believe, entrust (to)
**creo** (1), to create, appoint, bear, give birth to
**cresco** (3), **crevi, cretum,** to grow, increase, develop
**crevi,** *see* **cresco**
**crimen, -inis** (*n*), charge, accusation
**cruciatus, -us** (*m*), torture
**crucio** (1), to torture
**crudelis, -is, -e,** cruel
**crudelitas, -atis,** (*f*), cruelty
**crus, cruris** (*n*), leg
**cubiculum, -i** (*n*), bedroom
**cucurri,** *see* **curro**
**culpa, -ae** (*f*), blame, guilt
**culter, -tri** (*m*), knife
**cultor, -oris** (*m*), inhabitant
**cum** (+ *abl.*), with
**cum** (+ *indic.*), when
**cum** (+ *subj.*), when, since, although
**cum ... tum ...,** both ... and ...
**cunctatio, -onis** (*f*), hesitation
**cunctor** (1), **-atus sum,** to hesitate, delay
**cunctus, -a, -um,** all (together)
**cupa, -ae** (*f*), tub, cask
**cupiditas, -atis** (*f*), desire, greed
**cupidus, -a, -um** (+ *gen.*), desirous (of), eager (to)

**cupio** (3), **-ivi, -itum,** to want, wish, be anxious to

**cur,** why

**cura, -ae** (*f*), care, anxiety
    **curae esse** ( + *dat.*), to be a cause of anxiety (to)

**Curia, -ae** (*f*), Senate-House

**curo** (1), to look after, attend to

**curro** (3), **cucurri, cursum,** to run

**cursus, -us** (*m*), running, pace, course

**custodio** (4), to guard

**custos, -odis** (*m*), guard

## D

**damno** (1), to condemn

**de** ( + *abl.*), about, from
    **de improviso,** unexpectedly
    **de industria,** deliberately
    **de integro,** afresh, anew

**debeo** (2), to have to, I ought

**debilis, -is, -e,** feeble, weakened

**decedo** (3), **-cessi, -cessum,** to withdraw, retreat

**decem,** ten

**decet,** it is right

**decimus, -a, -um,** tenth

**decipio** (3), **-cepi, -ceptum,** to deceive

**declaro** (1), to indicate

**declinatio, -onis** (*f*), swerve

**decumana porta,** gate at the rear of a camp, the main gate

**decurro** (3), **-(cu)curri, -cursum,** to run down

**dedecus, -oris** (*n*), disgrace
    **dedecori esse** ( + *dat.*), to be a cause for disgrace (to), bring shame (upon)

**dedi,** *see* **do**

**dedo** (3), **dedidi, deditum,** to hand over
    **se dedere,** to surrender

**deduco** (3), **-duxi, -ductum,** to bring, escort, launch

**defendo** (3), **-fendi, -fensum,** to defend, keep safe

**defero, -ferre, -tuli, -latum,** to carry away, confer, report, bring before
    **rem deferre,** to report the matter

**defessus, -a, -um,** weary, tired

**deficio** (3), **-feci, -fectum,** to fail, run out, disappear

**deflecto** (3), **-flexi, -flexum,** to turn aside

**defunctus, -a, -um,** dead

**dehisco** (3), to yawn, gape open

**deicio** (3), **-ieci, -iectum,** to cast down

**dein,** then

**deinceps,** thereafter, one after another, successively, in turn

**deinde,** then

**delatum,** *see* **defero**

**delecto** (1), to please, delight

**deleo** (2), **-evi, -etum,** to destroy

**delibero** (1), to consider well

**delicatus, -a, -um,** soft, tender, harmless

**deligo** (1), to tie, bind

**deligo** (3), **-legi, -lectum,** to choose, select

**delphinus, -i** (*m*), dolphin

**delubrum, -i** (*n*), shrine, sanctuary

**demergo** (3), **-mersi, -mersum,** to plunge into

**demitto** (3), **-misi, -missum,** to lay down, send down

**demo** (3), **dempsi, demptum,** to take down, remove

**demolior** (4), **-itus sum,** to pull down, dislodge, remove

**demonstro** (1), to show, point out, describe

**demum,** at last

**denique,** in short, in fact

**densus, -a, -um,** dense

**depeculor** (1), **-atus sum,** to plunder

**depono** (3), **-posui, -positum,** to lay down, put aside

**depopulor** (1), **-atus sum,** to plunder, ravage, lay waste, devastate

**deporto** (1), to carry off, carry away

**deposco** (3), **depoposci,** to ask for, demand

**depositum, -i** (*n*), deposit

**deprehendo** (3), **-endi, -ensum,** to seize upon, catch, find

**desero** (3), **-serui, -sertum,** to desert, abandon

**desidero** (1), to long for, miss, feel the lack of

**designatus, -a, -um,** designate, (...)-elect (See page 124, note 77.)

**designo** (1), to mark out, designate

**desilio** (4), **-silui, -sultum,** to jump down

**desino** (3), **desii, desitum,** to cease, stop

**desisto** (3), **-stiti,** to cease, give up

**desolatus, -a, -um,** deserted

**desperatio, -onis** (*f*), despair

**despero** (1), to despair, give up hope

**despondeo** (2), **-spondi, -sponsum,** to promise, betroth

**destitutus, -a, -um,** left unsupported

**desum, deesse, defui,** to be lacking, wanting

**detineo** (2), **-tinui, -tentum,** to hold back

**detraho** (3), **-traxi, -tractum,** to take off, pull off

**detuli,** *see* **defero**

**deturbo** (1), to dislodge, blow down

**deus, -i** (*m*), a god

**devenio** (4), **-veni, -ventum,** to arrive at, reach

**devolvo** (3), **-volvi, -volutum,** to roll down

**dexter, -tra, -trum,** right

**dextera, -ae** (*f*), right hand
**di, deorum** (*m.pl*), gods
  **pro di immortales!** good heavens!
**dico** (3), **dixi, dictum,** to say, tell, speak
**dictator, -oris** (*m*), dictator
**dictito** (1), to say repeatedly
**dicto** (1), to dictate
**dies, diei** (*m*), day, daylight
  **in dies,** daily, every day
**differo, -ferre, distuli, dilatum,** to spread, carry in different directions, differ, postpone
**difficilis, -is, -e,** difficult
**difficultas, -atis** (*f*), difficulty
**diffido** (3), **diffisus sum** ( + *dat.*), to distrust, lack confidence (in)
**diffugio** (3), **-fugi,** to flee in different directions
**diffundo** (3), **-fudi, -fusum,** to spread out
**dignus, -a, -um** ( + *abl.*), worthy (of)
**dilabor** (3), **-lapsus sum,** to glide away
**dilacero** (1), to tear to pieces, tear apart
**dilatum,** *see* **differo**
**diligenter,** carefully, hard
**diligentia, -ae** (*f*), attention to duty, diligence, alertness, attentiveness
**diligo** (3), **-lexi, -lectum,** to love
**dimensus, -a, -um,** measured
**dimetior** (4), **-mensus sum,** to measure out
**dimico** (1), to fight
**dimitto** (3), **-misi, -missum,** to send away, let go, lose, dismiss
  **occasionem dimittere,** to let slip the opportunity
**diremptus, -a, -um,** separated
**dirus, -a, -um,** dreadful
**discedo** (3), **-cessi, -cessum,** to go away, leave
**discipulus, -i** (*m*), pupil
**disco** (3), **didici,** to learn
**discribo** (3), **-scripsi, -scriptum,** to divide, distribute
**discrimen, -inis** (*n*), danger, risk
**discursus, -us** (*m*), running to and fro
**dispello** (3), **-puli, -pulsum,** to disperse
**dispono** (3), **-posui, -positum,** to station at intervals
**disputo** (1), to dispute, argue
**dissimulo** (1), to keep secret
**distribuo** (3), **-ui, -utum,** to distribute, assign
**distuli,** *see* **differo**
**ditissimus, -a, -um,** richest
**diu,** for a long time
**divarico** (1), to set astride
**diversus, -a, -um,** facing in opposite directions, different, various
**dives, -itis,** rich
**divido** (3), **-visi, -visum,** to divide, separate
**divitiae, -arum** (*f.pl*), riches, wealth

**do** (1), **dedi, datum,** to give
  **dono dare,** to give as a gift
**doceo** (2), **-ui, doctum,** to teach
**doctus, -a, -um,** civilised
**doleo** (2), to grieve, mourn, feel pain
**dolor, -oris** (*m*), grief, pain, anguish, resentment
**dominus, -i** (*m*), master, lord
**domus, -us** (*f*), house, home
  **domum,** homewards
  **domo,** from home
  **domi,** at home, in his own community
**donec,** until, as long as
**dono** (1), to give, present
**donum, -i** (*n*), gift
**dubitatio, -onis** (*f*), hesitation, doubt
**dubito** (1), to doubt, hesitate
**dubius, -a, -um,** doubtful, uncertain
**ducenti, -ae, -a,** two hundred
**duco** (3), **duxi, ductum,** to lead, take, bring, think, consider, marry
**dum,** while
**dummodo,** provided that
**duo, duae, duo,** two
**duodecim,** twelve
**duodevicesimus, -a, -um,** eighteenth
**dux, ducis** (*m*), leader, general, guide

## E

**e, ex** ( + *abl.*), out of, from
**ecce!** look! see!
**ecquis? ecquid?** Is there anyone who (anything that)?
**edictum, -i** (*n*), decree
**editus, -a, -um,** lofty, rising
**edo** (3), **edidi, editum,** to cause
**edoceo** (2), **edocui, edoctum,** to inform, point out
**educo** (3), **eduxi, eductum,** to lead out, draw out
**effero, efferre, extuli, elatum,** to carry out, bring out
**effigies, -ei** (*f*), likeness, image
**effodio** (3), **-fodi, -fossum,** to dig up
**effringo** (3), **-fregi, -fractum,** to break open
**effugio** (3), **-fugi,** to escape
**effulgeo** (2), **-fulsi,** to shine forth
**effundo** (3), **-fudi, -fusum,** to pour out
**effusus, -a, -um,** let loose, hurried
**egi,** *see* **ago**
**ego,** I
**egredior** (3), **egressus sum,** to go out, leave, disembark
**eheu!** alas!
**eicio** (3), **eieci, eiectum,** to throw out
**elatum,** *see* **effero**
**elephantus, -i** (*m*), elephant
**eligo** (3), **elegi, electum,** to choose

**eludo** (3), **elusi, elusum,** to mock, baffle, make sport of

**emendo** (1), to improve, reform

**emergo** (3), **emersi, emersum,** to come forth, emerge

**emineo** (2), **-ui,** to stand out, be obvious

**eminus,** from a distance

**emitto** (3), **emisi, emissum,** to send out

**emo** (3), **emi, emptum,** to buy

**emotus, -a, -um,** moved

**emptor, -oris,** (*m*), buyer

**en!** look! see!

**enim,** for

**enoto** (1), to take notes

**eo,** to that place, there

**eodem,** to the same place

**eo magis,** all the more

**epistola, -ae** (*f*), letter

**eques, -itis** (*m*), horseman
   **equites, -um** (*m.pl*), horsemen, cavalry, the *equites* (knights)

**equester, -tris, -tre,** equestrian, on horseback

**equidem,** for my part

**equitatus, -us** (*m*), cavalry

**equus, -i** (*m*), horse

**ergo,** therefore

**eripio** (3), **eripui, ereptum,** to snatch from, rescue

**erro** (1), to wander, be wrong, be mistaken

**error, -oris** (*m*), error, mistake

**eruditus, -a, -um,** learned, scholarly

**erumpo** (3), **erupi, eruptum,** to burst out, break out

**eruptio, -onis** (*f*), sortie

**essedarius, -i** (*m*), chariot-warrior

**et,** and, also
   **et... et...,** both... and...

**etiam,** also, even

**etiamsi,** even if

**etsi,** although

**evado** (3), **evasi, evasum,** to go out, escape

**eveho** (3), **evexi, evectum,** to carry out, raise aloft

**evenio** (4), **eveni, eventum,** to turn out, happen

**eventus, -us** (*m*), outcome

**everto** (3), **everti, eversum,** to overturn, overthrow, outflank

**evocator, -oris** (*m*), recruiter, recruiting officer

**evoco** (1), to call out, summon

**exanimatus, -a, -um,** breathless

**excedo** (3), **-cessi, -cessum,** to go out, leave

**exceptus, -a, -um,** excepted, apart from

**excerpo** (3), **-cerpsi, -cerptum,** to make extracts from

**excido** (3), **-cidi,** to fall out of

**excipio** (3), **-cepi, -ceptum,** to receive, catch

**excito** (1), to stir, rouse, raise, waken

**excludo** (3), **-clusi, -clusum,** to shut out

**excuso** (1), to make excuses, excuse
   **se excusare,** to apologise for

**excutio** (3), **-cussi, -cussum,** to shake off

**exemplum, -i** (*n*), example, precedent

**exeo, -ire, exii, exitum,** to go out, leave

**exercitus, -us** (*m*), army

**exesus, -a, -um,** eaten away

**exhaurio** (4), **-hausi, -haustum,** to take away, remove

**exigo** (3), **-egi, -actum,** to spend

**exiguitas, -atis** (*f*), shortness

**exiguus, -a, -um,** small

**existimo** (1), to think, consider

**exitium, -i** (*n*), destruction
   **exitio esse** ( + *dat.*), to be a cause of destruction (to), destroy

**exitus, -us** (*m*), end, death

**exorior** (4), **-ortus sum,** to rise up, begin

**expedio** (4), to make ready, release, free, obtain, secure

**expeditus, -a, -um,** unencumbered, without baggage

**expello** (3), **-puli, -pulsum,** to drive out, expel

**expendo** (3), **-pendi, -pensum,** to spend

**experimentum, -i** (*n*), trial, experience

**experior** (4), **expertus sum,** to experience

**expertus, -a, -um,** having experienced

**explico** (1), to explain

**explorator, -oris,** (*m*), scout

**exploro** (1), to reconnoitre

**expono** (3), **-posui, -positum,** to lay open, make available, display, explain, land (troops), disembark

**exprimo** (3), **-pressi, -pressum,** to express

**expugno** (1), to capture, assault, take by storm

**expuli,** *see* **expello**

**exsilio** (4), **-ui,** to jump out of

**exsisto** (3), **-stiti,** to come into being

**exspecto** (1), to wait for, expect

**exstinctus, -a, -um,** exstinguished

**exstinguo** (3), **-stinxi, -stinctum,** to put out, eliminate, destroy

**exsto** (1), **-stiti,** to stand out

**extemplo,** at once, immediately

**exterritus, -a, -um,** thoroughly frightened

**extorqueo** (2), **-torsi, -tortum,** to twist out, wrest away from

**extra** ( + *acc.*), outside

**extraho** (3), **-traxi, -tractum,** to drag out, pull out

**extremus, -a, -um,** last, ultimate

**extuli,** *see* **effero**

**exuro** (3), **-ussi, -ustum,** to burn up

# F

faber, fabri (*m*), engineer
fabrico (1), to make, build
facile, easily, without difficulty
facilis, -is, -e, easy
facilitas, -atis (*f*) easiness, ease
facinus, -oris (*n*), crime, disgraceful deed
facio (3), feci, factum, to do, make
  iter facere, to journey, travel, march
factum, -i (*n*), deed
facultas, -atis (*f*) opportunity
falcarius, -i (*m*), sickle-maker
fallo (3), fefelli, falsum, to deceive
falx, falcis (*f*), sickle, grappling-hook
fama, -ae (*f*), report, rumour, reputation,
  fame
fames, -is (*f*), hunger
familiaris, -is, -e, (belonging to a) family,
  household
famosus, -a, -um, famous, notorious
fanum, -i (*n*), shrine, temple
fas, lawful, right
fateor (2), fassus sum, to confess, claim
fauces, -ium (*f.pl*), jaws, throat,
  mountain-pass
faustus, -a, -um, favourable, fortunate
fax, facis (*f*), torch, firebrand
fefelli, *see* fallo
feliciter, well, happily, with good luck
  feliciter evenire, to turn out well
felix, -icis, happy, lucky
femina, -ae (*f*), woman
fere, almost, roughly
ferme, almost, approximately
fero, ferre, tuli, latum, to carry, bring
ferociter, fiercely
ferox, -ocis, fierce
ferramentum, -i (*n*), metal tool
ferrum, -i (*n*), iron, axe, sword
ferus, -a, -um, wild
fervefacio (3), -feci, -factum, to make red-
  hot (blazing)
fessus, -a, -um, tired out
festino (1), to hurry
fictus, -a, -um, pretended, imagined, false
fidelis, -is, -e, faithful
fides, -ei (*f*), faith, loyalty, trust, pledge
  fidem dare, to promise, give one's word
  fidem fallere, to break one's word
  fidem praestare, to maintain good faith,
  serve loyally
  in fidem recipere, to accept into
  submission
fiducia, -ae (*f*), confidence
figura, -ae (*f*), shape
filia, -ae (*f*), daughter
filius, -i (*m*), son
fingo (3), finxi, fictum, to form, imagine

finis, -is (*m*), end
  fines, -ium (*m.pl*), borders, territory
finitimus, -a, -um, neighbouring
finitimus, -i (*m*), neighbour
fio, fieri, factus sum, to happen, be done,
  become
firmiter insistere, to get a firm foothold
firmo (1), to strengthen
firmus, -a, -um, strong, reliable
flagitium, -i (*n*), disgraceful deed
flamen, -inis (*m*), priest
  flaminem prodere, to nominate a priest
flamma, -ae (*f*), flame
flecto (3), flexi, flexum, to turn
fleo (2), flevi, fletum, to weep
fluctus, -us (*m*), wave
flumen, -inis (*n*), river
fluo (3), fluxi, fluxum, to flow
foede, shamefully, horribly, treacherously
foedus, -a, -um, horrible, horrid
folium, -i (*n*), leaf
foramen, -inis (*n*), hole
fores, -um (*f.pl*), door, double doors
forma, -ae (*f*), shape
formido, -inis (*f*), fear
formidulosus, -a, -um, terrifying
forte, perchance, by chance, as it happened
fortis, -is, -e, brave, strong
fortiter, bravely
fortuna, -ae (*f*), luck, fortune, good
  fortune
forum, -i (*n*), market-place, forum
fossa, -ae (*f*), ditch
fragor, -oris (*m*), noise, din
frango (3), fregi, fractum, to break
frater, fratris (*m*), brother
fraus, fraudis (*f*), trick, treachery
fregi, *see* frango
fremitus, -us (*m*), uproar, commotion
frenatus, -a, -um, bridled
frequens, -entis, packed, in full force, "en
  masse"
frequenter, frequently, commonly
frequentia, -ae (*f*), a crowded assembly
frigidus, -a, -um, cold
frigus, -oris (*n*), cold
frons, frontis (*f*), forehead, front
  a fronte, in front
frumentum, -i (*n*), corn, crops
fuga, -ae (*f*), flight
  in fugam dare, to put to flight
  fugam capessere, to take to flight
  fugae se mandare, to take to flight
fugio (3), fugi, to flee, run away, escape
fugitivus, -i (*m*), runaway slave
fulgor, -oris (*m*), glare, flashes
fulgur, -uris (*n*), lightning
fultus, -a, -um, propped up, wedged
fumus, -i (*m*), smoke

**funda, -ae** (*f*), sling
**funditor, -oris** (*m*), slinger
**fundus, -i** (*m*), farm, farm-house
**funis, -is** (*m*), rope
**fur, furis** (*m*), thief
**furo** (3), to be mad, rage
**furor, -oris** (*m*), madness, frenzy, excitement
**furtum, -i** (*n*), theft
**fustis, -is** (*m*), club, stick

## G

**galea, -ae** (*f*), helmet
**Galli, -orum** (*m.pl*), Gauls
**Gallia, -ae** (*f*), Gaul
**Gallicus, -a, -um,** Gallic
**Garumna, -ae** (*m*), the River Garonne
**gaudeo** (2), **gavisus sum,** to be glad, rejoice
**gaudium, -i** (*n*), joy
**gelu, -us** (*n*), frost, cold
**gemitus, -us** (*m*), groan
**gemo** (3), **-ui, -itum,** to groan
**gens, gentis** (*f*), race, family, clan
**genus, -eris** (*n*), kind, nature, family
**gero** (3), **gessi, gestum,** to wear, carry on, wage
    **bellum gerere,** to wage war
    **praeturam gerere,** to hold the praetorship
**gestator, -oris** (*m*), carrier
**gladiator, -oris** (*m*), gladiator
**gladius, -i** (*m*), sword
    **gladium stringere,** to draw a sword
**glans, glandis** (*f*), lead bullet
**gloria, -ae** (*f*), glory, fame
**gluten, -inis** (*n*), glue
**gradus, -us** (*m*), step
**Graecus, -a, -um,** Greek
**gratias agere** ( + *dat.*), to thank, give thanks (to)
**gratulatio, -onis** (*f*), thanksgiving
**gravis, -is, -e,** heavy, serious
**graviter,** heavily, seriously
**grex, gregis** (*m*), herd
**gubernaculum, -i** (*n*), helm, rudder
**gubernator, -oris** (*m*), helmsman, pilot
**gurges, -itis** (*m*), deep water
**gusto** (1), to taste, have a light meal

## H

**habeo** (2), to have, hold
**habitus, -us** (*m*), appearance, condition
**haereo** (2), **haesi, haesum,** to stick, cling
**haesito** (1), to doubt, hesitate
**harena, -ae** (*f*), sand
**haud,** not, by no means

**haurio** (4), **hausi, haustum,** to drain, swallow up
**Helvetii, -orum** (*m.pl*), the Helvetii
**herba, -ae** (*f*), grass
**heri,** yesterday
**hesternus, -a, -um,** of yesterday
**hetaeria, -ae** (*f*), club, fraternity
**hiberna, -orum** (*n.pl*), winter-quarters
**hic, haec, hoc,** this
**hic,** here
**hiemo** (1), to winter, spend the winter
**hiems, hiemis** (*f*), winter
**hilaris, -is, -e,** cheerful
**hinc,** from here
**hinc ... illinc ...,** on one side ... on the other ...
**historia, -ae** (*f*), story, account
**homo, -inis** (*m*), man, fellow, person
    **homines, -um** (*m.pl*), people
**honestus, -a, -um,** honourable
**hora, -ae** (*f*), hour
**horrendus, -a, -um,** terrifying, frightening
**horrens, -entis,** rough
**hortor** (1), **-atus sum,** to encourage, urge
**hostis, -is** (*m*), enemy
**huc,** here, hither
**huc illuc,** here and there, hither and thither
**humor, -oris** (*m*), moisture
**humus, -i** (*f*), earth

## I

**iaceo** (2), to lie, be situated
**iacio** (3), **ieci, iactum,** to throw
**iacto** (1), to allege, bandy about
**iaculum, -i** (*n*), javelin, dart
**iam,** now, already, by this time
    **iam diu,** for a long time now
    **iam pridem,** long since, long ago
**ianua, -ae** (*f*), door
**Ianuarius, -a, -um,** of January
**ibi,** there
**ictus, -us** (*m*), blow
**idem, eadem, idem,** the same
**identidem,** repeatedly, time and again
**ideo,** therefore
**idolon, -i** (*n*), ghost, apparition
**idoneus, -a, -um,** suitable
**Idus, -uum** (*f.pl*), Ides
**ieci,** *see* **iacio**
**igitur,** therefore
**ignarus, -a, -um,** not knowing, ignorant of, unaware(s)
**ignavia, -ae** (*f*), cowardice
**igneus, -a, -um,** fiery
**ignis, -is** (*m*), fire
**ignominia, -ae** (*f*), disgrace

**ignorantia, -ae** (*f*) ignorance
**ignoro** (1), to be ignorant of, not to know
**ignotus, -a, -um,** unknown
**illatum,** *see* **infero**
**ille, illa, illud,** that; he, she, it
**illic,** there
**illinc,** from there, on that side
**illo,** to that place, thither, there
**illuc,** to that place
**illustro** (1), to illumine, make clear
**imago, -inis** (*f*), likeness, apparition, ghost
**imber, imbris** (*m*), rain
**immemor, -oris,** unmindful, forgetful
**immensus, -a, -um,** endless
**immergo** (3), **-mersi, -mersum,** to plunge (oneself) into
**imminens, -entis,** imminent
**immineo** (2) (*+ dat.*), to threaten, be imminent
**immitto** (3), **-misi, -missum,** to send in
**immo,** in fact
    **immo vero,** on the contrary, in fact
**immobilis, -is, -e,** motionless, rooted to the spot
**immodicus, -a, -um,** excessive
**immortalis, -is, -e,** immortal
**impavidus, -a, -um,** unafraid, calm
**impedimenta, -orum** (*n.pl*), baggage
**impedio** (4), to hinder
**impeditus, -a, -um,** hampered, weighed down
**impello** (3), **-puli, -pulsum,** to drive on, induce, stimulate
**impendeo** (2) (*+ dat.*), to hang over, threaten
**impendo** (3), **-pendi, -pensum,** to weigh, spend
**imperator, -oris** (*m*), general, emperor
**imperatum, -i** (*n*), order
**imperitus, -a, -um** (*+ gen.*), inexperienced (in)
**imperium, -i** (*n*), command, empire, power
**impero** (1), to order, demand, levy
**impetro** (1), to have a request granted
**impetus, -us** (*m*), attack, advance
    **impetum facere,** to make an attack, attack
**impigre,** energetically
**impius, -a, -um,** unholy, wicked
**impleo** (2), **-plevi, -pletum,** to fill
**implicatus, -a, -um,** entangled, tangled up in
**imploratio, -onis** (*f*), prayer, appeal for help
**impono** (3), **-posui, -positum,** to put on
**improbus, -a, -um,** wicked, depraved
**improvisus, -a, -um,** unforeseen, unexpected
    **de improviso,** unexpectedly

**imprudentia, -ae** (*f*), imprudence, rashness, lack of foresight
**impune,** without punishment, scot-free
**imus, -a, -um,** lowest, the foot of, bottom of
    **ab imo pectore,** from deep down in his chest
**in** (*+ abl.*), in, on
**in** (*+ acc.*), into, towards, against
    **in dies,** daily
**inanimus, -a, -um,** inanimate
**inanis, -is, -e,** empty, empty-handed
**incalesco** (3), **-calui,** to grow warm, grow hot
**incautus, -a, -um,** incautious, heedless, not taking care
**incedo** (3), **-cessi, -cessum,** to march, advance
**incendium, -i** (*n*), fire
**incendo** (3), **-endi, -ensum,** to burn, set on fire
**incertus, -a, -um,** uncertain
**inchöo** (1), to begin, commence
**incido** (3), **-cidi, -cisum,** to carve, cut
**incido** (3), **-cidi, -casum,** to fall upon, come to light, light upon
**incipio** (3), **-cepi, -ceptum,** to begin
**incito** (1), to spur on, rouse, quicken
**inclino** (1), to lean, incline
**incognitus, -a, -um,** unknown
**incolo** (3), **-colui, -cultum,** to inhabit, dwell
**incolumis, -is, -e,** safe, unharmed
**inconsultus, -a, -um,** unthinking, rash
**incredibilis, -is, -e,** unbelievable, incredible
**incubo** (1), **-cubui, -cubitum,** to lie
**incultus, -a, -um,** unkempt
**incumbo** (3), **-cubui, -cubitum** (*+ dat.*), to apply oneself (to)
**incursus, -us** (*m*), attack
**incuso** (1), to accuse
**inde,** from there, then
**index, -icis** (*m*), informer
**indicium, -i** (*n*), sign, indication, proof
**indico** (1), to point out
**indignus, -a, -um** (*+ abl.*), unworthy (of), intolerable, shameful
**induco** (3), **-duxi, -ductum,** to induce, lead on
**induo** (3), **-dui, -dutum,** to put on
**inermis, -is, -e,** unarmed
**inerro** (1), to wander in
**inexplorato,** without reconnaissance
**infamis, -is, -e,** with a bad reputation, of ill repute
**infeliciter,** unhappily
**infelix, -icis,** unfortunate, unlucky, unhappy
**infero, -ferre, -tuli, illatum,** to bring in, import

**infestus, -a, -um,** hostile, deadly, murderous

**infirmus, -a, -um,** weak, shaky, disabled

**inflammo** (1), to set on fire, inflame

**inflexibilis, -is, -e,** inflexible

**informis, -is, -e,** shapeless, crude

**infra,** beneath, lower down

**infusus, -a, -um,** spread over

**ingens, -entis,** huge, great

**ingredior** (3), **-gressus sum,** to go on

**inhabito** (1), to live, dwell in

**inicio** (3), **-ieci, -iectum,** to throw upon

**inimicus, -a, -um,** hostile

**inimicus, -i** (*m*), personal enemy

**iniquitas, -atis** (*f*), inequality, injustice

**iniquus, -a, -um,** uneven, unjust

**initio,** at first

**iniungo** (3), **-iunxi, -iunctum,** to charge, impose

**iniuria, -ae** (*f*), injury, wrong-doing, act of injustice

**iniussu** ( + *gen.*), without the orders (of)

**iniustus, -a, -um,** unjust

**inlaesus, -a, -um,** unhurt, unharmed

**inligo** (1), to tie on, fasten

**inlunis, -is, -e,** moonless

**innitor** (3), **innixus sum** ( + *dat.*), to lean upon

**inno** (1), to float on, swim in

**innocens, -entis,** innocent, guiltless

**innoxius, -a, -um,** harmless

**innumerabilis, -is, -e,** innumerable, countless

**innuo** (3), **-ui, -utum,** to nod, give a sign

**innutritus, -a, -um,** reared, bred

**inquietus, -a, -um,** restless, disturbed

**inquit,** he/she says, said

**inrumpo** (3), **-rupi, -ruptum,** to burst in

**inscius, -a, -um,** not knowing

**inscribo** (3), **-scripsi, -scriptum,** to write in, register

**insequor** (3), **-secutus sum,** to pursue closely

**insertus, -a, -um,** wound round, wrapped round

**insideo** (2), **-sedi, -sessum** ( + *dat.*), to beset, occupy

**insidiae, -arum** (*f.pl*), ambush

**insidiator, -oris** (*m*), one who lies in ambush

**insidior** (1), **-atus sum** ( + *dat.*), to form an ambush, lie in wait (for)

**insigne, -is** (*n*), decoration
  **insignia, -ium** (*n.pl*), decorations, badges, feathered crests

**insignis, -is, -e,** conspicuous, easily recognised

**insilio** (4), **-ui,** to leap on

**insisto** (3), **-stiti** ( + *dat.*), to stand upon

**insono** (1), **-sonui,** to make a sound or noise

**instanter,** urgently, earnestly

**instituo** (3), **-ui, -utum,** to set up, erect

**institutum, -i** (*n*), practice, custom, regulation, arrangement

**insto** (1), **-stiti,** to press on

**instratus, -a, -um,** saddled

**instruo** (3), **-struxi, -structum,** to set in order, instruct, inform
  **aciem instruere,** to draw up a line of battle

**insuefactus, -a, -um,** trained

**insula, -ae** (*f*), island
  **insulam capere,** to reach the island

**insurgo** (3), **-surrexi, -surrectum,** to rise up

**integer, -gra, -grum,** whole, intact, with no injuries, honest, blameless
  **de integro,** anew, afresh

**intellego** (3), **-lexi, -lectum,** to realise, understand

**intempesta nocte,** at dead of night

**intendo** (1), **-tendi, -tentum,** to turn to, apply

**intentus, -a, -um** ( + *dat.*), intent (upon)

**inter** ( + *acc.*), among, between
  **inter se,** one another

**intercedo** (3), **-cessi, -cessum,** to intervene

**intercipio** (3), **-cepi, -ceptum,** to intercept

**intercurso** (1), to run between

**interdiu,** by day, during the day

**interdum,** sometimes

**interea,** meanwhile

**intereo, -ire, -ii, -itum,** to perish

**interficio** (3), **-feci, -fectum,** to kill

**interim,** meanwhile

**interior, -oris,** inner

**interitus, -us,** (*m*), destruction

**intermitto** (3), **-misi, -missum,** to interrupt, discontinue, pause, let pass

**internecio, -onis** (*f*), destruction, annihilation
  **ad internecionem redigere,** to annihilate, destroy utterly

**interpretor** (1), **-atus sum,** to interpret

**interrogo** (1), to ask questions

**interrumpo** (3), **-rupi, -ruptum,** to break through

**intersum, -esse, -fui** ( + *dat.*), to be between, lie between, engage (in), take part (in)

**intervallum, -i** (*n*), interval, distance

**intestinus, -a, -um,** internal

**intonsus, -a, -um,** shaggy, unshaven

**intra** ( + *acc.*), inside, within

**intro** (1), to enter

**introeo, -ire, -ii, -itum,** to enter

**intueor** (2), **intuitus sum,** to look at, see

**intuli,** *see* **infero**

**intus,** inside

**inusitatus, -a, -um,** unaccustomed, unusual
**invado** (3), **-vasi, -vasum,** to attack, invade
**invalesco** (3), **-valui,** to become stronger, increase
**inveho** (3), **-vexi, -vectum,** to carry in
**invehor** (3), **-vectus sum,** to sail in
**invenio** (4), **-veni, -ventum,** to come upon, find
**in vicem,** in turn
**invito** (1), to invite, summon
**invitus, -a, -um,** unwilling(ly)
**ipse, ipsa, ipsum,** -self
**ira, -ae** (*f*), anger
**irritatus, -a, -um,** provoked
**is, ea, id,** this, that; he, she, it
**iste, ista, istud,** that (of yours), that over there; that man
**ita,** in this way, so
**itaque,** and so, therefore
**item,** likewise, also, in the same way
**iter, itineris** (*n*), journey, march, way
  **iter facere,** to journey, travel, march
  **magnum iter,** a forced march
**iterum,** again
**iubeo** (2), **iussi, iussum,** to order
**iucundus, -a, -um,** pleasant, pleasing, enjoyable
**iudex, -icis** (*m*), judge
  **iudices, -um** (*m.pl*), members of the jury
**iudicium, -i** (*n*), judgment
**iudico** (1), to judge
**iugum, -i** (*n*), yoke, (mountain-)ridge
**iumentum -i** (*n*), beast of burden, pack-animal
**iungo** (3), **iunxi, iunctum,** to join
**Iuppiter Stator,** Jupiter the Protector
**iure,** rightly, justly
**ius, iuris** (*n*), law, a right
**iussi,** *see* **iubeo**
**iussu** ( + *gen.*), by order (of)
**iustus, -a, -um,** just
**iuvenis, -is** (*m*), young man
**iuvo** (1), **iuvi, iutum,** to help
**iuxta,** nearby

### K

**Kalendae, -arum** (*f.pl*), Kalends (first day of month)

### L

**labefacto** (1), to cause to fall, loosen
**labo** (1), to move, totter
**labor, -oris** (*m*), work, task, toil
**labor** (3), **lapsus sum,** to slip, stumble
**laboro** (1), to work, be hard pressed, be in difficulties
**lacrima, -ae** (*f*), tear

**lacrimo** (1), to weep, cry
**lacrimosus, -a, -um,** tearful
**lacus, -us** (*m*), lake
  **lacus Lemannus,** Lake Geneva
**laetitia, -ae** (*f*), happiness, joy
**laeva, -ae** (*f*), left hand
**laevus, -a, -um,** left
**lamentor** (1), **-atus sum,** to weep over
**lancea, -ae** (*f*), lance, spear
**languidus, -a, -um,** weak, faint, uncertain
**lapidatio, -onis** (*f*), stone-throwing
**lapis, -idis** (*m*), stone
**lapsus, -us** (*m*), fall
**Lares, -um** (*m.pl*), household gods
**large,** lavishly
**largitas, -atis** (*f*), extravagance, abundance
**lassitudo, -inis** (*f*), weariness
**late,** widely
**lateo** (2), to be hidden, lie hid
**latitudo, -inis** (*f*), width, breadth
**latro, -onis,** (*m*), robber, brigand
**latrocinium, -i** (*n*), robbery with violence, banditry
**latum,** *see* **fero**
**latus, -a, -um,** broad, wide
**latus, -eris** (*n*), side, flank
  **a lateribus,** on the flanks
**laudo** (1), to praise
**laus, laudis** (*f*), praise
  **laudi esse** ( + *dat.*). to be a reason for praising (someone)
**lavo** (1), **lavi, lavatum (lautum, lotum),** to wash
**laxo** (1), to loosen, open up
**lectica, -ae** (*f*), litter
**lectulus, -i** (*m*), small bed, cosy bed
**lectus, -i** (*m*), bed, couch
**legatus, -i** (*m*), ambassador, staff-officer, general
**legio, -onis** (*f*), legion
**legionarius, -a, -um,** legionary (soldier)
**legitimus, -a, -um,** legitimate
**lego** (3), **legi, lectum,** to read
**lenio** (4), to soothe, calm
**leniter,** gently
**lentus, -a, -um,** slow
**leo, leonis** (*m*), lion
**levis, -is, -e,** light
  **levis armatura,** light-armed infantry
**lex, legis** (*f*), law
**libellus, -i** (*m*), little book, pamphlet
**libenter,** gladly, willingly
**liber, libri** (*m*), book
**liber, -era, -erum,** free
**Liberalia, -ium** (*n.pl*), Festival of Liber (Bacchus)
**liberaliter,** kindly, courteously, generously
**libero** (1), to set free

**libertas, -atis** (*f*), freedom, liberty
**liburnica, -ae** (*f*), light vessel, galley
**licet** (2), **licuit** (+ *dat.*), it is allowed
  **mihi licet,** I am allowed
**lictor, -oris** (*m*), lictor, magistrate's
  attendant
**lignum, -i** (*n*), piece of wood, tree
**limen, -inis** (*n*), doorway, threshold
**lingua, -ae** (*f*), tongue, language
**linter, lintris** (*f*), boat
**linteum, -i** (*n*), linen, sail
**liquidus, -a, -um,** clear
**litterae, -arum** (*f.pl*), letter, dispatches
**litus, -oris** (*n*), shore, beach
**loco** (1), to place, pitch
**locus, -i** (*m*), place, ground
**longe,** by far, far, a long way
**longitudo, -inis** (*f*), length
**longus, -a, -um,** long
**loquor** (3), **locutus sum,** to speak, talk, say
**lorica, -ae** (*f*), breastplate, breastwork,
  parapet
**lorum, -i** (*n*), thong, rein
**lotus, -a, -um,** having washed (bathed)
**lubricus, -a, -um,** slippery
**luceo** (2), **luxi,** to shine
  **lucet,** it is daylight
**luctuosus, -a, -um,** mournful
**ludibrium, -i** (*n*), mockery, laughing-stock
  **ludibrio esse** (+ *dat.*), to be a laughing
  stock
**ludus, -i** (*m*), game, school
**lumen, -inis** (*n*), light, lamp
**luna, -ae** (*f*), moon
**luridus, -a, -um,** lurid, pale, sickly yellow
**lusus, -us** (*m*), game, sport, play
**lux, lucis** (*f*), light, daylight
  **prima luce,** at dawn

## M

**machinor** (1), **-atus sum,** to devise, plot
**macies, -ei** (*f*), emaciation, leanness
**macte** (+ *abl.*), blessings on!
**macto** (1), to reward, afflict, punish
**macula, -ae** (*f*), spot, stain, blemish,
  disgrace
**maculatus, -a, -um,** stained
**maculosus, -a, -um,** spotted, mottled
**magis,** more
  **eo magis,** all the more
**magistratus, -us** (*m*), magistrate, office of
  state
**magnitudo, -inis** (*f*), greatness, size
**magnopere,** greatly
**magnus, -a, -um,** great, big, loud
**maior, maius,** bigger
  **maiores natu,** the elders
**male,** badly

**maledico** (3), **-dixi, -dictum** (+ *dat.*), to
  curse
**maleficium, -i** (*n*), mischief, harm, wrong-
  doing
**malo, malle, malui,** to prefer
**malum, -i** (*n*), evil
**mancus, -a, -um,** ineffective
**mandatum, -i** (*n*), order
**mando** (1), to order, instruct, entrust,
  commit
  **se mandare,** to entrust oneself
**mane,** in the morning
**maneo** (2), **mansi, mansum,** to remain
**manes, -ium** (*m.pl*), spirits of the dead, the
  departed spirit of a person, ghost
**manipulus, -i** (*m*), maniple (third of a
  cohort)
**mansuetudo, -inis** (*f*), gentleness, tameness
**manus, -us** (*f*), hand, company, band (of
  soldiers)
**mare, -is** (*n*), sea
**maritimus, -a, -um,** sea, naval
**Massilia, -ae** (*f*), Marseilles
**mater, -tris** (*f*), mother
**materia, -ae** (*f*), material(s), timber
**matrimonium, -i** (*n*), marriage
  **in matrimonium ducere,** to marry
**matrona, -ae** (*f*), married woman
**Matrona, -ae** (*m*), the River Marne
**maturo** (1), to hasten
**maturus, -a, -um,** early, earlier
**maxime,** very, very much
**maximus, -a, -um,** largest, very big
**meatus, -us** (*m*), passage (of breathing)
**medicus, -i** (*m*), doctor
**mediocriter,** moderately, in small degrees,
  to a limited extent, slightly
**medius, -a, -um,** mid-, middle of
**mehercule!** by Hercules! my goodness!
**melior, -ius,** better
**membrum, -i** (*n*), limb
**memoria, -ae** (*f*), memory, recollection
  **in memoria tenere,** to remember
**memoro** (1), to declare, record
**mens, mentis** (*f*), mind, plan, intention
**mensa, -ae** (*f*), table
**mensis, -is** (*m*), month
**mentitus, -a, -um,** feigned, false
**mentum, -i** (*n*), chin
  **mento tenus,** up to the chin
**mercator, -oris** (*m*), merchant
**mergo** (3), **mersi, mersum,** to plunge, dive
**mergor** (3), **mersus sum,** to plunge oneself
  into
**metuo** (3), **-ui, -utum,** to fear
**metus, -us** (*m*), fear
**meus, -a, -um,** my
**miles, -itis** (*m*), soldier, courtier
**mille** (*pl.* **milia**), thousand

minae, -arum (*f.pl*), threats
minimus, -a, -um, smallest
ministra, -ae (*f*), female servant,
   deaconess
minor (1), -atus sum (+ *dat.*), to threaten
minus, less
miraculum, -i (*n*), wonder, strange sight
mirandus, -a, -um, wonderful
miror (1), -atus sum, to wonder, marvel at
mirus, -a, -um, wonderful, strange
miser, -era, -erum, unhappy, wretched
miserabiliter, pitifully, piteously
misereo (2), to feel pity
   me miseret, it distresses me, I pity
misericordia, -ae (*f*), pity
miseror (1), -atus sum, to pity, bewail
mitto (3), misi, missum, to send
mixtus, -a, -um, mixed
modicus, -a, -um, moderate, slight, modest
modo, only, just
modus, -i (*m*), way, means, manner
moenia, -ium (*n.pl*), (city) walls
moles, -is (*f*), mass, trouble, difficulty
molior (4), -itus sum, to toil, struggle,
   devise
moneo (2), to warn, advise
mons, montis (*m*), mountain
monstrum, -i (*n*), apparition, monster
montani, -orum (*m.pl*), mountain-dwellers
monumentum -i (*n*), monument
mora, -ae (*f*), delay
morbus, -i (*m*), disease, illness
morior (3), mortuus sum, to die
moror (1), -atus sum, to delay
mors, mortis (*f*), death
mos, moris (*m*), custom, tradition
   more solito, in the usual way, as usual
motus, -us (*m*), movement
moveo (2), movi, motum, to move
mox, soon
mulco (1), to beat, cudgel
muliebris, -is, -e, of a woman, womanly,
   female
mulier, -eris (*f*), woman
multitudo, -inis (*f*), large number, crowd,
   throng
multo (1), to punish
multus, -a, -um, much; (*plur.*) many
   multo (+ *comparative*), much
mundus, -i (*m*), world, universe
munimentum, -i (*n*), defence, protection
munio (4), to defend, fortify, build
munitio, -onis (*f*), fortification, defence
munus, -eris (*n*), gift
muralis, -is, -e, used in fighting from walls
murus, -i (*m*), wall
muto (1), to change

# N

nam, for
nanciscor (3), nactus sum, to obtain
narro (1), to tell
natio, -onis (*f*), tribe, nation
nato (1), to swim
natura, -ae (*f*), nature
natus, -a, -um, born, inborn, natural,
   naturally suited
nauta, -ae (*m*), sailor
navigabilis, -is, -e, navigable
navigo (1), to sail
navis, -is (*f*), ship
   navis longa, warship
   navis oneraria, merchant ship
   navem conscendere, to embark, go on
   board ship
navo (1), to do
   operam navare, to do one's best
ne (+ *subjunctive*), in case, lest, that,
   that ... not, to avoid, not to, not
-ne? (indicates a question)
ne multa, to cut a long story short, in
   short
ne ... quidem, not even
nebula, -ae (*f*), mist
nec, and ... not, nor
   nec ... nec ..., neither ... nor ...
necessarii, -orum (*m.pl*), relations
necessarius, -a, -um, necessary
necesse est, it is necessary
necessitas, -atis (*f*), necessity
neco (1), to kill
necopinatus, -a, -um, unexpected
nefarius, -a, -um, abominable,
   unprincipled, wicked
neglego (3), -lexi, -lectum, to neglect,
   ignore
nego (1), to say that ... not, deny
negotium, -i (*n*), business, trouble,
   difficulty
   nihil negotii est, it is no great task
nemo, nullius, no one
nempe, certainly, surely
nequaquam, by no means, in no way
neque, and ... not, nor
   neque ... neque ..., neither ... nor ...
nequiquam, in vain
neuter, -tra, -trum, neither
nex, necis (*f*), death
niger, -gra, -grum, black
nihil, nothing
   nihil movere, to make no impression on
   nihilo, by nothing
   nihilo minus, nonetheless, by no means
nimis, too much
nimium, too much
nimius, -a, -um, excessive, too much, too

**nisi**, if ... not, unless, except
**nitor** (3), **nisus sum (nixus sum)**, to strive
**nix, nivis** (*f*), snow
**no** (1), to swim
**nobilis, -is, -e**, noble, famous
**nobilitas, -atis** (*f*), nobility, rank, the nobles
**nocens, -entis**, guilty
**noctu**, by night
**nocturnus, -a, -um**, of the night, nightly, nocturnal
**nomen, -inis** (*n*), name
**nominatim**, by name
**nomino** (1), to name
**non**, not
    **non modo ... sed etiam ...**
    **non modo ... verum etiam ...**
    **non solum ... sed etiam ...**
    not only ... but also ...
**nondum**, not yet
**nonne?** surely?
**nonnulli, -ae, -a**, some, several
**nonnumquam**, sometimes
**nonus, -a, -um**, ninth
**nos**, we, us
**noscito** (1), to recognise
**nosco** (3), **novi, notum**, to get to know
**noster, -tra, -trum**, our
    **nostri, -orum** (*m.pl*), our men
**noto** (1), to mark, note, point out
**notus, -a, -um**, known
**novem**, nine
**novi**, *see* **nosco**
**novissime**, last
**novissimus, -a, -um**, last, final
    **novissimum agmen**, the rear-guard
**novus, -a, -um**, new
    **novus homo**, a "new man" (See note on M. Tullius Cicero on page 100.)
**nox, noctis** (*f*), night
    **nocte intempesta**, at dead of night
**nubes, -is** (*f*), cloud
**nubilus, -a, -um**, cloudy
**nudo** (1), to lay bare, expose, strip
**nudus, -a, -um**, bare, naked
**nullus, -a, -um**, no
**num**, surely ... not? whether, if
**numerus, -i** (*m*), number
**numquam**, never
**nunc**, now
**nuntio** (1), to announce, report
**nuntius, -i** (*m*), messenger, message, announcement
**nuper**, recently, lately
**nupta, -ae** (*f*), bride
**nuptialis, -is, -e**, (of a) wedding
**nusquam**, nowhere
**nuto** (1), to totter
**nutus, -us** (*m*), nod

# O

**ob** ( + *acc*.), on account of
**obductus, -a, -um**, covered
**obedienter**, obediently
**obeo, -ire, -ii, -itum**, to meet
**obicio** (3), **-ieci, -iectum**, to throw in the way of
**obliquus, -a, -um**, slanting
**oblisus, -a, -um**, crushed
**obliviscor** (3), **oblitus sum** ( + *gen*.), to forget
**obrigesco** (2), **-rigui**, to grow stiff
**obscure**, obscurely, secretly, vaguely
**obscurus, -a, -um**, obscure, dark
**observo** (1), to watch
**obses, -sidis** (*m*), hostage
**obsideo** (2), **-sedi, -sessum**, to besiege, blockade
**obsidio, -onis** (*f*), siege
**obsigno** (1), to sign
**obsisto** (3), **-stiti, -stitum**, to resist, bar the way
**obstinatio, -onis** (*f*), obstinacy
**obsto** (1), **-stiti, -statum**, to block the way, oppose
**obstringo** (3), **-strinxi, -strictum**, to bind
**obstructus, -a, -um**, blocked up
**obstruo** (3), **-struxi, -structum**, to block up
**obtempero** (1) ( + *dat*.), to obey
**obtero** (3), **-trivi, -tritum**, to crush, trample
**obtineo** (2), **-tinui, -tentum**, to hold, keep possession of
**obtrunco** (1), to kill
**obversor** (1), **-atus sum** ( + *dat*.), to be near, hover about
**obviam** ( + *dat*.), in the way (of)
**obvius, -a, -um**, meeting
**occasio, -onis** (*f*), opportunity, chance
    **occasionem dimittere**, to let slip the opportunity
**occido** (3), **-cidi, -cisum**, to kill
**occulte**, secretly
**occultus, -a, -um**, hidden, secret
**occupatus, -a, -um**, busy
**occurrit** ( + *dat*.), it occurs (to me, etc.)
**occurro** (3), **-curri, -cursum** ( + *dat*.), to attack
**occurso** (1), to run up to, meet
**octavus, -a, -um**, eighth
**octo**, eight
**oculus, -i** (*m*), eye
**odi, -isse**, to hate
**odio esse** ( + *dat*.), to be an object of hatred
**odor, -oris** (*m*), scent, smell
**officium, -i** (*n*), official ceremony, duty
    **officium praestare**, to do one's duty
**offirmo** (1), to strengthen
**olim**, once upon a time, one day

**omen, -inis** (*n*), omen, sign
**omitto** (3), **-misi, -missum,** to say nothing of, omit
**omnino,** altogether
**omnis, -is -e,** all, every
**onerarius, -a, -um,** carrying burdens, transporting freight
   **navis oneraria,** merchant-ship
**oneratus, -a, -um,** weighed down, burdened
**onus, -eris** (*n*), burden, load
**onustus, -a, -um,** laden, loaded
**operam navare,** to do one's best
**operio** (4), **operui, opertum,** to cover
**opertus, -a, -um,** covered
**opinio, -onis** (*f*), opinion, expectation
**opinor** (1), **-atus sum,** to think, suppose
**oportet te** ( + *infin.*), you must
**oppidum, -i** (*n*), town
**oppletus, -a, -um,** filled, completely covered
**opportune,** conveniently
**opprimo** (3), **-pressi, -pressum,** to crush, overwhelm
**opprobrium, -i** (*n*), insult
**oppugnatio, -onis** (*f*), attack
**oppugno** (1), to attack
**(ops) opem, opis, ope** (*f*), help
**optimus, -a, -um,** best, excellent, very good
   **optimum factu,** the best thing to do
**optio, -onis** (*f*), choice
**opus, -eris** (*n*), work
**opus est** ( + *abl.*), there is need (of)
**ora, -ae** (*f*), shore, coast
   **ora maritima,** sea-shore, sea-coast
**oratio, -onis** (*f*), speech
   **orationem habere,** to deliver a speech
**orbis, -is** (*m*), circle
   **orbis terrarum,** the world, earth
**ordino** (1), to arrange, draw up
**ordo, -inis** (*m*), rank
**orior** (4), **ortus sum,** to rise, begin
**ornamentum, -i** (*n*), decoration, ornament
**orno** (1), to decorate, equip
**oro** (1), to beg, pray
**os, oris** (*n*), face
**os, ossis** (*n*), bone
**osculor** (1), **-atus sum,** to kiss
**ostendo** (3), **-tendi, -tentum,** to show, point out
**ostento** (1), to point out
**ostium, -i** (*n*), entrance, river-mouth
**otium, -i** (*n*), leisure

## P

**pacatus. -a, -um,** pacified, friendly
**paco** (1), to pacify, subdue

**pactum, -i** (*n*), method, plan, way
**paene,** almost
**paenitentia, -ae** (*f*), repentance
**paenula, -ae** (*f*), long cape with no sleeves
**paenulatus, -a, -um,** wearing a cape
**palam,** openly, in public
**paludamentum, -i** (*n*), military cloak
**palus, -udis** (*f*), swamp, marsh
**pando** (3), **pandi, passum,** to open, spread out
**pannus, -i** (*m*), cloth, rag
**paratus, -a, -um,** prepared, ready
**parens, -entis** (*m/f*), parent
**pareo** (2) ( + *dat.*), to obey
**paro** (1), to prepare
**pars, partis** (*f*), part, direction
**particeps, -ipis** ( + *gen.*), sharing (in), taking part (in)
**partim,** partly
**partio** (4), to divide
**parvus, -a, -um,** small
**passim,** everywhere, in every direction, in all directions
**passus, -us** (*m*), step, pace
   **mille passus,** mile
   **duo milia passuum,** two miles
**passus sum,** *see* **patior**
**pastus, -us** (*m*), food
**pateo** (2), to lie open, extend, be exposed
**patefacio** (3), **-feci, -factum,** to lay open, expose
**patens, -entis,** open
**pater, -tris** (*m*), father
   **patres conscripti** (*m.pl*), senators
**patesco** (3), **patui,** to be open
**patientia, -ae** (*f*), endurance, patience
**patior** (3), **passus sum,** to allow, suffer, endure
**patria, -ae** (*f*), native land
**patrius, -a, -um,** of one's native land
**pauci, -ae, -a,** few
**paulatim,** gradually
**paulisper,** for a short time
**paulo,** a little
**paulum,** little, a little
**pauper, -eris,** poor
**pavens, -entis,** terrified
**pavor, -oris** (*m*), fear, panic, fright
**pax, pacis** (*f*), peace
**pectus, -oris** (*n*), chest, breast
**pecunia, -ae** (*f*), money
**pecus, -oris** (*n*), cattle, herd of cattle, flock
**pedes, -itis** (*m*), foot-soldier, infantry
**pedestris, -is, -e,** on foot
**pedetentim,** step by step, gradually
**peditatus, -us** (*m*), infantry
**pedites, -um** (*m.pl*), infantry
**pellicio** (3), **-lexi, -lectum,** to allure, entice
**pello** (3), **pepuli, pulsum,** to drive, push back, beat

**pendeo** (2), **pependi,** to hang
**pepuli,** *see* **pello**
**per** ( + *acc.*), through, along, over
  **per se,** as far as they were concerned
**perago** (3), **-egi, -actum,** to accomplish
**perangustus, -a, -um,** very narrow
**percello** (3), **-culi, -culsum,** to terrify
**percrebresco** (3), **-crebrui,** to spread,
  become known
**percunctor** (1), **-atus sum,** to make
  enquiries, ask
**perdo** (3), **-didi, -ditum,** to lose, destroy
**perditus, -a, -um,** lost, corrupt, villainous
**perduco** (3), **-duxi, -ductum,** to lead
  through
**peremptus, -a, -um,** killed, slain
**pereo, -ire, -ii, -itum,** to pass away, be
  lost, perish
**perfacilis, -is, -e,** very easy
**perfero, -ferre, -tuli, -latum,** to convey,
  report, endure
**perficio** (3), **-feci, -fectum,** to finish,
  accomplish
**perforo** (1), to bore through
**perfrigidus, -a, -um,** very cold
**perfugio** (3), **-fugi,** to flee for refuge, desert
**perfundo** (3), **-fudi, -fusum,** to sprinkle
**perfusus, -a, -um,** drenched
**pergo** (3), **perrexi, perrectum,** to go on,
  proceed
**periclitor** (1), **-atus sum,** to run risks
**periculosus, -a, -um,** dangerous
**periculum, -i** (*n*), danger, trial
  **periculo esse** ( + *dat.*), to be a source of
  danger (to), endanger
**perlatum,** *see* **perfero**
**perlego** (3), **-legi, -lectum,** to read through
**permaneo** (2), **-mansi, -mansum,** to remain
  to the end, persist
**permitto** (3), **-misi, -missum,** to allow, grant
**permotus, -a, -um,** deeply moved,
  persuaded
**permoveo** (2), **-movi, -motum,** to rouse,
  affect, move deeply
**permulti, -ae, -a,** very many
**pernicies, -ei** (*f*), destruction, disaster
**perparvulus, -a, -um,** very small,
  diminutive, tiny
**perpauci, -ae, -a,** very few
**perpetuus, -a, -um,** continual, continuous,
  unbroken
  **in perpetuum,** for ever
**perrexi,** *see* **pergo**
**perrumpo** (3), **-rupi, -ruptum,** to burst
  through
**persevero** (1), to persist, persevere
**perspicio** (3), **-spexi, -spectum,** to examine,
  observe
**persuadeo** (2), **-suasi, -suasum** ( + *dat.*), to
  persuade

**perterritus, -a, -um,** terrified
**pertinacia, -ae** (*f*), persistence, obstinacy
**pertineo** (2), **-ui** (**ad** + *acc.*), to concern,
  apply (to)
**pertraho** (3), **-traxi, -tractum,** to drag over
**pertrecto** (1), to stroke
**pertuli,** *see* **perfero**
**perturbo** (1), to confuse, throw into
  confusion
**pervagor** (1), **-atus sum,** to wander,
  spread
**pervenio** (4), **-veni, -ventum** (**ad** + *acc.*), to
  reach, arrive at
**pervigilo** (1), to spend the night awake
**pes, pedis** (*m*), foot
  **pedem referre,** to retreat
**pestilens, -entis,** unhealthy, haunted
**pestis, -is** (*f*), pest, plague, destruction
**petitio, -onis** (*f*), attack
**peto** (3), **-ivi, -itum,** to seek, make for,
  attack
**philosophus, -i** (*m*), philosopher
**pigritia, -ae** (*f*), weariness, lethargy
**pilum, -i** (*n*), javelin
**pinna, -ae** (*f*), pinnacle, battlements
**pinus, -i** (*f*), pine-tree
**pirata, -ae** (*m*), pirate
**piscor** (1), **-atus sum,** to fish
**placet** (2), **-uit** ( + *dat.*), it pleases, it is
  decided (by)
**placo** (1), to pacify, appease
**plane,** openly, clearly
**planus, -a, -um,** flat, level
**plenus, -a, -um,** full
**plures, -ium,** more, several
**plurimus, -a, -um,** very much, (*pl.* very
  many)
**plus, pluris,** more
**poena, -ae** (*f*), penalty, punishment
  **poena capitis,** death penalty
**Poenus, -a, -um,** Carthaginian
**pollex, -icis** (*m*), thumb
**polliceor** (2), **pollicitus sum,** to promise
**pondus, -eris** (*n*), weight
**pono** (3), **posui, positum,** to place, put
**pons, pontis** (*m*), bridge
**poposci,** *see* **posco**
**popularis, -is, -e,** fellow-countryman
**populus, -i** (*m*), people, nation, district
**porrigo** (3), **-rexi, -rectum,** to stretch out
**porro,** furthermore
**porta, -ae** (*f*), gate
  **porta decumana,** gate at rear of camp,
  main gate
**porticus, -us** (*f*), covered walk, colonnade
**porto** (1), to carry
**portus, -us** (*m*), harbour
  **portum tenere,** to reach harbour
**posco** (3), **poposci,** to demand, beg, ask
  for

**possum, posse, potui,** to be able

**post,** behind

**post** (+ *acc.*), after

**postea,** afterwards

**posteri, -orum** (*m.pl*), future generations

**posterus, -a, -um,** next, following
  **postero die,** on the following day

**posthac,** after this

**postis, -is** (*m*), doorpost

**postquam,** after, when

**postremo,** at last, finally

**postridie,** on the next day

**posui,** *see* pono

**potens, -entis,** powerful

**potestas, -atis** (*f*), power, opportunity

**potior** (4), **potitus sum** (+ *abl.*), to gain
  possession (of)

**potius,** rather

**potui,** *see* possum

**prae** (+ *abl.*), because of

**praebeo** (2), to offer, give, supply, provide

**praecedo** (3), **-cessi, -cessum,** to excel,
  surpass, precede

**praeceps, -cipitis,** headlong, head-first,
  precipitous

**praecipio** (3), **-cepi, -ceptum** (+ *dat.*), to
  instruct, order, anticipate

**praecipito** (1) to hurl headlong

**praeclarus, -a, -um,** famous

**praeditus, -a, -um,** (+ *abl.*), endowed,
  honoured

**praedo, -onis** (*m*), robber

**praedor** (1), **-atus sum,** to pillage, plunder

**praeeo, -ire, -ii, -itum,** to go ahead

**praefectus, -i** (*m*), officer

**praefero, -ferre, -tuli, -latum** (+ *dat.*), to
  prefer, regard more highly
  **se praeferre** (+ *dat.*), to surpass

**praegredior** (3), **-gressus sum,** to go in
  front

**praelatum,** *see* praefero

**praemitto** (3), **-misi, -missum,** to send on
  ahead

**praemium, -i** (*n*), reward, prize, bribe

**praenuntius, -i** (*m*), forewarning,
  harbinger

**praeruptus, -a, -um,** steep

**praescribo** (3), **-scripsi, -scriptum,** to
  direct, prescribe

**praesens, -entis,** present, on the spot,
  immediate, in person, prompt

**praesidium, -i** (*n*), garrison
  **praesidio esse** (+ *dat.*), to be a means of
  protection (to), protect

**praesto** (1), **-stiti, -statum** (+ *dat.*), to be
  superior (to), display, fulfil
  **fidem praestare,** to maintain good faith,
  serve loyally, keep a promise
  **officium praestare,** to do one's duty

**praetendo** (3), **-tendi, -tentum,** to stretch in
  front

**praeter** (+ *acc.*), except, past, along

**praeterea,** besides, moreover

**praeterquam quod,** apart from what

**praetor, -oris** (*m*), praetor

**praetorius, -a, -um,** of the praetor,
  praetorian, of the governor

**praetuli,** *see* praefero

**praetura, -ae** (*f*), praetorship
  **praeturam gerere,** to hold the
  praetorship

**praeustus, -a, -um,** burnt at the end, burnt
  to a point

**praevaleo** (2), **praevalui,** to prevail

**pravus, -a, -um,** depraved, warped

**preces, -um** (*f.pl*). prayers, pleas

**precor** (1), **-atus sum,** to pray

**premo** (3), **pressi, pressum,** to press, crush,
  trouble, put under pressure, pursue

**pretiosus, -a, -um,** precious

**pretium, -i** (*n*), price, bribe

**pridie,** on the previous day

**primi ordines,** senior centurions

**primipilus, -i** (*m*), chief centurion

**primo,** at first, first

**primus, -a, -um,** first

**princeps, -cipis** (*m*), emperor, leading
  citizen, leader

**prior, -oris,** first, previous, former

**pristinus, -a, -um,** previous, former

**prius,** previously

**priusquam,** before

**privatus, -a, -um,** private

**privo** (1) (+ *abl.*), to deprive (of)

**pro** (+ *abl.*), in front of, instead of, in
  proportion to, as, for

**proagorus, -i** (*m*), mayor, chief-magistrate

**probo** (1), to approve

**procedo** (3), **-cessi, -cessum,** to step
  forward

**proclivis, -is, -e,** steep, sloping down

**proconsul, -is** (*m*), proconsul

**procul,** far, far off, from afar

**procumbo** (3), **-cubui, -cubitum,** to fall

**procurro** (3), **-curri, -cursum,** to run
  forward

**prodesse,** *see* prosum

**prodo** (3), **-didi, -ditum,** to betray

**produco** (3), **-duxi, -ductum,** to bring
  forward

**proelior** (1), **-atus sum,** to fight

**proelium, -i** (*n*), battle
  **proelium committere,** to join battle

**profectio, -onis** (*f*), departure

**profecto,** certainly, assuredly

**proficiscor** (3), **profectus sum,** to set out

**profiteor** (2), **professus sum,** to declare,
  promise, offer

**profligo** (1), to overcome, rout, dislodge
**profundus, -a, -um,** deep
**progredior** (3), **progressus sum,** to go forward, advance
**prohibeo** (2), ( + *infin.*), to prevent (from)
**proicio** (3), **-ieci, -iectum,** to throw, cast
**proinde,** accordingly
**prolabor** (3), **-lapsus sum,** to fall down
**promiscuus, -a, -um,** common, ordinary
**promissus, -a, -um,** allowed to grow long
**promissum, -i** (*n*), promise
**promitto** (3), **-misi, -missum,** to promise
**promuntorium, -i** (*n*), peak, height
**propello** (3), **-puli, -pulsum,** to drive away
**prope** ( + *acc.*), near
**prope,** nearby, almost
**propero** (1), to hasten
**propono** (3), **-posui, -positum,** to display, set before
**propraetor, -oris** (*m*), propraetor
**proprius, -a, -um,** special, peculiar
**propter** ( + *acc.*), on account of
**propterea quod,** because, inasmuch as
**propulso** (1), to repel, ward off
**proripio** (3), **-ripui, -reptum,** to snatch forth, rush forward
  **se proripere,** to rush out
**proruo** (3), **-rui, -rutum,** to cast down
**proscribo** (3), **-scripsi, -scriptum,** to advertise, put up for sale
**prosequor** (3), **-secutus sum,** to pursue
**prospecto** (1), to look out at
**prospectus, -us** (*m*), view
**prosterno** (3), **-stravi, -stratum,** to overthrow, lay low
**prosum, prodesse, profui** ( + *dat.*), to benefit
**protinus,** at once, immediately
**proturbo** (1), to harass, throw into confusion
**prout,** as if
**provehor** (3), **-vectus sum,** to go forward
**provincia, -ae** (*f*), province
**provolo** (1), to rush out, dart forward
**proxime,** next, most recently
**proximus, -a, -um,** nearest, last
**prudentia, -ae** (*f*), good-sense, discretion, skill
**publice,** officially, at public expense
**publicus, -a, -um,** public
**pudet** (2), **-uit,** to shame, make ashamed
  **me pudet,** I am ashamed
**pudor, -oris** (*m*), shame
**puer, -i** (*m*), boy
  **pueri, -orum** (*m.pl*), children
**pugillares, -ium** (*m.pl*), writing-tablets
**pugio, -onis** (*m*), dagger
**pugna, -ae** (*f*), battle, fight
**pugno** (1), to fight
**pulsum,** *see* **pello**

**pumex, -icis** (*m*), pumice-stone
**Punicus, -a, -um,** Carthaginian
**punio** (4), to punish
**pupa, -ae** (*f*), doll
**puppis, -is** (*f*), stern, ship
**purgo** (1), to make clean, cleanse, purify
**puteus, -i** (*m*), well
**puto** (1), to think
**putrefactus, -a, -um,** rotted, rotten

## Q

**qua,** where
**quacunque,** wherever
**quadraginta,** forty
**quadriduum, -i** (*n*), (a period of) four days
**quadringenti, -ae, -a,** four hundred
**quadriremis, -is** (*f*), quadrireme (vessel with four oarsmen in each 'room')
**quae cum ita sint,** since this is so, this being so, in the circumstances
**quaero** (3), **quaesivi, quaesitum,** to ask, look for, question
**quaeso,** I beseech you, please
**quaestor, -oris** (*m*), quaestor
**qualis, -is, -e,** of what kind
**quam,** than
**quam!** how!
**quam** ( + *superlative*), as ... as possible
  **quam primum,** as soon as possible
**quamdiu,** how long, as long as
**quamlibet,** however much
**quam ob rem,** therefore
**quamquam,** although
**quandocunque,** whenever
**quantum,** how much
**quantus, -a, -um,** how big, how much
  **quanto ... tanto ...,** the more ... the more ...
**quare,** therefore, why
**quartus, -a, -um,** fourth
**quasi,** as if
**quasso** (1), to shake violently
**quatenus,** how far
**quatio** (3), *no perf.*, **quassum,** to shake
**-que,** and
**qui, quae, quod,** who, which
**quia,** because
**quicunque, quaecunque, quodcunque,** whoever, whatever
**quid,** what, why
  **quid plura?** to cut a long story short
**quidam, quaedam, quoddam,** a certain, (*pl*) some
**quidem,** indeed
  **ne ... quidem,** not even
**quies, quietis** (*f*), peace, quiet, rest
**quiesco** (3), **quievi, quietum,** to rest, sleep
**quiete,** quietly
**quin** ( + *subjunctive*), without

**quindecim,** fifteen
**quin etiam,** moreover
**quingenti, -ae -a,** five hundred
**quinquaginta,** fifty
**quintus, -a, -um,** fifth
**quintus decimus,** fifteenth
**quiritatus, -us** (*m*), wailing
**Quirites,** citizens
**quis, quid,** who, which, what
**quisquam,** anyone
**quisque,** each
**quo,** where to
  **quo usque,** up to what point, how far
**quo** (*comparative + subjunctive*), in order
  that
**quoad,** as long as, until
**quod,** because
**quod si,** but if
**quominus** ( *+ subjunctive*), so that ... not,
  from
**quomodo,** how
**quoniam,** since
**quoque,** also
**quot,** how many
**quoties,** how many times, how often

## R

**raeda, -ae** (*f*), coach, carriage
**raedarius, -i** (*m*), coachman, driver
**ramus, -i** (*m*), branch
**rapidus, -a, -um,** swift
**rapio** (3), **rapui, raptum,** to snatch, seize
**raptim,** hurriedly
**rarus, -a, -um,** thinly scattered, rare
**ratio, -onis** (*f*), plan, method, way,
  reasoning, logic
**ratis, -is** (*f*), raft
**ratus, -a, -um,** thinking (*see* **reor**)
**recedo** (3), **-cessi, -cessum,** to retire,
  retreat, go back
**recens, -entis,** recent, fresh
**recipio** (3), **-cepi, -ceptum,** to receive, take
  back, recover
  **se recipere,** to retreat, withdraw,
  recover
**recito** (1), to read aloud, recite
**reclamo** (1), to object loudly, protest
**recognosco** (3), **-novi, -nitum,** to review,
  recall to mind, revise
**recte,** rightly (in moral sense)
**rector, -oris** (*m*), driver, mahout
**rectus, -a, -um,** straight, direct
**recubo** (1), to lie, recline
**recupero** (1), to recover
**recurro** (3), **-curri, -cursum,** to run back
**recuso** (1), to refuse
**reddo** (3), **-didi, -ditum,** to give back,
  return

**redeo, -ire, -ii, -itum,** to go back, return
**redigo** (3), **-egi, -actum,** to reduce
  **ad internecionem redigere,** to destroy
  utterly, annihilate
**redintegro** (1), to renew
**reditio, -onis** (*f*), return
**refero, -ferre, rettuli, relatum,** to bring
  back
  **pedem referre,** to retreat, withdraw
**reficio** (3), **-feci, -fectum,** to repair,
  rebuild, refresh, revive
**refugio** (3), **-fugi,** to flee back
**refuto** (1), to refute, disprove
**regio, -onis** (*f*), region, district, land
**regnum, -i** (*n*), kingdom, kingship, kingly
  power
**rego** (3), **rexi, rectum,** to rule, command
**regredior** (3), **regressus sum,** to go back,
  return
**reicio** (3), **reieci, reiectum,** to throw back,
  throw aside, throw off
**relatum,** *see* **refero**
**religio, -onis** (*f*), religious belief,
  scruple(s), respect for the gods
**religiosus, -a, -um,** showing reverence,
  scrupulous
**religo** (1), to fasten
**relinquo** (3), **-liqui, -lictum,** to leave
**reliquus, -a, -um,** remaining, rest of
**reluceo** (2), **-luxi,** to blaze, shine out
**remaneo** (2), **-mansi,** to stay behind,
  remain
**remitto** (3), **-misi, -missum,** to send back
**removeo** (2), **-movi, -motum,** to remove,
  get rid of
**remus, -i** (*m*), oar
**renovo** (1), to renew
**renuntio** (1), to report
**reor** (2), **ratus sum,** to think
**repagula, -orum** (*n.pl*), bolts, bars
**repello** (3), **reppuli, repulsum,** to drive
  back, beat back
**repens, -entis,** sudden
**repente,** suddenly
**repentinus, -a, -um,** sudden
**repeto** (3), **-petivi, -petitum,** to seek again,
  revive, renew
**reperio** (4), **repperi, repertum,** to find out,
  discover
**repleo** (2), **-plevi, -pletum,** to fill (up),
  replenish
**reppuli,** *see* **repello**
**reprimo** (3), **-pressi, -pressum,** to hold in che
**repudio** (1), to reject, refuse
**requiro** (3), **-quisivi, -quisitum,** to search
  for, question
**res, rei** (*f*), thing, matter, affair, situation
  **rem gerere,** to campaign, fight
  **rem bene gerere,** to succeed

**rescindo** (3), **-scidi, -scissum,** to cut away, break down

**resido** (3), **-sedi,** to sit down, sink down, abate

**resina, -ae** (*f*), resin

**resisto** (3), **-stiti** ( + *dat.*), to resist

**resolvo** (3), **-solvi, -solutum,** to unfasten

**resorbeo** (2), to suck back

**respicio** (3), **-spexi, -spectum,** to look back, look round at

**respondeo** (2), **-spondi, -sponsum,** to reply

**responsum, -i** (*n*), reply, answer

**respublica, reipublicae** (*f*), the state

**restituo** (3), **-stitui, -stitutum,** to set up again, restore

**retinaculum, -i** (*n*), cable

**retineo** (2), **-tinui, -tentum,** to hold back

**retro,** back

**rettuli,** *see* **refero**

**revello** (3), **-velli, -vulsum,** to wrench off, pull down

**revenio** (4), **-veni, -ventum,** to come back, return

**re vera,** really, in actual fact

**reverto** (3), **-verti,** to return (*perf. part.* **reversus**)

**revoco** (1), to recall, call back

**revolvo** (3), **-volvi, -volutum,** to roll back

**rex, regis** (*m*), king

**rexi,** *see* **rego**

**Rhenus, -i** (*m*), Rhine

**Rhodanus, -i** (*m*), Rhône

**rideo** (2), **risi, risum,** to laugh, laugh at

**rigens, -entis,** stiff

**rima, -ae** (*f*), crack

**ripa, -ae** (*f*), bank (of river)

**rite,** properly, duly

**robur, -oris** (*n*), strength, the flower of the army (i.e. the most experienced troops)

**robustus, -a, -um,** strong

**rogo** (1), to ask

**Roma, -ae** (*f*) Rome

**Romanus, -a, -um,** Roman

**ruina, -ae** (*f*), ruin, downfall

**rupes, -is** (*f*), rock, crag

**ruptus, -a, -um,** broken

**rursus,** again

## S

**sacra, -orum** (*n.pl*), rites

**sacramentum, -i** (*n*), oath

**saepe,** often

**saevio** (4), to rage

**sagitta, -ae** (*f*), arrow

**sagittarius, -i** (*m*), archer, bowman

**sagulum, -i** (*n*), (small military) cloak

**saltus, -us** (*m*), pass, gorge

**salus, -utis** (*f*), safety

**saluti esse** ( + *dat.*), to be a means of safety (to), be the salvation (of), save

**saluto** (1), to greet, welcome, pay respects to

**salvus, -a, -um,** safe

**sanctus, -a, -um,** sacred, holy

**sane,** very

**sanguis, -inis** (*m*), blood

**sarcina, -ae** (*f*), pack, (*pl*) baggage

**satietas, -atis** (*f*), sufficiency, glut

**satis,** enough

**satisfacio** (3), **-feci, -factum** ( + *dat.*), to satisfy, make amends, do one's duty

**saxum, -i** (*n*), rock

**scala, -ae** (*f*), ladder

**scapha, -ae** (*f*), light boat, small boat

**scelus, -eris** (*n*), crime

**scientia, -ae** (*f*), knowledge

**scio** (4), to know

**scribo** (3), **scripsi, scriptum,** to write, describe

**scutum, -i** (*n*), shield

**se,** himself, herself, itself, themselves

**secedo** (3), **-cessi, -cessum,** to go away, withdraw

**secerno** (3), **-crevi, -cretum,** to separate

**secretum, -i** (*n*), seclusion

**secundum** ( + *acc.*), in accordance with

**secundum flumen,** alongside the river

**secundus, -a, -um,** favourable

**securitas, -atis** (*f*), lack of concern

**secus,** otherwise

**secutus,** *see* **sequor**

**sed,** but

**sedecĭm,** sixteen

**sedeo** (2), **sedi, sessum,** to sit

**sedes, -is** (*f*), seat, (*pl*) foundations

**segniter,** lazily, sluggishly

**sella, -ae** (*f*), seat, official chair

**semel atque iterum,** once or twice

**semen, -inis** (*n*), seed

**sementis, -is** (*f*), (seed-)sowing

**semper,** always

**senatus, -us** (*m*), senate

**senatus consultum,** decree of the senate

**senectus, -tutis** (*f*), old age

**senesco** (3), **senui,** to grow old, fail

**senex, senis** (*m*), old man

**sententia, -ae** (*f*), opinion

**sentio** (4), **sensi, sensum,** to feel, notice, realise

**sepelio** (4), **-ivi, sepultum,** to bury

**septem,** seven

**septimus, -a, -um,** seventh

**Sequana, -ae** (*m*), the River Seine

**sequor** (3), **secutus sum,** to follow

**sermo, -onis** (*m*), conversation, chatter, gossip

**serpo** (3), **serpsi, serptum,** to creep, spread

**servilis, -is, -e,** servile, slavish

**servo** (1), to save, keep, protect
**servulus, -i** (*m*), young slave
**servus, -i** (*m*), slave
**sessum,** *see* **sedeo**
**seu ... seu ...,** whether ... or ...
**sex,** six
**sexaginta,** sixty
**sexus, -us** (*m*), sex
**si,** if
  **si modo,** if only
  **si quis,** if anyone
**sic,** thus, in this way
**sica, -ae** (*f*), dagger
**sicco** (1), to dry
**siccus, -a, -um,** dry
**Sicilia, -ae** (*f*), Sicily
**Siculi, -orum** (*m.pl*), Sicilians
**sicut,** just as
**sigillum, -i** (*n*), statuette
**signifer, -eri** (*m*), standard-bearer
**significo** (1), to make a sign, indicate
**signum, -i** (*n*), standard, signal, statue
  **signa convertere,** to wheel, turn
  **signa inferre,** to advance
  **signa movere,** to break camp
  **signa tollere,** to break camp
**silentium, -i** (*n*), silence
**sileo** (2), **silui,** to be silent
**silva, -ae** (*f*), wood
**similis, -is, -e,** like, similar
**similitudo, -inis** (*f*), likeness
**simul,** at the same time
  **simul ... simul ...,** both ... and ...
**simulac,** as soon as
**simulacrum, -i** (*n*), statue, image
**simulatque,** as soon as
**sin,** but if
**sine** ( + *abl.*), without
**singularis, -is, -e,** single, one by one,
  remarkable, extraordinary
**singuli, -ae, -a,** singly, one at a time, one
  each
**sinister, -tra, -trum,** left
**sinistra, -ae** (*f*), left hand
**sino** (3), **sivi, situm,** to allow
**sinus, -us** (*m*), bay
**sisto** (3), **stiti, statum,** to check, stop
**sive ... sive ...,** whether ... or ...
**sivi,** *see* **sino**
**socius, -i** (*m*), companion, ally, accomplice
**sol, solis** (*m*), sun
  **solis occasus,** sunset
**solatium, -i** (*n*), consolation, solace
  **pro solatio,** as compensation
**solea, -ae** (*f*), sandal
**soleo** (2), **solitus sum,** to be accustomed
**solitudo, -inis** (*f*), loneliness, solitude,
  exile
**sollemnis, -is, -e,** customary, annual

**sollicito** (1), to rouse, attract
**sollicitus, -a, -um,** anxious
**solor** (1), **-atus sum,** to comfort, relieve
**solum, -i** (*n*), (solid) ground
**solus, -a, -um,** alone
**solutus, -a, -um,** free, freed from
**solvo** (3), **solvi, solutum,** to loosen, free,
  set sail
  **navem solvere,** to set sail
**somnus, -i** (*m*), sleep
**sonans, -antis,** sonorous, loud
**sonus, -i** (*m*), sound, noise
**sordidus, -a, -um,** dirty
**soror, -oris** (*f*), sister
**sparsus, -a, -um,** scattered
**spatiosus, -a, -um,** spacious
**spatium, -i** (*n*), space, interval
**species, -ei** (*f*), appearance
**spectaculum, -i** (n), spectacle
**spectator, -oris** (*m*), spectator
**speculor** (1), **-atus sum,** to watch, observe
**sperno** (3), **sprevi, spretum,** to despise
**spero** (1), to hope
**spes, spei** (*f*), hope
**sprevi,** *see* **sperno**
**spiritus, -us** (*m*), breath, blast
**spolio** (1), to loot, pillage, strip
**squalor, -oris** (*m*), filth
**stabilis, -is, -e,** steady
**stagnum, -i** (*n*), pool, lagoon
**statim,** immediately, at once
**statio, -onis** (*f*), guard-post, outpost
**stativus, -a, -um,** standing
  **stato die,** on a fixed day
**statua, -ae** (*f*), statue
**statum,** *see* **sto**
**statuo** (3), **-ui, -utum,** to decide
**status, -us** (*m*), condition, position
**sterno** (3), **stravi, stratum,** to spread,
  scatter, slaughter
**steti,** *see* **sto**
**stilus, -i** (*m*), pen
**stipo** (1), to surround, hem in
**stirps, stirpis** (*f*), stalk, root
**stiti,** *see* **sisto**
**sto** (1), **steti, statum,** to stand
**stomachus, -i** (*m*), wind-pipe
**stramentum, -i** (*n*), straw, thatch
**stratus, -a, -um,** scattered, slaughtered
**stravi,** *see* **sterno**
**strepitus, -us** (*m*), noise, din
**studeo** (2), **-ui** ( + *dat.*), to study
**studium, -i** (*n*), zeal, eagerness, study
**stulte,** foolishly
**stultus, -a, -um,** foolish
**suadeo** (2), **suasi, suasum** ( + *dat.*), to
  advise
**sub,** under
**subdo** (3), **-didi, -ditum,** to plunge into

**subeo, -ire, -ii, -itum,** to undergo, enter, approach, take on (its) back

**subiaceo** (2), **-ui,** to lie under

**subicio** (3), **-ieci, -iectum,** to subject, subdue, place under

**subito,** suddenly

**subitus, -a, -um,** sudden

**sublatum,** *see* **tollo**

**subministro** (1), to supply

**submitto** (3), **-misi, -missum,** to send up

**submoveo,** *see* **summoveo**

**subrideo** (2), **-risi,** to smile

**subsellium, -i** (*n*), bench

**subsequor** (3), **-secutus sum,** to follow closely

**subsidium, -i** (*n*), help
  **subsidio esse** (*+ dat.*), to be a help (to), help

**subsisto** (3), **-stiti,** to stay, remain

**subtraho** (3), **-traxi, -tractum,** to remove, take away

**succendo** (3), **-cendi, -censum,** to set on fire

**succido** (3), **-cidi,** to fall

**succurro** (3), **-curri, -cursum** (*+ dat.*), to come to the assistance (of)

**sudis, -is** (*f*), stake

**suffragium, -i** (*n*), vote

**sulpur, -uris** (*n*), sulphur

**summa, -ae** (*f*), chief point, whole of

**sumministro** (1), to supply

**summoveo** (2), **-movi, -motum,** to dislodge

**summus, -a, -um,** the greatest, the top of

**sumo** (3), **sumpsi, sumptum,** to take, pick up, assume

**sumptus, -us** (*m*), expense

**sunt qui,** there are some (men) who

**super** (*+ acc.*), above

**superior, -oris,** higher

**supero** (1), to overcome, defeat, cross

**superpono** (3), **-posui, -positum,** to place above, lay on top

**superstes, -stitis,** surviving

**superstitio, -onis** (*f*), superstition, religious belief

**supersum, -esse, -fui,** to remain, be left, survive

**suppeto** (3), **-petivi, -petitum,** to be sufficient

**supplicium, -i** (*n*), punishment

**supplico** (1), (*+ dat.*), to pray (to)

**suppono** (3), **-posui, -positum,** to place under

**supra,** above

**surgo** (3), **surrexi, surrectum,** to rise, get up

**sursum,** upwards

**suscipio** (3), **-cepi, -ceptum,** to undertake

**suspensus, -a, -um,** hanging, suspended

**suspicio, -onis** (*f*), suspicion

**suspicor** (1), **-atus sum,** to suspect

**suspirium, -i** (*n*), sigh

**sustento** (1), to hold out, sustain, maintain

**sustineo** (2), **-tinui, -tentum,** to hold off, sustain

**sustuli,** *see* **tollo**

**suus, -a, -um,** his, her, its, their (own)

# T

**tabulae, -arum** (*f.pl*), records

**Tabularium, -i** (*n*), Public Records Office

**taceo** (2), to be silent

**tacitus, -a, -um,** silent, silently

**tactum,** *see* **tango**

**taedet** (2), **-uit** (*+ acc.*), to weary
  **me taedet** (*+ gen.*), I am tired (of)

**taedium, -i** (*n*), weariness

**talis, -is, -e,** such, of such a kind

**tam,** so
  **tam ... quam ...,** as ... as ...

**tamen,** however

**tamquam,** as if, as though

**tandem,** at length, at last

**tandem** (in a question), pray tell me

**tango** (3), **tetigi, tactum,** to touch

**tantum,** only

**tantum ... quantum ...,** as much ... as

**tantus, -a, -um,** so great

**tarde,** slowly

**tardo** (1), to slow down

**tardus, -a, -um,** slow

**tectum, -i** (*n*), roof, house, building

**tegimentum, -i** (*n*), cover, case

**tego** (3), **texi, tectum,** to cover

**telum, -i** (*n*), weapon

**temere,** rashly, unthinkingly, without good reason

**temperantia, -ae** (*f*), restraint, moderation, self-control, self-restraint

**tempero** (1), to refrain

**tempestas, -atis** (*f*), storm, weather

**templum, -i** (*n*), temple

**tempus, -oris** (*n*), time
  **brevi tempore,** in a short time

**tendo** (3), **tetendi, tensum,** to stretch, exert oneself, aim

**tenebrae, -arum** (*f.pl*), darkness

**teneo** (2), **-ui, tentum,** to hold, keep, confine

**tener, -era, -erum,** tender, young

**tenuatus, -a, -um,** thinned out

**tenuis, -is, -e,** weak, feeble, frail, slight, slender, delicate

**tenus** (*+ abl.*), as far as
  **mento tenus,** up to the chin

**tergum, -i** (*n*), back
  **a (ab) tergo,** in the rear, from behind

**terra, -ae** (*f*), earth, land

**terreo** (2), to terrify

terribilis, -is, -e, terrifying
terror, -oris (*m*), terror
tertius, -a, -um, third
testudo, -inis (*f*), "tortoise", shelter
tetendi, *see* tendo
tetigi, *see* tango
thermae, -arum (*f.pl*), public baths
thesaurus, -i (*m*), treasure
tigris, -is (*m/f*), tiger, tigress
timeo (2), to fear
timor, -oris (*m*), fear
titubo (1), to stumble, stagger
titulus, -i (*m*), notice
toga praetexta, toga with purple edging
tollo (3), sustuli, sublatum, to lift, raise,
    remove
tormentum, -i (*n*), war-engine, catapult,
    torture
torrens, -entis (*m*), torrent
torreo (2), torrui, tostum, to scorch, roast
torridus, -a, -um, parched, shrivelled
tortus, -a, -um, twisted
tot, so many
totus, -a, -um, whole of
tractatus, -us (*m*), handling
trado (3), -didi, -ditum, to hand over
    tradunt, they say
tragula, -ae (*f*), javelin, spear
traho (3), traxi, tractum, to drag
traicio (3), -ieci, -iectum, to put across,
    take across, cross
traiectus, -us (*m*), crossing
trano (1), to swim across
tranquillitas, -atis (*f*), peace, quiet
trans ( + *acc.*), across
transcendo (3), -scendi, -scensum, to cross
    over
transeo, -ire, -ii, -itum, to cross, pass
    through
transfero, -ferre, -tuli, -latum, to transfer
transfigo (3), -fixi, -fixum, to pierce
    through
transgredior (3), -gressus sum, to cross
transitus, -us (*m*), crossing
transmitto (3), -misi, -missum, to cross
    over
transporto (1), to carry across
tremor, -oris (*m*), shaking, quaking
trepidatio, -onis (*f*), fear, fright
trepido (1), to panic, be excited
trepidus, -a, -um, alarmed, panic-stricken
tres, tres, tria, three
tribunal, -alis (*n*), tribunal, platform for
    magistrates
tribunus, -i (*m*), tribune
    tribunus militum, tribune of the soldiers,
    military tribune
tribuo (3), -ui, -utum, to grant, give,
    bestow

triduum -i (*n*), (period of) three days
triennium, -i (*n*), (period of) three years
tristis, -is, -e, sad, sorrowful
trucido (1), to slay, butcher
truncatus, -a, -um, cut off
trunco (1), to cut off
truncus, -i (*m*), headless body, tree-trunk
tu, you
tuba, -ae (*f*), trumpet
tueor (2), tuitus sum, to protect
tuli, *see* fero
tum, then, at that moment
tumultus, -us (*m*), confusion, attack,
    uprising
tumulus, -i (*m*), mound
tunc, then, at that moment, at that point
tunica, -ae (*f*), tunic
turba, -ae (*f*), crowd
turbo (1), to throw into confusion
turbulentus, -a, -um, stormy
turpis, -is, -e, shameful
turpitudo, -inis (*f*), disgrace, shame
turris, -is (*f*), tower
tus, turis (*n*), frankincense
tutus, -a, -um, safe, out of harm's way
tuus, -a, -um, your
tyrannus, -i (*m*), tyrant


## U

ubi, where, when
ubinam, where (on earth)
ubique, everywhere
ulciscor (3), ultus sum, to avenge, take
    vengeance on
ullus, -a, -um, any
ulterior, -oris, farther
ultra, beyond
ultus, *see* ulciscor
ululatus, -us (*m*), howling, wailing, cry (of
    mourning)
umerus, -i (*m*), shoulder
una, together
unde, whence, from where/which
undecimus, -a, -um, eleventh
undique, from all directions, everywhere
unicus, -a, -um, only, alone of its kind,
    unique
universus, -a, -um, entire, all together
unus, -a, -um, one
urbanus, -a, -um, of the city
urbs, urbis (*f*), city
urgeo (2), ursi, to press hard, press, put
    under pressure
usque ad ( + *acc.*), right up to
usura, -ae (*f*), use, enjoyment
usus, -us (*m*), use, experience
    usui esse ( + *dat.*), to be of use (to), be
    useful (to)

**ut** ( + *indic.*), when, as, how
  **ut primum,** as soon as
**ut** ( + *subjunctive*), so that, that, to
**uter, utris** (*m*), bag made of animal hide,
  skin bag
**uter, utra, utrum,** which of two
**uterque,** each of two
  **utrique** (*m.pl*), both sides
**utilis, -is, -e,** useful
**utor** (3), **usus sum** ( + *abl.*), to use, employ
**utroque,** on both sides
**uxor, -oris** (*f*), wife

## V

**vacuefacio** (3), **-feci, -factum,** to empty,
  vacate
**vacuus, -a, -um,** empty
**vado** (3), to go
**vadum, -i** (*n*), ford, shallow water
**vagor** (1), **-atus sum,** to wander
**vagus, -a, -um,** wandering
**valeo** (2), to be strong, be well, be able
**valetudo, -inis** (*f*), state of health, good or
  bad health
**validus, -a, -um,** strong
**vallum, -i** (*n*), rampart (with palisade)
**valvae, -arum** (*f.pl*), folding-doors
**vanesco** (3), to vanish, die away
**varius, -a, -um,** different, various, varied
**vasa, -orum** (*n.pl*), cooking utensils,
  equipment, baggage
**vastus, -a, -um,** huge, violent
**-ve,** or
**vectis, -is** (*m*), crow-bar, lever
**vehementer,** violently, furiously
**vehiculum, -i** (*n*), vehicle, carriage
**vel,** or
**velut,** as if, as though
**veneo, -ire, -ii, -itum,** to be up for sale
**veneror** (1), **-atus sum,** to revere, worship
**venia, -ae** (*f*), pardon
**venio** (4), **veni, ventum,** to come
  **in mentem venire** ( + *dat.*), to think of,
  occur (to)
**ventus, -i** (*m*), wind
**verbero** (1), to beat
**verbum, -i** (*n*), word
**vere,** truly, rightly
**vereor** (2), **veritus sum,** to fear
**vero,** truly, even
**versor** (1), **-atus sum,** to move about, be
  involved in, go about among, be
  associated with, to be
**verto** (3), **verti, versum,** to turn, change
**verum,** but, but yet, however
**verus, -a, -um,** true
  **vera dicere,** to tell the truth
**vester, -tra, -trum,** your

**vestigium, -i** (*n*), trace, foot-print
**vestimentum, -i** (*n*), garment, (*pl*) clothes
**vestis, -is** (*f*), clothing
**vexillum, -i** (*n*), standard
**vexo** (1), to annoy, tease, harass
**via, -ae** (*f*), road, street
**viator, -oris** (*m*), traveller
**vibratus, -a, -um,** quivering
**vibro** (1), to brandish
**vice alterna,** alternately
  **in vicem,** in turn, in response
**vici,** *see* **vinco**
**victima, -ae** (*f*), victim
**victor, -oris** (*m*), victor, conqueror
**victoria, -ae** (*f*), victory
**victum,** *see* **vinco** and **vivo**
**vicus, -i** (*m*), village
**video** (2), **vidi, visum,** to see
**videor** (2), **visus sum,** to seem
**vigil, -is** (*m*), watchman
**vigilanter,** carefully, vigilantly
**vigilia, -ae** (*f*) watch (guard-duty during
  night)
**vigilo** (1), to keep watch, lie awake
**viginti,** twenty
**vilitas, -atis** (*f*), cheapness
**villa, -ae** (*f*), country-house, farm
**vincio** (4), **vinxi, vinctum,** to bind, tie up
**vinclum,** contracted form of **vinculum**
**vinco** (3), **vici, victum,** to conquer,
  overcome
**vinculum, -i** (*n*), chain, bond
**vindico** (1), to claim, punish
**vinum, -i** (*n*), wine
**vir, viri** (*m*), man
**vires, -ium** (*f.pl*), strength
**virga, -ae** (*f*), stick, rod
**viridis, -is, -e,** green
**virtus, -utis** (*f*), courage, valour
**vis, (vim, vi)** (*f*), force
**vita, -ae** (*f*), life
**vitis, -is** (*f*), vine-wood staff (carried by a
  centurion)
**vitium, -i** (*n*), vice, fault
**vito** (1), to avoid
**vivo** (3), **vixi, victum,** to live
**vivus, -a, -um,** alive, living
**vix,** scarcely, with difficulty
**vixdum,** scarcely yet
**voco** (1), to call
**volo, velle, volui,** to wish, be willing
**voluntas, -atis** (*f*), wish, willingness, goodwill
**vos,** you
**votum, -i** (*n*), vow, prayer
**vox, vocis** (*f*), voice
**vulnero** (1), to wound
**vulnus, -eris** (*n*), wound
**vultus, -us** (*m*), face, countenance,
  expression

# CHRONOLOGICAL CHART

| PERIOD | HISTORICAL EVENTS | |
|---|---|---|
| **MONARCHY**<br>753–509 BC | 753 BC<br>509 BC | **Romulus** founded Rome (according to legend)<br>**Tarquinius Superbus,** the seventh and last king of R…<br>was expelled (according to legend) |
| *REPUBLIC*<br>509–31 BC | 500–200 BC<br><br>264–202 BC<br><br>202 BC<br><br>133–122 BC<br><br>157–86 BC<br><br>138–78 BC<br>106–48 BC<br><br><br><br>102–44 BC<br><br>63 BC<br><br>58–51 BC<br>49 BC<br>48 BC<br>44 BC<br>31 BC | Rome extended her power through Italy and the<br>  Mediterranean<br>Rome's wars with her main rival Carthage (First an…<br>  Second Punic wars)<br>Defeat of **Hannibal,** leader of the Carthaginians, at<br>  Zama<br>Democratic reforms at Rome. The power of the Ser…<br>  reduced<br>**Marius,** Roman general, creator of professional Ro…<br>  army<br>**Sulla:** reforms in law and administration<br>**Pompey the Great:** Roman general who defeated th…<br>  pirates and made conquests in the Eastern<br>  Mediterranean. At first, he was Caesar's ally; late…<br>  his rival<br>**Julius Caesar:** conquered Gaul and became dictato…<br>  Rome after defeating Pompey<br>**Cicero** was consul and put down the conspiracy of<br>  Catiline<br>Caesar's conquest of Gaul and landings in Britain<br>Caesar crossed the River Rubicon and invaded Ital…<br>Caesar defeated Pompey at Pharsalus<br>Murder of Caesar<br>**Octavian** defeated **Mark Antony** at Actium |
| *EMPIRE*<br>31 BC–AD 180 | 27 BC<br><br>c.4 BC<br>27 BC–AD 68<br><br>AD 64<br>AD 68–69<br><br><br>AD 69–96<br>AD 79<br><br>AD 96–180 | Octavian became the first emperor of Rome and to…<br>  the title **Augustus**<br>Birth of **Jesus Christ**<br>The Julio-Claudian Emperors: **Augustus, Tiberius,**<br>  **Caligula, Claudius, Nero**<br>The Great Fire of Rome<br>The year of the four emperors: **Galba, Otho, Vitelli…**<br>  **Vespasian**<br><br>The Flavian Emperors: **Vespasian, Titus, Domitian**<br>The eruption of Vesuvius and destruction of Pomp…<br>  and Herculaneum<br>"The Five Good Emperors": **Nerva, Trajan, Hadri…**<br>  **Antoninus Pius, Marcus Aurelius** |
| *THE DECLINE<br>AND FALL OF<br>THE EMPIRE*<br>AD 180–410 | AD 192–306<br><br>AD 313<br><br>AD 330<br><br>AD 410 | In this period there were 33 emperors, many of wh…<br>  were assassinated<br>**Constantine,** the first Christian Emperor, issued th…<br>  Edict of Milan allowing Christians to worship fr…<br>Constantine founded Constantinople: beginning of<br>  two Empires – Eastern and Western<br>Rome was sacked by Alaric the Goth |

*Note.* Some of the above dates (particularly those referring to dates of birth) are approximate